Testimonials

The Souls of Queer Folk is an original! Dr. Joel Davis Brown weaves together compelling stories, fresh ideas, unexpected evidence, and beautiful prose, delivering a transformational understanding of LGBTQ+ culture. Each page of this book offers doses of inspiration and an enhanced sense of what is possible when it comes to your own leadership practice. This book is a must-read for anyone looking to break out of the mold of conformity and architect the kind of inclusive leadership our world so desperately needs today.

Rhodes Perry
CEO of Rhodes Perry Consulting and Bestselling Author
of *Belonging at Work* and *Imagine Belonging*

Adversity is a crucible that has created generations of LGBTQ+ leaders who are different from leaders who do not identify as part of the queer community. Joel's latest book, *The Souls of Queer Folk,* affirms that Queer people have something special to bring to leadership that we can—and often do—leverage to be better leaders.

This book gives names to those special qualities. It provides a roadmap to help all leaders understand LGBTQ+ leaders better and will help all leaders—LGBTQ+ or not—bring those skills to their own leadership practice. *The Souls of Queer Folk* reflects our best qualities as LGBTQ+ leaders and fills a glaring hole in the vast field of leadership teachings that I didn't realize was there until I read the book.

Ann Dunkin
Public Sector IT Executive & Former Chair,
Hewlett Packard Global PRIDE Council

In his new book, *The Souls of Queer Folk,* Joel offers readers a beautiful portrait of LGBTQ+ culture, highlighting the intrinsic values, extraordinary gifts, and diverse talents of a community that often goes unnoticed and underappreciated. Deeply researched and analytically rigorous, Joel's book is also deeply personal, reflecting his own journey with vulnerability, courage, and humor.

The Souls of Queer Folk is a book that will give every reader a better understanding of LGBTQ+ culture and a deeper appreciation for the values, norms, and lived experiences of LGBTQ+ people. Brown's book offers readers practical strategies and new frameworks for leading with authenticity and self-mastery.

John Sage
CEO, Pivotal Ventures

I met Joel at a Diversity Collegium event honoring Dr. Price Cobbs. Price wanted the opportunity to engage younger DEI professionals, and Joel was one of them. It was very clear to me that Joel had the kind of deep-thinking capability that Price enjoyed. The Souls of Queer Folks reflects this attribute of Joel's. It is no surprise that Joel invoked his intercultural mindset to present Queer Folks in terms of cultural values, for what better core concept is there for people to understand their common humanity. To advance these cultural values as a model of "a new brand of transformational leadership" for everyone is Joel's genius, and an example of the LGBTQ+ cultural genius™ he talks about. This book should be required reading in every MBA program, and a must read for every leader. Not only will readers gain a much deeper understanding of Queer folks, they will also learn how to improve their leadership.

Barbara R. Deane
Co-Director, Institute for Sustainable Diversity & Inclusion, Seattle, WA

I had the pleasure of meeting Dr. Davis Brown through the Diversity Collegium, a pioneering DEI think tank. My first impression of Joel was that he was someone who would bring innovative ideas and elevate the field. Over the years, this has proven to be true, and this book is another stellar example. Written in a voice that is lyrical yet practical, the book introduces a new platform based on qualitative and quantitative research to not only verify and understand the culture of LGBTQ+ people, but to learn how the identified values are critical to leadership development in our new reality. What I especially appreciated is that the book's architecture is one of head, heart, and hands. A research-based intellectual platform is supported with storytelling to engage the heart and practical "how to" recommendations to put one's understanding into action. It is groundbreaking work that individuals, organizations, and societies can benefit from immensely.

Kay Iwata
President, K. Iwata Associates, Inc.

Joel Davis Brown's new book, *The Souls of Queer Folk*, is an unexpected and newly explored analysis of the life skills many LGBTQ+

people develop in order to cope in the world and lead authentic lives. But, Joel posits, these life skills are indeed also leadership skills grown out of oppression by a marginalized community. Joel builds a reasoned and logical case for his premise that these skills can be applied in anyone's life and, in fact, are the leadership skills we need now to function in our fractured society. The application lessons at the end of many of the chapters are special gems for self-inquiry and personal development. I highly recommend this book, both as a critical examination of LGBTQ+ culture and, more specifically, as a guide to the leadership qualities necessary for our world.

Steven Humerickhouse
Executive Director, The Forum on Workplace Inclusion,
Augsburg University

I first crossed paths with Dr. Joel Davis Brown four years ago when he was delivering a workshop to our Executive MBA students at Berkeley Haas School of Business. Over the years, I continued to have the good fortune and pleasure of witnessing him at work across a variety of topics. In that time, we have connected personally and professionally as fellow changemakers in the field of diversity, equity, and inclusion practitioners. Joel's authentic interest in my work and my well-being has been notable. This authenticity comes across in how he generously and carefully guides along the reader as he lays out his thesis for *The Souls of Queer Folk*. His book offers the reader an opportunity to contemplate one's authenticity in the workplace, and the possibility of true freedom and self-actualization that comes with this liberation, if we follow the path laid out for us by LGBTQ+ elders and ancestors.

Élida M. Bautista, PhD
Chief DEI Officer, UC Berkeley Haas School of Business

As I reviewed this book, I heard Joel providing his wisdom and asking for a paradigm shift that allows straight and cisgender people to recognize the wisdom of the LGBTQ+ community. As a leader, understanding the importance of identity, meaning, and belonging in self and others is critical. Joel lays out a path for doing so at a time when there are many who want to turn the clock back.

Juan T. Lopez
President, Amistad & Associates Consulting
Founder of D2000 Think Tank

The SOULS
OF QUEER FOLK

The SOULS
OF QUEER FOLK

How Understanding
LGBTQ+ Culture Can Transform
Your Leadership Practice

DR. JOEL A. DAVIS BROWN

PYP **Publish** Your Purpose

For permission requests, write to the publisher, addressed "Attention: Permissions Coordinator," at the address below.

Publish Your Purpose
141 Weston Street, #155
Hartford, CT, 06141

PYP **Publish** Your Purpose

The opinions expressed by the Author are not necessarily those held by Publish Your Purpose.

Ordering Information: Quantity sales and special discounts are available on quantity purchases by corporations, associations, and others. For details, contact the publisher at orders@publishyourpurposepress.com.

Edited by: Malka Wickramatilake, Gina Sartirana
Cover design by: Cornelia Murariu
Typeset by: Medlar Publishing Solutions Pvt Ltd., India

Printed in the United States of America.

ISBN: 979-8-88797-001-1 (hardcover)
ISBN: 979-8-88797-000-4 (paperback)
ISBN: 979-8-88797-002-8 (eBook)

Library of Congress Control Number: 2022921691

First edition, January 2023.

Publish Your Purpose is a hybrid publisher of non-fiction books. Our authors are thought leaders, experts in their fields, and visionaries paving the way to social change—from food security to anti-racism. We give underrepresented voices power and a stage to share their stories, speak their truth, and impact their communities. Do you have a book idea you would like us to consider publishing? Please visit PublishYourPurpose.com for more information.

Dedication

For Mom: The best teacher and leader I have ever had.
When someone asked me why I wanted to write a book on
leadership development, it was because I saw your sterling
example of leadership every single day.

For Aunt Margaret: My second mama and kindred spirit.
The first elder to be my LGBTQ+ ally. You encouraged me
to be myself and never let go of my spirit of adventure.
I miss you in ways that defy description.

For Aunt Mickey: My third mama and guide,
who taught me to love creativity and embrace my spirituality
in my own way. God is love and love is you (wink).

For Dr. Price Cobbs: Author of *Black Rage*, and
my mentor who encouraged me to write this book.
I hope you get to read it in the heavens.

This book is dedicated to LGBTQ+ people worldwide, no matter
if you are living bodaciously, struggling in isolation, questioning
your value, fighting for the right to exist peacefully, or simply
telling your honest damn truth. Your story is mine. Let us find
our truth together and set the universe ablaze…

All my relations…

Acknowledgments

*"If I have seen a little further it is by standing
on the shoulders of giants..."*
—Sir Isaac Newton

In that vein and with that understanding...

I want to salute my close circle of family and friends (110 people, to be exact) for their support, even as I labored away from them in relative isolation for weeks and months at a time.

I want to honor those who have transitioned to the other side, specifically my uncle "Captain" Harold P. Davis, my aunt (and second mom) Margaret Miller Holmes, Auntie Ivy Jewel (my guardian angel), and the titans... my grandparents Hugh Davis Sr., Addie L. Davis, Lillie C. Davis, and Lois Gantt.

In the end, this book would not have been possible without the support of the Davis family, whose love has sustained me from the moment I drew breath. They have poured all of their hopes and aspirations into me, and in turn, I have used every bit of grit, strength, and patience during this process to honor them faithfully.

To my siblings and best friends: Damon & Regina. My "roll-dawgs." We will always be Earth, Wind, & Fire. Thank you for your love and support and our NATO Alliance. May the Universe have mercy on anyone that causes any of us to invoke "Article 5."

I want to acknowledge the Brown Family for their prayers, love, and support, especially Aunt Georgia, Mabel, Will, Dad, San, Kim, and Kyllan.

I want to thank my mentors and spiritual guides for keeping me on the righteous path. I want to thank my highest self for manifesting this book.

I want to thank the wonderful team at Publish Your Purpose press, specifically "JT," Bailly "B-Diddy" Morse, and my editors Malka and Gina, for helping to bring this book to fruition. It means a lot when you have a competent publisher that actually has a heart, a worldview, and a code of ethics.

And last but not least, I want to thank the kindred spirits and community of warriors, advocates, and tireless leaders—past or present—who have fought globally to protect the humanity and beauty of LGBTQ+ people. In those moments when I felt confused, tired, and fatigued, I remembered the Ghanian word Sankofa, which says in essence: "It is not wrong to go back for that which you have forgotten." In honoring that word, I thought about the legion of LGBTQ+ scholars, citizens, and activists who came before us. If we pay attention, those ancestors and transcestors still have much to teach us...and in the endless moments that framed this project, they certainly taught me.

Always in love... always in solidarity.

Joel

Dear Reader & Curious Soul,

Thank you for going on this ride with me. To make your journey easier, let me share with you how your reading experience will unfold.

Section I frames the discussion. It sets the tone and provides the philosophical and intellectual rationale for why this book was written. Like any proud chef greeting their patrons before serving a good meal, it provides the context for and outlines the scope of what you will be reading. It will whet your appetite and warm you up before the adventure begins.

In Section II, we spend some time reviewing the research that serves as the basis for this book. If you are a nerd like me, you will enjoy reading the synopsis of the ethnographic research I conducted to learn more about the cultural values of the LGBTQ+ community. If you are not a nerd, I promise you will wish you were after digesting Chapter 2.

Section III is for those savvy individuals who want to become transformational leaders. Unfortunately, we know that not everyone wants to be a transformational leader. Some people are content being authoritarian, top-down, uninspiring, individualist leaders. However, if you are interested in a leadership style that is more humanistic, collectivist, poetic, and groundbreaking, Section III is a leadership manifesto or "guidepost" of LGBTQ proportions. Section III provides the leading-edge Queer insight to help you be a leader who creates a positive legacy. Your employees, communities, clients, and peers will thank you for it.

By the time you get to Section IV, you will be ready to learn how to avoid the miscalculations and missteps that prevent everyday people and leaders alike from leveraging LGBTQ+ wisdom. I encourage you to take Section IV to heart, as there are reasons why Queer global wisdom has been obscured until now. Section IV will give you the insight and tools to harness LGBTQ+-inspired leadership lessons in a thoughtful and discerning way.

And finally, Section V is like a montage at the end of a movie that replays the best moments of a feature film. It summarizes the key points from the discussion, but it doesn't stop there: Section V issues a personal challenge to you to decide who you want to be as a leader. Before you can have thoughtful actions, you have to have the requisite understanding to know how to support people. And before you can have the requisite understanding to support people, you must possess the right consciousness to recognize that any actions you take to support others will also reflect how you truly see yourself. Prior to possessing the consciousness to see yourself truly, you must be willing to examine your "beingness" in all its varied dimensions. Once you do that, then you are on the path to being a great(er) leader.

As you read this book, I encourage you to engage it with a curious mind *and* an open heart. This is not a book that is meant to be read once or to sit idly on a dusty shelf. Give it life. Read it whenever you need inspiration. Consult it whenever you have questions, doubts, or concerns in your leadership practice. Share it when you find that it can create meaning for others. This book was channeled to help produce greater joy, love, and wisdom in the world, and it can't do that without you embodying the best of who you are and seeing the best in others. Know that this book may not teach you as much as it may *remind* you of who you are.

Step outside of your comfort zone. Stretch your mind. Commit to being a better leader than you were yesterday. And as I always say, "Have fun." This book was a labor of love for me. I hope that reading it will be an exercise in joy for you.

Love, peace, and soul,

JADB

Table of Contents

SECTION 3: LGBTQ+ LEADERSHIP: THE VALUE OF QUEER FOLK

SECTION 4: BARRIERS TO RECOGNIZING LGBTQ+ CULTURAL GENIUS™

SECTION 5: CONCLUSION

Preface

After writing nearly 100,000 words, I must say it feels odd to have the opportunity to offer a personal reflection and yet struggle to find the right words. To reduce my feelings and experiences to several pages seems trite and difficult, especially as I think about what started this journey, who sustained me during the journey, and of course, the journey itself.

Writing a book was never my goal. I did not seek to be an author. I am a writer and a poet, but I resist doing things for the sake of achievement. I only write or speak up when I think something needs to be said that isn't being said. In my estimation, the point of sharing anything in the public sphere is to tell the world something it didn't know before.

Over the years, I kept waiting for someone to write about the LGBTQ+ community in a revelatory way. It seemed that all the notions about who we were had already been decided, and I didn't find that reality particularly satisfying. No one really seemed curious about the community, including some community members. No one seemed willing to take a step back and question the assumptions, the stereotypes, and the grand conclusions that had been made about us or maintained about us. When I shared my frustrations with some close friends and asked them why no one wanted to engage in this conversation, they said, "Perhaps because you're the one who's supposed to be leading that conversation."

Admittedly, as a curly-headed Black boy from the north side of Milwaukee, the thought never occurred to me to do that. But then I remembered: the conversation is not about me—it's about the struggles, stories, pain, joy, despair, and triumph of the community. I didn't need to do anything except move out of the way and center the experiences of my tribe. As I felt the words and ideas churning inside of me, I knew my passion for this topic would express itself fully if given the chance, and hence, a book was born.

Writing a book is an incredible journey that comes with a lot of responsibility. I've always found it interesting how writing a book can give a stamp of approval to what someone says, even if what they say is fallacious or deeply problematic.

Because of that trend, I didn't take this project lightly. Writing is an opportunity to tell a story. Too often, however, that latitude has been inaccessible to those who are marginalized. For far too many years, the power of the narrative has been misdirected at those who do not have power. And authorship has been denied to certain people because they did not have a scholarly title, cultural profile, or academic pedigree that was palatable to those with the power to make publication possible. At some point, maybe I'll write a book about that too.

But in no uncertain terms, being a researcher, a sociologist, and an author comes with great duty. They require dexterity, skill, compassion, and heart. They require insight and accountability. I thought I understood that before I began this journey, but I understand that responsibility even more now. To be an author requires care and compassion to ensure you get the story right. As an author, it is critically important to make sure that when you write about a marginalized community, your writing doesn't cause further marginalization.

As for me, I have always wanted to tell the truth about LGBTQ+ people. As I followed my curiosity and started to "pull the thread," I also had to unravel my assumptions and notions about our place in the world. I had to be honest about my inferences and biases as a middle-class, "millennial-esque," cisgender, African American, gay man from the Global North. I had to do the work myself, and I rested comfortably in the realization that, as with any human being, there would always be more work to do.

Being LGBTQ+ has never been a simple answer, but I know this: our community is multi-faceted and wonderfully gifted in so many ways. If we are serious about resolving the issues plaguing our world now—war, climate change, poverty, extremism, displacement, and repression—then LGBTQ+ people cannot be kept on the sidelines. We must be at the table. We must have a dedicated seat. And in some instances, we must be the ones leading and designing the conversation. I hope this book will serve that purpose.

INTRODUCTION

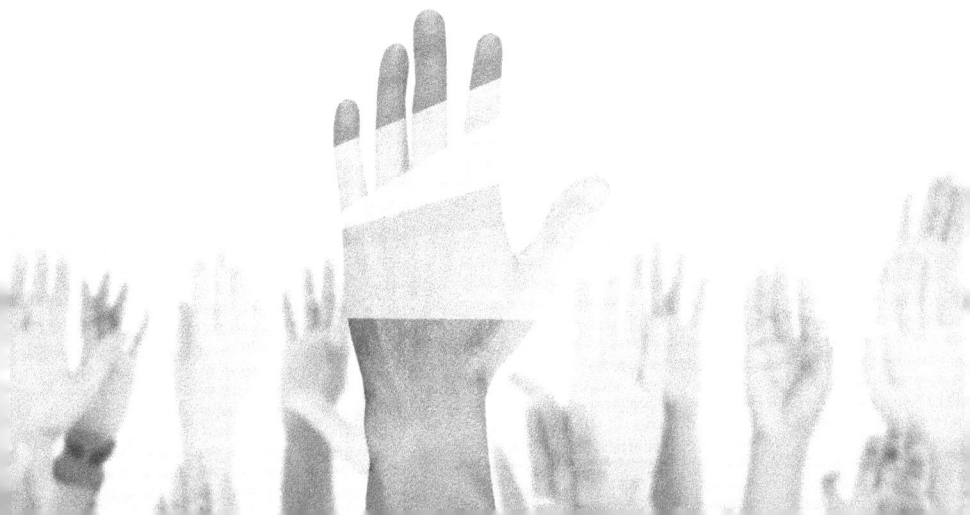

"*The way we see the world shapes the way we treat it. If a mountain is a deity, not a pile of ore; If a forest is a sacred grove, not timber; if other species are biological kin, not resources; or if the planet is our mother, not an opportunity - then we will treat each other with greater respect. Thus is the challenge, to look at the world from a different perspective.*"

David Suzuki

CHAPTER 1

The Leadership Quandary

The Inquisitive one asks:
Is truth supposed to be for a show?
Are you more interested in what you believe?
and less of what you know?

It seems people believe too much
and know too little
Love is playing second fiddle
in this kingdom of hard minds
Once upon a time
Aristophenes said:
Whirl is King
Having driven out Zeus
and today…
It seems souls reek
and minds are too loose
But I can't be an island onto myself
True love doesn't act with stealth

it is bold in its voyage
So I skate from the shadows
I skim treetops
I rattle cages
I slip into the pages
of dirty manifestos
where zealots would choose to strike fear
the world's heartbeat is what I hear
I come to commune
knowing I can't be immune
My hope is that together…soon
We shall all find…
Peace
in 360.

As I reflected on the state of global leadership, I wrote the foregoing poem 20 years ago as I witnessed the confluence of socio-political events at the turn of the century. And as the notion of leadership continues to dangle before us as we push further into the 21st century, the question of what constitutes good leadership is no less a fascinating proposition today than it was in yesteryear. Ironically, the more we see misdirection and poor guidance, the more we can recognize good leadership.

To explain, let me offer some examples of how stewardship can fluctuate between two extremes. While poor leadership can assume the worst qualities of narcissism and treat dissent as an affront to reason or as an assault on the world order, good leadership embraces timely feedback and values differing opinions. Whereas poor leadership surrounds itself with like-minded and "like-looking" sycophants in order to glorify its narrow view of the world, strong leadership creates a tent that welcomes people from a variety of backgrounds and relishes global-mindedness. Further, while poor leadership is beset by scandal and the "wheeling and dealing" machinations of the self-interested, effective leadership possesses a moral compass that is purposeful, deeply rooted, and socially conscious. The unfortunate thing, however, is that if you have spent any amount of significant time on this planet, you have probably witnessed, been exposed to, or had to overcome poor leadership at some point in your personal or professional life.

Now, if I were a pessimistic or morbid fellow, I would probably begin and end this book right here without any further discussion and write a maudlin epitaph on leadership. In that case, we could treat the current state of leadership as a fixed and immutable phenomenon and conclude our analysis with some trite statement indicating that leadership is in some existential crisis. I wouldn't blame you if the notion sounds appealing, but that probably wouldn't be good leadership on my part, either.

So, as I thought about leadership and, more importantly, the prospect of transformational leadership—the kind that changes hearts and minds and speaks to the better angels of our nature—I found myself looking for new sources of inspiration. Those revelations came from a place that, while familiar, would certainly be unexpected to the masses of people who study, seek, and advise on the subject of leadership development. What I discovered in a parallel journey is that a source for, and example of, transformational leadership lies in a special place otherwise known as the…The Lesbian, Gay, Bisexual, Transgender, and Queer (LGBTQ+) community.[1]

At this point, you probably believe you've been set up. Let me make an attempt at transcribing your thoughts.

Come again?

---

[1] In most contexts, I use the full acronym for the community: 2SLGBTQIA+. 2SLGBTQIA references the Two Spirit, Lesbian, Gay, Bisexual, Transgender, Queer, Intersex, and Asexual community. However, in order to make this book more readable, I shortened the acronym and used the term Queer to speak to the entire community. Using this cultural shorthand was not done with the intention of rendering any community invisible. If my decision has hurt anyone, I apologize and welcome the space to dialogue.

Puh-leeze.

That can't be!

But fellow homo sapiens, seekers of knowledge, and leaders du jour, remember: you can't be curious and judgmental at the same time. If you remain curious and open to new ways of learning, I can assure you: a review of the LGBTQ+ community and its cultural values footprint is but one gateway—albeit an important one—to transforming and revolutionizing your leadership practice.

Now, as a proud and self-respecting member of the LGBTQ+ community, you may assume that I am biased or following some agenda to interject some off-brand topic into the all-important subject of leadership. But…nothing could be further from the truth.

This revelation about the souls of Queer folk and their impact on leadership began many years ago when I was a child on the north side of Milwaukee. As I slowly became aware of my gayness, I started to ask what seemed like humble questions: What does it mean to be me? And what does it mean to be LGBTQ+? Not surprisingly, the latter question is one that has been asked in other forms by various people. In 2015, the *New Republic* published an article entitled "What Will Gay Culture Look Like in 2035?"[2] Some of the answers were fairly predictable. Many of the LGBTQ+ people interviewed believed that Queer sensibilities would become more mainstream. As the interviewees theorized, LGBTQ+ people will become so accustomed to being integrated into society that the idea that this population was ever ostracized will seem like a distant social memory. Other respondents hoped for an era where cis-heterosexuality would not be presumed to be the norm. Yet, a few others predicted a less utopian outcome and warned of cultural invisibility as LGBTQ+ people become part of the great melting pot of assimilation.

---

[2] Chee, A. (2015, June). What will gay culture look like in 2035? *New Republic.* Retrieved from https://newrepublic.com/article/122120/what-will-gay-culture-look-203

At the very least, it was a positive thing that the Queer[3] people interviewed envisioned a reality in which Queer people were still a recognizable part of society. However, for all the talk about LGBTQ+ culture in 2035, I finished the article still wondering what exactly is LGBTQ+ culture today.

Apparently, others have struggled with the same question. Author David Halperin asked plaintively in his 2012 *New York Times* column: "Are gay people simply indistinguishable from normal folk?"[4] And while Halperin did not explicitly ask about culture per se, the subtext of his column is the open-ended question of whether LGBTQ+ culture really exists, and if it does, is it more than a colorful iteration of pre-defined, already-existing heterosexual culture? Bruce Bawer, author of *A Place at the Table: The Gay Individual in American Society*, asked in his 2013 *Forbes* column, "Just What Is 'Gay Culture' In 2013?" Activist and blogger James Owen also queried about the substance of LGBTQ+ culture and cautioned LGBTQ+ people that, in their quest to gain social acceptance, they must not forsake the essential question of "who they are" as opposed to "what they do."[5] The basic values of the LGBTQ+ community seem muddled, and my curiosity as a social scientist, an intellectual, and a gay man compelled me to unearth those fundamental values.

Perhaps the problem with this question of LGBTQ+ culture is that the answer seems too obvious. In a world where LGBTQ+ people have become increasingly more visible, it may be easy to assume that the question of Queer culture is a foregone conclusion. Alternatively,

---

[3] For the purposes of this book, I use LGBTQ+ and Queer interchangeably. Queer is an umbrella term that is intended to encompass the entire community.

[4] Halperin, D. (2012, June). Normal as Folk. *New York Times.* Retrieved from http://www.nytimes.com/2012/06/22/opinion/style-and-the-meaning-of-gay-culture.html?mcubz=3

[5] Owen, J. (2015, June 26). "Beyond Sex: What Is Gay?" *Huffington Post,* Retrieved from http://www.huffingtonpost.com/james-owens/beyond-sex-what-is-gay_b_6951926.html

given that sexuality and gender identity appear to be the most salient difference between LGBTQ+ people and their heterosexual, cisgender counterparts, it may be fairly convenient for laypeople to reduce LGBTQ+ culture to sex, sexuality, and gender non-conformity.

While sex and sexuality are not unimportant, the suggestion that LGBTQ+ culture is simply about sexuality—particularly when one invokes LGBTQ+ culture and, more specifically, LGBTQ+ cultural values—seems incomplete. While gender norms are complex, assuming that LGBTQ+ culture is simply a predisposition towards asking people to honor different pronouns (as one example) is problematic. Therefore, I *initially* began my research to address the question that society and perhaps even LGBTQ+ people have taken for granted: What does it mean to be LGBTQ+ from an ethnographic standpoint?

Throughout my research study, which spanned several years, I discovered some important information:

- LGBTQ+ people are more than the caricatures that mainstream society would portray us to be.
- LGBTQ+ people are perhaps more culturally significant than even those of us who identify as LGBTQ+ gave ourselves credit for.
- LGBTQ+ people are as culturally rich and layered as any other cultural group on the planet.

I also discovered cultural values that, while not exclusive to our community, are positioned and aggregated in such a way within the LGBTQ+ ethos that they create a unique, powerful, and original cultural portrait that must be illuminated. Ours is a cultural narrative that must be described with greater integrity and responsibility.

Yet, in the process of attempting to elevate our culture in a new way, something else happened too: I also realized that LGBTQ+ culture is a demonstrably generative way to inspire leaders and to develop new and more effective forms of leadership. LGBTQ+ people are not just the latest entrants to the ball of would-be intercultural groups, simply looking to popularize the field of diversity and inclusion. By virtue of our lived experience, we are also teachers, conductors, and mentors for how a society plagued by poor stewardship can be a world guided by transformational leadership. That is the mission of this book: to demonstrate how the values of the LGBTQ+ community are instructive for leaders everywhere and serve as the foundation for a new brand of global transformational leadership.

That being said, being a transformational leader is more than just memorizing leadership competencies. It requires our leaders to transform themselves in a way that balances self-interest with the collective good, chooses inspiration over the short-term appeal of reveling in pain, and recognizes that intellect and pragmatism must also be powered with compassion. Transformational leadership is a consciousness and a calling. Transformational leadership is about being-ness, not just doing-ness. You must be able to face and lead *yourself* in order to be a great leader.

But in a world where leaders are seemingly doing twice as much work with half as many resources as their predecessors, the "how to" aspect of becoming a transformational leader can seem elusive or too complex to master in any discernible way. Let's face it friends: leadership is hard. And…according to a Gallup survey in 2020 and 2021, leadership burnout is only getting worse. Leadership burnout occurs when leaders experience high levels of mental, emotional, and physical work-related stress that impairs their ability to fulfill their obligations. Managers are experiencing high levels of stress and anxiety, and the rate of depression among managers has increased in recent years.[6] According to the American Psychological Association's 2021 Work and Well-being Survey, nearly 3 out of 5 employees reported

---

[6] Harter, J. (2021, November 18). Manager Burnout Is Only Getting Worse. Gallup. https://www.gallup.com/workplace/357404/manager-burnout-getting-worse.aspx

symptoms of burnout, including lack of interest, motivation, or energy (26%), as well as a lack of effort at work (19%). Meanwhile, 36% of those survey reported cognitive weariness, emotional exhaustion (32%), and physical fatigue (44%), a 38% increase since 2019. What's more, only 1 out of 4 managers strongly agree that they are able to maintain a healthy balance between work and their personal commitments. And unfortunately, analysts expect the current leadership trends to continue among massive shifts in the labor market.[7] Given these dynamics, it's hard to imagine that leaders have the wherewithal to be transformational when the proverbial ground they are standing on feels relatively unstable. As more and more people quit their jobs in the era of the Great Resignation,[8,9] leaders are facing more pressure to transform their working environments for existing workers while creating an appealing and inclusive workforce for prospective employees. Leaders are finding themselves in a catch-22 situation where they're being asked to be the very transformational leaders that their teetering work environments won't allow.

Therefore, to support current and burgeoning leaders and to ensure that any fledgling attempts to be positively-impactful and transformational are successful, our job as thought leaders is to provide modern, relevant, and generative frameworks for our leaders to be the stalwarts the world needs them to be. Cultural genius is the social, intellectual, and leadership acumen that social groups (particularly minoritized communities) develop by virtue of their cultural pathway. Fortunately, by virtue of their cultural genius™, LGBTQ+ people have provided a cultural blueprint and powerful case study that not only exhibits transformational leadership, but also teaches every leader *how* to begin that journey of personal growth.

---

[7] *Id.*

[8] According to the US Department of Labor, there were 11.5 million workers who quit their jobs during Q2 of June 2021.

[9] U.S. Bureau of Labor Statistics. (2022) Table 4. [Quit levels and rates by industry and region, seasonally adjusted]. *Economic News Release.* https://www.bls.gov/news.release/jolts.t04.htm

Naturally, there will be some who, when introduced to this book, will chafe at the notion that the LGBTQ+ community holds value, much less that the community can teach them anything valuable about leadership. There will be some who will try to reduce the book's theme to cultural egoism, and some who will assert that this book is the latest in embellished progressive propaganda designed to re-engineer society and eradicate traditional values.

Such thinking would not only be rash but foolhardy. Not only would those naysayers be ignoring the increasing visibility and ubiquity of the LGBTQ+ community, they would also be dismissing the import of the lessons that the community is trying to impart. And given the depth, magnitude, and breadth of the challenges we face as a society in the 21st century, we as a species cannot afford to leave any wisdom on the table, even if it comes from a community that is still irrationally discriminated against and massively misunderstood. The leadership wisdom inherent in LGBTQ+ cultural values should not be determined by the relative obscurity in which they have unfolded, but by the persistent results they have undeniably created. Despite the sum weight of the church, the political system, and the social craze to eliminate LGBTQ+ sensibilities and influence, the community remains a fixture in our social fabric. LGBTQ+ people have changed the world in qualitative and quantifiable ways, which is in no small part due to the values we adhere to in our cultural journey on a customary basis.

Some may also argue that the book is an attempt at respectability politics or believe that the book is explicitly aimed at the cis-heterosexual community. I am not interested in proving to the world that LGBTQ+ people are just like everyone else. We are not like everyone else, which is why I believe our culture is a fascinating, compelling, and instructive tale of how to be a powerful leader and defy the odds. And, while I would love to believe that all Queer people understand their superhuman talents, I know far too well that there is tremendous opportunity for other LGBTQ+ people to see their light as well. If you are LGBTQ+, this book is an invitation to your own party.

So if you're like my righteous friends who asked me pointedly: "What will I get out of this book?" I hope you receive (if nothing else): 1) an illuminated sense of the LGBTQ+ community, 2) a holistic view of LGBTQ+ culture, 3) a healthy dose of Queer wisdom, and a 4) sturdy prescription for transforming your leadership practice.

Accordingly, this book has the following path and format. In Section I, I will provide some background on why this topic of LGBTQ+ leadership is timely, especially given the political and social perils that LGBTQ+ people continue to face in the global landscape. My hope is that, at the very least, this book will help our society see our gifts and talents—not as caricatures or social avatars—but as three-dimensional human beings who possess beauty, knowledge, and wisdom. The purpose of this book is not to deify LGBTQ+ people; however, it wasn't written to demonize them either. Instead, by providing an unobstructed but elevated view of the community, I am simply laying bare the quiet truths and simple beauty that have existed for quite some time.

From there, I will frame the opportunity to use the LGBTQ+ community as a leadership case study. Admittedly, LGBTQ+ people may seem like unlikely leadership role models, given the profound lack of understanding as to what LGBTQ+ cultural values are. Mainstream society presents what I call the Queer paradox— the seeming *visibility* of Queer or LGBTQ+ people in modern society with the apparent *unfamiliarity* with the community's intrinsic values as a whole. If more people understood what the LGBTQ+ community stands for culturally, they would recognize the value we bring to society and treat this community with the dexterity, curiosity, and respect that an inquiry of this nature richly deserves.

Thirdly, I will share the cultural values that are part of the fabric of the community. Those values were derived from research conducted in two parts over three years. The data was based on personal interviews and an American national survey of members of the LGBTQ+ community. The research identified 15 cultural values that, when reviewed and identified, fell into nine primary value categories or meta-themes that captured the essence of LGBTQ+ culture and the souls of Queer folk.

In turn, those nine meta-themes illustrate that LGBTQ+ people possess a cultural genius™ that, when extracted, can be beneficial to the world. Those key themes or considerations provide knowledge and insight that can help leaders in any part of the world enhance and embellish their leadership practice. The insights and cultural best practices gleaned from Queer wisdom form the basis of Section III, which contains lessons in LGBTQ+ leadership.

In Section IV, I identified several key factors which may impede a leader's ability to receive or appreciate the cultural genius™ of the LGBTQ+ community. Whether it's the twin forces of heterosexism or cisgenderism, the homogenization of the LGBTQ+ community, or the circular reasoning employed by religious fanatics, leaders who fall victim to these dynamics will miss the cultural genius™ of the LGBTQ+ community. Regardless of whether the leadership opportunity is in one's community, one's enterprise, one's place of employment, or one's family, leaders who succumb to anti-LGBTQ+ bias will fail to take advantage of the best practices, leadership acumen, and sage advice that LGBTQ+ people have to offer to the world.

Finally, I concluded the book with a reminder of how LGBTQ+ cultural genius™ can create a new generation of leaders and a metamorphosized brand of leadership. Workplaces will be havens for belonging and ingenuity, communities will become beacons of collaborative inquiry and healing, and the unheralded leaders in our midst will let go of their under-sized ambition and use their peculiar and brilliant sensibilities to change the world.

And maybe, in the process of those factions rescuing leadership from the ominous place where it sits right now, there will be no more "fairies" or degenerates or "alphabet people." Maybe I will be the last "homosexual" whose book you read, and maybe your LGBTQ+ peers will be the last sordid strangers you meet. Just maybe, instead of being outcasts or the colorful and fun people you know as neighbors or the distant people you share a community culture with, perhaps we can start to see LGBTQ+ people as full-fledged dynamos, who, while not perfect, have a lot to teach our leaders and a lot to offer this world. It is my hope and prayer to transform leadership and liberate our views of the LGBTQ+ community. It is time that we fully and unapologetically start to do both.

CHAPTER 2

Why LGBTQ+ Culture Is Important

If LGBTQ+ culture is important from a leadership perspective, then we must account for the crucible that has helped to forge Queer culture. In my formative years as a gay man, I always felt that my sexuality, or my social difference from my cis-heterosexual counterparts, had much more to do with cultural values than superficial affectations. My "gayness" not only disrupted many of the social norms and values I grew up with, but also changed my worldview. Even if I did not have sex or pursue any physical attraction to a member of the same sex, I sensed that being a Queer man still created a different cultural reality. As I attended LGBTQ+ events or mingled in LGBTQ+ circles, I talked about these ideas with a number of friends. Although many agreed, I did not have the inclination to pursue the analysis further until I saw how many people lambasted the idea of LGBTQ+ culture, even some who were members of the LGBTQ+ community.

Notably, even diversity and inclusion practitioners (those who advise individuals and organizations on how to understand different cultures) suffer from this disquieting belief that gayness or Queerness do not exist and are not worth further examination. Early in my career, I was paired with a colleague to facilitate a three-day diversity workshop at a naval installation. At the time, the diversity issues that surfaced in the military included race and ethnicity, religion, disability, gender, gender identity, age, and sexual orientation. As we prepped for the first day of training and discussed the objectives for the course, we agreed that we would ask the workshop participants to identify how the recruitment of marginalized groups could actually benefit the agency. Imagine my surprise when my colleague turned to me and said, "Do you mind handling the sexual orientation and gender identity discussions? I am not sure what Queerness means or how that really ties into the overall business purpose here." I was fairly disappointed but not surprised.

Researching and rethinking LGBTQ+ culture seems like the natural culmination of historical events that span decades. It was only 50 years ago that homosexuality was labeled a psychiatric illness, and many gay people were forced to repress who they were.[10] Even in 2022, 1 out of 3 LGBTQ+ people suffered from some form of discrimination,[11] the most unheralded form of discrimination being microaggressions. Microaggressions are the brief and commonplace daily verbal, behavioral, and environmental indignities, whether intentional or unintentional, that communicate hostile, derogatory, or negative slights and insults to members of a marginalized group.[12] When we examine discrimination at the interpersonal level, LGBTQ+ people suffer from microaggressions in every facet of life, whether at work, in the community, on social media, or among

---

[10] Life Before Stonewall. (1994, July 3). *Newsweek*. Retrieved from http://www.newsweek.com/life-stonewall-189962

[11] Sue, 2010.

[12] Sue, Capodilupo, et al., 2007.

their family. Typical examples of microaggressions include cis-heteronormative language such as references to lesbian or gay people as "homosexuals" or references to transgender people as "transgenders" or "the transgenders." Calling lesbian or gay people "homosexuals" sounds "clincal" or "scientific" and denies gays and lesbians their cultural heritage and identity. Referring to transgender people as "transgenders" or "the transgenders," like an alien life form or the new family who just moved in down the block, denies transgender people their humanity. But in truth, microaggressions take many forms, including: a) over-sexualization, b) homophobia/transphobia/biphobia, c) assumptions of "sinfulness," d) assumption of abnormality, e) cis-heterosexist language /terminology, f) denial of individual heterosexism/cisgenderism, g) and endorsement of cis-heteronormative culture and behaviors. These phenomena underline the systemic reality that Queer people are not fully liberated people in our global society.

Fortunately, due to the organizing efforts of groups like the Daughters of Bilitis and the Mattachine Society, as well as the watershed events of the Compton Cafeteria Riot in 1966 and the Stonewall Riots in 1969, LGBTQ+ people now enjoy unprecedented freedom.[13] In addition, recent times have seen LGBTQ+ people secure rights that probably seemed unthinkable to previous generations. As an example, same-sex marriage is now legal in 30 countries,[14] and the majority of Americans support same-sex marriage.[15]

However, discrimination against LGBTQ+ people in the workplace is still a major social concern. For example, 55% of LGBTQ+ workers in Singapore reported being discriminated against at work.[16] In South Africa, the monthly earnings of LGBTQ+ men

---

[13] Kazin, Dissent, 2013.

[14] Same Sex Marriage Around the World, Pew Center, 2019.

[15] McCarthy, Gallup, 2021.

[16] Wong, S. (2022, September 20). *55% experienced workplace discrimination in Singapore: AWARE survey.* yahoo!news. https://news.yahoo.com/workplace-discrimination-singapore-aware-survey-130324125.html

are 30% lower than that of their cis-hetero counterparts.[17] In the U.K., 1 out of 3 employers has admitted they are "less likely" to hire a transgender person and 43% are unsure if they would recruit a transgender worker.[18] In a nationally-representative survey in the U.S., the Williams Institute at the UCLA School of Law reported that over 45.5% of LGBTQ+ workers experienced unfair treatment, including harassment, bias, and termination.[19] The study showed that over 50% of LGBTQ+ people hid their identities from their supervisors to avoid discrimination, and over a quarter of respondents hid their identities from their co-workers.[20] Moreover, over one in four LGBTQ+ respondents reported experiencing discrimination at some point in their lives.[21]

Unfortunately, the reach of LGBTQ+ stigmatization and discrimination extends far outside the workplace, and there is still a lack of comprehensive U.S. federal legislation protecting LGBTQ+ people from discrimination in all walks of life. Studies in the late 2010s show nearly a third of LGBTQ+ participants avoided speaking about LGBTQ+ issues in social settings, and at least 16% of the LGBTQ+ people interviewed reported moving away from their families or cutting people out of their lives to avoid discrimination.[22]

---

[17] UCLA School of Law Williams Institute. (2019, December 9). LGBT Discrimination costs South African more than $300 million per year. Retrieved from https://williamsinstitute.law.ucla.edu/press/cost-discr-south-africa-press-release/

[18] Crossland. (2018, November 18). "Transphobia rife among UK employers as 1 in 3 won't hire a transgender person." Crossland. Retrieved from https://www.crosslandsolicitors.com/site/hr-hub/transgender-discrimination-in-UK-workplaces

[19] Sears, B., Mallory, C., Flores, A., and Conron, K. (2021). LGBTQ People's Experience of Workplace Discrimination and Harassment. Williams Institute. UCLA School of Law. https://williamsinstitute.law.ucla.edu/wp-content/uploads/Workplace-Discrimination-Sep-2021.pdf

[20] Id.

[21] Id.

[22] Singh, S. & Durso, L. E. (2017, May 2). Widespread Discrimination Continues to Shape LGBT People's Lives in Both. Subtle and Significant Ways.

Further, 23% of LGBTQ+ people avoid social situations for fear of anti-LGBTQ+ bias, and roughly 18–19% of respondents stated that discrimination affected their decisions of where to live or shop.[23] The effects of discrimination also extended to healthcare, where more than half of LGBTQ+ people have reported being discriminated against by medical providers.[24]

Outside of the United States, the environment for LGBTQ+ people appears even more precarious. In Kenya, for example, the murder of non-binary, Queer people like Sheila Lumumba is sparking new discussions about the discrimination that LGBTQ+ people routinely face in the country.[25] In Russia, the largest LGBTQ+ organization has been dissolved,[26] and activists are still being targeted under the country's "gay propaganda" law preventing anyone from publicizing or publicly commenting on "non-traditional" sexual relations.[27] Even worse, LGBTQ+ people in countries such as Saudi Arabia, Yemen, and Iran face an almost certain death sentence for same-sex activity.[28] Regardless of nationality, it seems that the majority of LGBTQ+ people in the world face significant legal, political, and humanitarian challenges to being treated as full-fledged members of their respective societies.

As a result, I believe a critical examination of LGBTQ+ culture would not only help to reduce discrimination against LGBTQ+ people, but would also help to create more positive environments for LGBTQ+ people to live, work, attend school, pursue leisure or recreational activities, and exist like any other liberated group in

---

Center for American Progress. Retrieved from https://www.Americanprogress.org/issues/lgbt/news/2017/05/02/429529/widespread-discrimination-continues-shape-lgbt-peoples-lives-subtle-significant-ways/

[23] Singh & Durso, 2017.

[24] Singh & Durso, 2017.

[25] Ogola, BBC, 2022.

[26] Bellamy-Walker, NBC News, 2022.

[27] "Russia: Court Rules," 2016.

[28] Weinthal, Jerusalem Post, 2021.

the world. Positive regard for LGBTQ+ people could support and embellish diversity efforts that are now taking place in commerce, which shows that diversity benefits business.[29] In turn, I believe diversity efforts that humanize LGBTQ+ people would benefit U.S. society—and, I would argue, the world as a whole—by increasing innovation, sponsoring critical thinking, promoting adaptability, teaching global-mindedness, and inciting new forms of leadership.[30] Such is the promise of Queer leadership. Yet, as long as the culture of LGBTQ+ people is minimized, dismissed, and under-studied, the lives of LGBTQ+ people (and the community as a whole) will remain undervalued on a global scale.

In reviewing the social ethos with respect to LGBTQ+ rights, a reasonable question emerges: Why do various constituencies across the world feel so threatened by the advancement of LGBTQ+ rights? The short answer is that LGBTQ+ culture represents a threat to the existing cherished norms around sexuality and gender,[31] and negative attitudes towards "gay" sex and gender roles have existed as far back as ancient Greece.[32] In other words, anti-gay, anti-LGBTQ+, and anti-transgender attitudes are not new. Yet, in the North American context, LGBTQ+ people appear to represent some visceral threat.[33] George Weinberg, the psychologist who coined the term homophobia, believed that society saw gayness/Queerness as

[29] Hunt, V., Yee, L., Prince, S., & Dixon-Fyle, S. (2018). *Delivery through diversity.* New York, NY: McKinsey & Co.

[30] Hewlett, S. A., Marshall, M., & Sherbin, L. (2013, December). How diversity can drive innovation. *Harvard Business Review.* Retrieved from https://hbr.org/2013/12/how-diversity-can-drive-innovation

[31] Herek, G. M. (1984). Beyond "Homophobia": A social psychological perspective on attitudes towards Lesbians and Gay men. *Journal of Homosexuality, 10*(10), 1–21. doi:10.1300/J082v10n01_01

[32] Fone, B. (2000). *Homophobia: A history.* New York, NY: St. Martin's Press.

[33] Herek, G. M. (2004). Beyond "Homophobia": Thinking about sexual prejudice and stigma in the twenty-first century. *Sexuality Research & Public Policy, 1*(2), 6–24.

a menace rather than as an intriguing community worthy of study. As a result, it is perhaps understandable that society has not really heralded the Queer cultural experience in any sustained way other than to say that it is distinct or somehow different. LGBTQ+ people are still underrepresented in the media, government, politics, and arts and entertainment, and even today, 70+ countries around the world deem LGBTQ+ relationships illegal and ripe for persecution.[34]

These circumstances raise the following questions:

How do LGBTQ+ people overcome daily microaggressions where people are suggesting that trans people are living in an imaginary world or that bisexual people are confused?

How can lesbian women and gay men be seen "soul-fully" when they are still referred to in clinical and "othering" terms as homosexuals?

How do LGBTQ+ people deal with social stigma, comedians tripping over themselves to poke fun at the community, or stereotypes where every LGBTQ+ person is presumed to be cisgender, white, or male?

The question for me or for anyone when they hear these statistics or observe these dynamics should be: how is this community able to survive despite such daunting circumstances? What has allowed this community to persevere with little to no mainstream social support throughout history? How has this community been able to thrive with threadbare resources among an unrelenting wave of hostility?

The answer is quite simple: no group could survive what the LGBTQ+ community has gone through unless it possessed some level of intrinsic transformational leadership acumen. The LGBTQ+ community has a special mojo or leadership quality, by virtue of its cultural journey, that allows it to demonstrate exceptional

---

[34] Fenton, S. (2017, December 6). The 74 countries where it's illegal to be gay. *The Independent*. Retrieved from http://www.independent.co.uk/news/world/gay-lesbian-bisexual-relationships-illegal-in-74-countries-a7033666.html

leadership. In other words, the LGBTQ+ community has a cultural genius™ that if studied, could help the world to deal with its most vexing issues and create a society that is more self-actualized, more harmonious, and more healthy than what we see now.

Therefore and appropriately, it is important to frame LGBTQ+ culture properly, given that it is growing as a cultural force and an identifiable community across the globe.[35] At the time of publication, one in five members of Generation Z (those born between 1999 and 2003) identify as LGBTQ+, with the number expected to rise in succeeding generations.[36] Therefore, regardless of whether LGBTQ+ people are being celebrated or disenfranchised, the health and status of the community has emerged as a preeminent global issue.[37] In order to portray the community in a more even-handed way, honor the changing cultural face of the world, and avail ourselves of a timely leadership prescription, the LGBTQ+ community and its culture merit study and understanding.

---

[35] Human Rights Campaign. (2015, December 10). 2015: A year in review of LGBTQ equality worldwide. Retrieved from https://www.hrc.org/blog/2015-a-year-in-review-of-lgbt-equality-worldwide

[36] Doherty, E. (2022). *The number of LGBTQ-identifying adults is soaring.* Retrieved from Axios: https://www.axios.com/2022/02/17/lgbtq-generation-z-gallup

[37] Lavers, M. K. (2016, December 29). Top 10 international stories of 2016. *The Washington Blade.* Retrieved from http://www.washingtonblade.com/2016/12/29/top-10-international-stories-2016/

CHAPTER 3

Understanding Culture and the Beauty of LGBTQ+ "Cultural Genius™"

If you were to ask 100 leaders where they learned how to be a great leader, I imagine you would get a number of responses, most of which might point to some business school as the source for great leadership advice. Unfortunately, what many of us fail to realize is that oftentimes, our leadership ideology is developed way before any of us think to enter an MBA program or conference room, should those options even be appealing or available to us. More to the point, leadership competency can and is developed in family systems, geographic neighborhoods, and social communities. Yet, what is often under-recognized is the instructive value that our cultural pathways provide us in becoming better leaders. Particularly if you come from a minoritized[38] community, one's cultural pathway can instill a number of values and practices that can help any individual navigate a complex environment beset by leadership challenges. What this demonstrates is that leadership wisdom need not come from "on high." It exists in the fierce spaces where LGBTQ+ people exist and attend to their own liberation every single day.

Nonetheless, understanding the essence of culture and what it has to teach us can still feel confusing if we have never been taught explicitly about the concept of culture, or if we have never been taught the value of our *own* culture. And frankly, despite what may be said about the LGBTQ+ community from external forces, nowhere is the need to define culture more important than within the group itself. If a group does not understand its own culture, or when its culture is defined negatively, the lack of understanding and social recognition may inhibit the personal growth and sociability of members within that community. To fully illuminate the impact of negative social attitudes on Queer people, Iudici and Verdecchia[39] studied the effects of stigmatization on gay cultural identification among a mixed cohort of 35 gay men and lesbian women in northern Italy. Using a qualitative methodology, the researchers interviewed the participants about their personal histories. After each participant's story was generated, several themes emerged: among them was the idea that being gay was a normal and healthy part of human life. However, Iudici and Verdecchia noted that negative labels about being gay not only had an undesirable impact on the participants' self-acceptance as gay people (internal or otherwise) but also "hindered and slowed down the achievement of [self-acceptance]."[40]

---

[38] I use the word "minoritized" to reflect the understanding that marginalization is not passive; it occurs because forces in society act to relegate certain groups to second-class citizenship status.

[39] Iudici, A. & Verdecchia, M. (2015). Homophobic Labeling in the Process of Identity Construction. *Sexuality & Culture* 19, 737–758.

[40] Iudici & Verdecchia, 2015, p. 754.

Other authors have written about minority stress, or the psychological burden that cultural groups such as the LGBTQ+ community face as a result of social stigmatization.[41,42,43,44] As such, social identification with a marginalized group or culture has real psychological implications.

As we discuss the impact of social stigmatization on minoritized cultural groups and their sense of cultural appreciation, it begs the question, "What is culture?" Culture is a set of beliefs or standards, shared by a group of people, which help the individuals to decide what is, what can be, how to feel, what to do, and how to go about doing it.[45] Culture consists of the various standards for perceiving, evaluating, believing and participating in the world phenomena around us, and those standards are interpreted in a manner acceptable to its members.[46] Culture is derived from lived experience—intentionally or organically—and is informed by the images and meanings transmitted from past generations or contemporaries, or formed by

[41] DiPlacido, J. (1998). Minority stress among lesbians, gay men, and bisexuals: A consequence of heterosexism, homophobia, and stigmatization. In G. M. Herek (Ed.), *Psychological perspectives on lesbian and gay issues, Vol. 4. Stigma and sexual orientation: Understanding prejudice against lesbians, gay men, and bisexuals.* Thousand Oaks, CA: Sage Publications Inc. doi:10.4135/9781452243818.n7

[42] Maylon, A. K. (1982). Psychotherapeutic implications of internalized homophobia in gay men. *Journal of Homosexuality, 7*(2–3), 59–69. doi:10.1300/J082v07n02_08

[43] Meyer, I. H. (1995). Minority Stress and Mental Health in Gay Men. *Journal of Health and Social Behavior, 36*(1), 38–56. doi:10.2307/2137286

[44] Williamson, I. (2000). Internalized homophobia and health issues affecting lesbians and gay men. *Health Education Research, 15*(1), 97–107. doi:10.1093/her/15.1.97

[45] Goodenough, W. H. (1981). Culture, language, and society, 2nd Ed. Menlo Park, CA: Benjamin/Cummings Pub. Co.

[46] Goodenough, W. H. (1957). Cultural Anthropology and Linguistics. *In* P. L. Garvin, ed., Report of the Seventh Annual Round Table Meeting on Linguistics and Language Study. Washington, Georgetown University Monograph Series on Languages and Linguistics No. 9.

individuals themselves.[47] Although culture has a personal dimension in terms of what people feel, believe, and notice about the world around them, culture is not entirely individual. In specific instances, human beings operate in certain cultural patterns that are representative of distinct categories of people.[48] Further, although culture is negotiated by its members, it is also refined by the relationship between different classes of people and bounded by the structural forces and material conditions that are mediated, in part, by the powers that dominate society.[49] In other words, culture is determined both by the social scripts shared among people, as well as by the historical forms of oppression that govern society. The seminal question for this book relates to the collective mental model that LGBTQ+ people have with respect to themselves and the world in which they exist.

By illuminating the cultural values of the Queer community, the exercise can benefit the LGBTQ+ population in order to be more culturally determinative and can help the community continue to take its rightful place in framing and describing its *own* culture. These changes would prove beneficial instead of having the cultural ethos framed by others who do not understand or respect LGBTQ+ culture. A West African proverb tells us, "The lion's story will never be known as long as the hunter is the one to tell it." From a cultural perspective, the power of self-determination is a form of communal power that allows us to tell our story in ways that reflect who we really are.[50] In their article, "Claiming a Homosexual Identity,"

---

[47] Schwartz, S. H. (1999). A theory of cultural values and some implications for work. *Applied Psychology: An International Review, 48*(1), 23–47.

[48] Geertz, C. (2017). *The Interpretation of cultures.* New York, NY: Basic Books, Inc.

[49] Giroux H. (1983). *Theory and resistance in education.* South Hadley MA: Bergin and Garvey.

[50] Chirkov, V. I., Ryan, R. M., Kim, Y., & Kaplan, U. (2003). Differentiating autonomy from individualism and independence: A self-determination theory perspective on internalization of cultural orientations and well-being. *Journal of Personality and Social Psychology, 84,* 97–110. doi:10.1037/0022-3514.84.1.97

Cross and Epting[51] asserted that for the gay individual, power comes from being able to privately affirm oneself and disassociate from norms that do not fit one's self-image. If taken one step further, we should recognize that the power for the LGBTQ+ community lies in its ability to extol its cultural values and underline its cultural narrative. The ability for any community to have the agency and freedom to tell its story should not be under-estimated, and this book lends itself to the ongoing dialogue to help the LGBTQ+ community be seen as more than just an amorphous and acultural social entity.

However, the process of understanding, defining, and spotlighting one's culture not only benefits members of one's cultural community but also those who are outside of the community as well. Beyond the psychological considerations, understanding the cultural values of any social group can help global citizens work more effectively together and engage each other. For example, sociologists have developed frameworks and theories for helping leaders understand cultural differences, regardless of whether it was Banks and McGee Banks (noting how culture references values, beliefs, and worldviews);[52] Geertz (describing that culture consists of inherited beliefs that help people make meaning out of life);[53] or Kroeber & Kluckhorn (showing that culture helps drive the ceaseless interactions between the community and the individual and the individual and the environment).[54] All in all, these definitions of culture gave texture to the cultural ethos that many cultures operated in and clarified the meaning produced and exchanged between members

---

[51] Cross, M., & Epting, F. (2005). Self-obliteration, self-definition, self-integration: Claiming a Homosexual identity. *Journal of Constructivist Psychology, 18*(1), 53–63. doi.10.1080/10720530590523071

[52] Banks, J., & McGee-Banks, C. (1989). Multicultural Education: Issues and Perspectives (8th ed.). London, England: Wiley.

[53] Geertz, C. (2017). *The Interpretation of cultures.* New York, NY: Basic Books, Inc.

[54] Kroeber, A. L., & Kluckhorn, C. (1952). *Culture: A critical review of concepts and definitions.* Cambridge, MA: Peabody Museum of Archaeology and Ethnology.

of various ethnic groups.[55] Put differently, in the progeny of ethnographic and intercultural studies that surfaced in the late 20th century, sociologists understood that researching, identifying, and deconstructing cultural values could not only improve intercultural understanding, but promote greater cross-cultural communication and group performance in any context.

Moreover, as researchers unearthed and unmasked cultural values—the abstract and invisible beliefs that guide people in their relationship with the world—those values could be useful in understanding a specific culture or cultural group and helping leaders to lead more effectively from a macro level. In his study of organizational culture, Edgar Schein[56] defined culture as the composite of artifacts, espoused values, and basic values.[57] Whereas the top layer or most observable aspects of culture are the "artifacts" such as dress, food, and language, the espoused values and the fundamental values are those intangible qualities or beliefs accepted and endorsed by a given community.[58] While the artifacts encapsulate meaning, the espoused values and the basic values are the very truths and principles that cultures live by, both past and present. Espoused values tend to incorporate conscious goals, strategies, and philosophies, whereas basic values speak to more existential ideas about truth, the world, and human nature. Our fundamental values reflect those deeply-embedded values that are hard to describe, even for insiders in the community, but form the very essence of the culture.[59] Although many may possess the ability to identify the individual and outward expressions (or artifacts) of LGBTQ+ culture (a conversation that once again may fall susceptible to "behavior") or be

---

[55] Hall, S., & du Gay, P. (1996). *Questions of Cultural Identity*. London: Sage Publications.

[56] Schein, E. (2017). *Organizational culture and leadership* (5th ed.). Hoboken, New Jersey: Wiley & Sons, Inc.

[57] Ibid.

[58] Ibid.

[59] Ibid.

able to relay the espoused values of the community, what is far more interesting and what has been far less conveyed are those basic values that are at the heart of LGBTQ+ culture. Further, once those values have been excavated, they have an educational and edifying component for everyone—including leaders, professionals, and global citizens—should we choose to pay attention. The question, of course, is: Are we paying attention? Do we see *their* value? And are we ready to apply those values to the world at large? As rich and as germane as LGBTQ+ values are, I certainly hope so.

Undoubtedly, the exercise of using cultural insight and cultural genius™ to further leadership development has been done before, albeit in different contexts. For example, in *Salsa, Soul, and Spirit*, Juana Bordas[60] shared how communities of color were introducing a new social covenant into the United States that would challenge the traditional values of rugged individualism and competition. As African Americans, Latinos, and Native Americans continue to increase their social prominence in America, Bordas noted that communities and organizations needed to adopt a new leadership model that reflected these new sensibilities. For example, communities of color value egalitarianism when it comes to making decisions.[61] Also, communities of color champion activism and see themselves as "protectors" of the common good.[62] Further, communities of color believe in servant leadership, where leaders embody humility and togetherness to lead their communities forward.[63] As Bordas highlighted the cultural distinctions among sectors of the American population, she signaled that organizations would have to transform their organizational models in order to stay relevant in the 21st century. More importantly, Bordas illuminated the cultural values of

---

[60] Bordas, J. (2012). *Salsa, soul, & spirit: Leadership for a multicultural age*. San Francisco, CA: Berrett-Koehler.

[61] Bordas, J. (2012). *Salsa, Soul, & Spirit: Leadership for a Multicultural Age*. San Francisco, CA: Berrett-Koehler.

[62] Ibid.

[63] Ibid.

various ethnic groups and made the argument that those values are critical to operating in the global marketplace.

Therefore, the importance of studying various cultural groups lies not just in learning who they are and what they stand for, but in learning new skills in order to lead our communities and organizations, *especially if our communities and institutions are now being led, supported, and driven by members of those particular groups.* And… ironically, Queer wisdom is informed by people from every other cultural group, including BIPOC communities, Women, Immigrants, People with Disbilities, Spiritualists and Religious Devotees, and people from different generational cohorts, but LGBTQ+ cultural genius™ adds the <u>additional perspective</u> of sexual minorities and gender non-conforming people. Queer leadership draws from the community well and it would behoove us to drink from that fountain of wisdom. The only difference between the LGBTQ+ community and those communities that have been given the platform to teach, inspire, and model new leadership is time, intention, and opportunity. Whereas fields such as sociology and anthropology are replete with ethnographic studies that focus on nation-states and racial/ethnic minorities, the academic literature, by comparison, is lacking when it comes to LGBTQ+ cultural values. This fact not only underscores the opportunity to illuminate LGBTQ+ culture, but also to accord it the cultural visibility and mainstream respect that has been given to other social groups. And now that we understand what culture is, what culture imparts, and why culture is important, we can use cultural genius™ and human capital to reimagine how we live, work, and engage with each other. Understanding culture and the cultural imprint of the LGBTQ+ community is integral for organizations to stay relevant to gender and sexual minorities. Yet, recognizing the genius of Queer culture is necessary for <u>any</u> enterprise to maintain its vitality, become a heart-centered institution, and remain as an employer of choice.

CHAPTER 4

How LGBTQ+ Culture Is a Study in Transformational Leadership

Based on the leadership opportunities that abound, the ubiquity of LGBTQ+ culture across the world, and the instructive value that the culture has, the purpose of this book is to help facilitate a greater and deeper understanding of LGBTQ+ culture and spawn new thinking about transformational leadership. In order to achieve the foregoing, this book necessarily aims to build upon existing research (which has focused primarily on gay identity formation, gay male coping strategies, and gay sexuality) in order to foster a greater understanding and appreciation of LGBTQ+ culture.

Consequently, a greater appreciation of Queer culture could reduce discrimination against LGBTQ+ people since a lack of cultural understanding about the cultural values of another group can lead to intercultural bias.[64] By some measures in the United States,

---

[64] Fiske, S. T. (2002). What we know about bias and intergroup conflict, the problem of the century. *Current Directions in Psychological Science, 11*(4), 123–128. doi:10.1111/1467-8721.00183

queerness and LGBTQ+ rights are steadily becoming more accepted. For example, according to Gallup, acceptance of same-sex relationships is at an all-time high at 70%.[65] However, there are still significant gaps in providing the Queer community full protection under the law. As an example, the U.S. federal government provides legal protections for LGBTQ+ people in matters related to employment, but those protections do not extend to housing, medical care, public accommodations, education, federally-funded programs, credit, or jury service.[66] Moreover, leaders and activists should not be fooled into thinking that Americans respect *all* subgroups within the larger LGBTQ+ community (particularly transgender or non-binary people), understand LGBTQ+ cultural values, or could fully and correctly identify LGBTQ+ cultural values if given the opportunity. Acceptance of a cultural group does not equate with understanding their cultural sensibilities, and a more robust and honest accounting of LGBTQ+ culture could transform how society looks at LGBTQ+ people, and in turn, how society treats the population.

If we want to transform the world, the opportunity rests in changing not only how we regard LGBTQ+ people, but how we lead, support, and nurture all people at every position and at all levels within society. Fortunately for us, LGBTQ+ leadership is available to us in this critical moment, and who could better understand this world—its frailties or complexities, its imperfections and its deepest yearnings—than those who operate at the edge of society? From its struggle and sacrifice, the LGBTQ+ community presents to society a precious love offering: wisdom from the margins and beauty from the shadowy places within.

---

[65] McCarthy, J. (2021, June 8). Record-high 70% in U.S. Support Same-Sex Marriage. *Gallup*. Retrieved from https://news.gallup.com/poll/350486/record-high-support-same-sex-marriage.aspx

[66] Newport, F. (2021, March 29). American Public Opinion and the Equality Act. *Gallup*. Retrieved from https://news.gallup.com/opinion/polling-matters/340349/american-public-opinion-equality-act.aspx

As it stands, the world related to transformational leadership appears to be vague and tepid. A transformational leader is a person who recognizes their power and wields their power in an adaptive way to inspire and liberate others. Today's professionals and leaders want to be "transformational," but they don't know exactly what that means, or how to be transformational, or from where to get their guidance. Leaders are tired of lectures and articles that skim the surface on leadership development but fail to deliver any real examples or practical solutions. More importantly, leaders are overwhelmed because with all of the competing demands in the day, they seldom have time to think about transformational leadership when their first goal is to survive in a daily "work grind" that chews people up and spits them out indiscriminately. Ironically, global leaders socialize, live, and work among LGBTQ+ people every day (and many are part of the LGBTQ+ community) and never realized that the answers to their leadership dilemmas exist right before them: within the LGBTQ+ community, a socially visible but largely misunderstood community that presumably inhabits almost every corner of the world. Much like the Queer-oriented, Indigenous "Two Spirit" people who have served as spiritual advisors in many First Nation communities across North America, LGBTQ+ people can serve as humanistic guides for the world and usher in a new era of leadership.

The issues that LGBTQ+ people face are a microcosm of the issues that leaders face daily, and the impact and influence of LGBTQ+ people extends globally. Therefore, the intent of this book is two-fold: 1) to show who LGBTQ+ people are to the world, and 2) to show why LGBTQ+ values and lived experiences should be instructive for leaders and organizations everywhere. If leaders study and learn from the LGBTQ+ cultural example, they will become "F.I.R.E.starters"[67]—people who create an energetic "blaze" that

---

[67] F.I.R.E = Fearless or Fabulous, Inclusive or Insightful, Resourceful or Resilient, Empathetic or Equity-Minded.

can light up the world—and exhibit a model of leadership that can jumpstart their own journey to greater self-realization and create environments where people leverage their talents on behalf of the greater good.

Although LGBTQ+ people are the protagonists or subject matter experts in this leadership development book, that does not mean that the lessons the community shares (metaphorically speaking) are any less significant or that the collective wisdom demonstrated is any less credible. In other words, LGBTQ+ positionality within the social hierarchy should not give this conversation less sway. In fact, given the marginalization and disenfranchisement that LGBTQ+ people continue to face (particularly transgender youth and transgender women of color), the leadership lessons imparted within bear more substance and carry even more authority. The LGBTQ+ leadership principles apportioned herein have saved people from discrimination, bias, trauma, social alienation, serious injury, and yes... death. These leadership principles may have been invoked by your friends, neighbors, loved ones, or even yourself. If the principles articulated in the pages of this book can protect LGBTQ+ people— who are mired in animus and repression worldwide—in some small measure, then they can certainly help you be a better mentor, manage a project, make better decisions, or communicate with your peers more effectively. Learning from the LGBTQ+ community is not a risk if you value your community, career, or enterprise. And based on the miraculous things our community has done and the high-minded goals I'm sure you want to achieve, you (and we) can't really afford to not heed the cultural wisdom and leadership advice of LGBTQ+ people.

If we don't take advantage of the opportunity to rethink stewardship and our role within it, leadership and leadership transformation will continue to flounder as we struggle to overcome the problems of the 21st century. Our workplaces will lack connection, empathy, and innovation and our communities will continue to be polarized. Leaders will become more disillusioned and transformational leadership will continue to exist as a buzzword instead of as a generative word that inspires feeling, reflection, and tangible action. This manuscript is like a recipebook for preparing a great meal. And who doesn't want to eat something delicious, healthy, and filling? The star chefs are the members of the Queer community, and everyone can eat heartily if they follow the prescriptions offered inside. If leaders study the LGBTQ+ community and learn from its wisdom, they can obtain practical, time-tested, and thoughtful strategies that have been forged by the community since time immemorial. To possess greater global wisdom, you don't have to be Queer, just Queer-minded: open to new possibilities and poised to begin an adventure of growth and exploration. Leaders will benefit from the gritty and resilient social acumen that LGBTQ+ people have developed at the margins of society to support their own survival and livelihood. They will be able to transform themselves, their families, their communities, their organizations, and in turn, the globe. They will not only realize their potential, but remember their gifts, talents, and purpose for the world. They will find new ways of thinking, *being*, acting, and engaging that will move us from our collective social malaise to a place of greater connectivity, harmony, and balance. They can become the leaders we have always needed and the leaders our world has called for. Let's examine the source for what the transformational journey will look like.

THE SOULS
OF QUEER FOLK:
IDENTIFYING LGBTQ+
CULTURAL VALUES

CHAPTER 5

The Research

In his poem "Impasse," Queer author Langston Hughes described how many marginalized communities may feel in sharing their cultural narrative with those of the privileged majority:

"I could tell you
If I wanted to
What makes me
What I am.

But I don't
Really want to—
And you don't
Give a damn."[68]

---

[68] Hughes, L. (1967). *The panther & the lash (Vintage classics)*. New York, NY: Vintage Books.

And...who can blame any minoritized person for feeling this way? Although LGBTQ+ people enjoy greater social visibility and freedom in today's society than at any other time in history, the community still suffers from a perception problem as to what the LGBTQ+ community values and represents beyond the stereotypes perpetuated in society.[69] Even in today's day and age, it seems fair to ask the question: Do people within and outside the community know or understand what LGBTQ+ culture means? And even if LGBTQ+ people and their allies understand what the culture signifies from a values perspective, it seems important at this time—given the increased focus on Queer liberation—to create a clear picture and coherent narrative of what LGBTQ+ culture encapsulates. We must remember one truism:

> We are one community but many people.

Beyond the superficial descriptions that focus on same-sex sexual attraction and gender non-conformity, the community still suffers from relative cultural obscurity. Accordingly, a more focused discussion on LGBTQ+ cultural values could help laypeople and academicians alike uncover the souls of Queer folk and truly understand how Queer people navigate the world.

From a reductionist standpoint, LGBTQ+ culture is reduced in mainstream circles to only being viewed as gay male culture and from an elementary standpoint, gayness is equated with same-sex desire. If you identify as LGBTQ+, your culture is presumed to begin with romantic attraction to a member of the same sex and end with "breaking" traditional gender norms. However, just like dark skin by itself does not tell the story of African American culture, same-sex attraction (or gender non-conformity) does not tell the full cultural story of being LGBTQ+. Instead, same-sex attraction has become the centerpiece for a set of socially constructed cultural values, beliefs, and

---

[69] Halperin, D. (2014). *How to be Gay*. Boston, MA: Belknap Press.

sensibilities that, in their totality, are said or thought of as constituting Queerness. This constructivist and incomplete view of Queerness and the LGBTQ+ experience is what I explore more throughout this book.

As a result, the theoretical starting place for the ethnographic research began by asking: What are the fundamental cultural values of the LGBTQ+ community? Some critics would suggest that any attempt to study LGBTQ+ cultural values creates the risk that all LGBTQ+ people will be typecast in some broad or unflattering way. In some of my research presentations, I certainly heard those concerns articulated by supportive but cautious members of the community. It is important to remember that culture is, as sociologist Helen Spencer-Otay[70] calls it, a "fuzzy" concept. Culture is negotiated at both the individual and collective level, and while cultural groups may have some values in common, they are unlikely to share completely identical sets of attitudes and beliefs. More correctly, members of cultural groups like the LGBTQ+ community are likely to share "family resemblances" (Spencer-Otay, 2012) that create familiarity and likeness but are nonetheless differentiated by personal identity.[71] As such, members of the Queer community share similarities in terms of behaviors, norms, and beliefs.

Some would also argue that the intersectionality within the community makes the idea of LGBTQ+ culture less coherent. As an example, the idea that a Queer Latina and a cisgender, white gay male share a common cultural heritage might be laughable to some given the different components of their cultural identity. Yet, the same argument could be made of any cultural group. I identify as American (for my friends in Central and South America, "Usonian")[72] and even though I am sometimes reluctant to admit it,

---

[70] Spencer-Otay, H. (2012) What is culture? A compilation of quotations. *GlobalPAD Core Concepts.*

[71] Ibid.

[72] Usonian is a term to refer to people who are citizens of or native to the U.S. In the Western Hemisphere (specifically Central America and South America),

there are distinct characteristics and beliefs that I share with other Americans who live in vastly different regions than I do. While one can never suggest that there is an absolute set of features that can definitively distinguish *any* group from another, culture matters and shared cultural norms exist despite our claims to suggest otherwise. The LGBTQ+ community is no different from any other cultural group whose members belong to different cultural groups within the larger human mosaic and whose values and norms also influence our cultural composition. Nonetheless, the diversity among LGBTQ+ people should not dissuade us from regarding the LGBTQ+ community as a distinct and discernible cultural group. As has been done with cultural groups worldwide, I think it is important to recognize the themes and values that make Queer people recognizable and draw LGBTQ+ people together.

Similar to the Latino-identity model developed by Ferdman and Gallegos,[73] I recognized that Queerness and one's affiliation to LGBTQ+ culture would have different degrees and levels of intensity and subscription depending on the person. Admittedly, I was most interested in unmasking how those with the greatest level of identity-affiliation and cultural subscription saw and understood LGBTQ+ values. By initially focusing on gay leaders and self-identified LGBTQ+ people, I hoped to identify a more robust and detailed understanding of how Queer people understand LGBTQ+ culture than what is typically described in the literature.

The cultural questions I posed are not unique or exclusive in their source. Some may argue that LGBTQ+ culture has already

---

many people outside of the U.S. refer to themselves as Americans and resent the term "American" being used exclusively to refer to people who reside in the United States.

[73] Ferdman, B. M. & Gallegos, P. I. (2001). Racial identity development and Latinos in the United States. In C. L. Wijeyesinghe, B. W. Jackson, III (Eds.), *New perspectives on racial identity development: A theoretical and practical anthology.* New York, NY: New York University Press.

been adroitly defined and that LGBTQ+ experiences, imagery, and sex are in fact, definitive and sufficient elements to describe the culture. Yet, understanding culture requires us to be more probative. First, the experiences of LGBTQ+ people (such as attending Gay Pride) do not explicitly or intelligently state values. For example, one can be proud of group identification without being clear about what membership in that group entails. Second, with respect to LGBTQ+ imagery, given that LGBTQ+ people are still socio-political minorities, I would argue that much of the imagery is so abstract that it needs to be translated in a culturally portable way so that it can be useful for Queer people to navigate the world consciously. Third, although the idea of sexual liberation is a key value, I sincerely doubt that it is the *only* value or even the most prominent value for a majority of LGBTQ+ people. Unfortunately, the cultural underpinnings of LGBTQ+ ethos (apart from sex) seem to be assumed and expediently agreed upon without careful analysis of the underlying ideas or precepts. Strangely, this question has not been examined thoroughly as cisgender heterosexuals (and some LGBTQ+ people) have been content to assign an identity based on unquestioned concepts around normativity instead of looking more closely at cultural values. Fortunately, now is the time to start seeking more definitive and nuanced answers for a community that exists in every part of the world and without whom the world as we know it would not exist.

As a result, I conducted a study to illuminate the community's cultural values. I performed a mixed methods study using quantitative and qualitative research methods to understand a research problem.

In the qualitative survey, I posed the research question: According to lesbian, gay, bisexual, transgender, and queer leaders and allies in the San Francisco Bay Area, what are the fundamental cultural values of the Queer community? My hope was that the study could begin to generate a clearer understanding of LGBTQ+ values and lay the foundation for greater inclusion of and equity towards LGBTQ+ people in larger society. Qualitative studies are useful when trying to understand culture or how specific communities make sense of the world. They draw upon the experiences of certain constituencies by using immersion, interviews, and observation to record the community members' feelings, ideas, and impressions.[74]

The subjects in the qualitative study were split into two categories: 1) self-identified Queer people in the San Francisco Bay Area who were working on LGBTQ+ socio-political initiatives or working for Queer organizations and 2) allies of Queer people who by virtue of their jobs or activism, regularly interacted with and/or navigated the LGBTQ+ community. The participants discussed the basic cultural values in the community in order to generate a rich and thoughtful dialogue about the contours of Queer culture. The cohort of participants was considerably diverse, with the interviewees ranging from ages 18 to 81. Further, the respondents were diverse based on religion, political affiliation, and ethnicity, with nearly 60% of the participants identifying as people of color and nearly 20% of the participants having been raised outside of the United States.

I focused my study on Queer leaders and their allies, since those populations would have a critical vantage point in navigating, observing, and interacting with LGBTQ+ people and Queer culture. A designated leader needed to show an active commitment to a public Queer cause, organization, social group, or community initiative; their title or level of prestige was irrelevant. An ally was considered any non-LGBTQ+ person who either worked for an LGBTQ+ organization or had volunteered for an LGBTQ+ initiative in the past two years. By interviewing allies of the Queer community who were non-LGBTQ+ identified, the ethnographic picture of Queer leaders in the Bay Area was enhanced and more expansive. In addition,

---

[74] Merriam, S. B., & Tisdell, E. J. (2016). *Qualitative Research: A Guide to Design and Implementation* (4th ed.). San Francisco, CA: Jossey-Bass.

with a cultural study that blends the views of both members and non-members, the cultural portrait of Queer communal values was strengthened considerably. In all, we gleaned that 15 cultural values are important to the community of Queer people from the first part of the study.

We then created a quantitative survey using a specific quote from the qualitative research that spoke to each of those 15 values. Through social media, an online survey asked members of the LGBTQ+ community to determine how strongly they identified with each of the value statements using a five-part Likert scale.[75] Respondents were asked to determine if they strongly agreed, agreed, were neutral, disagreed, or strongly disagreed with the statements provided in the quantitative survey.

The sample for the quantitative portion of the mixed methods study was much larger and more diverse, with 574 participants identifying as lesbian (20%), gay (46%), bisexual (13%), transgender (27%), and intersex (.52%). Unlike in the qualitative research, a greater percentage of respondents were not "out" or were not "out" to a large number of people (20%). The respondents were dispersed nationally[76] and displayed the wide range of socio-economic, racial, religious, and ethnic diversity that we saw in the qualitative study. For example, nearly 30% of the respondents were racial and ethnic minorities, and 70% of the respondents came from income brackets

---

[75] A Likert scale is a survey instrument which measures attitudes and opinions towards a question or a statement. Named after its inventor, psychologist Rensis Likert, the Likert scale asks individuals to respond to a collective set of responses by indicating whether they strongly agree (SA), agree (A), are neutral (N), disagree (DA), or strongly disagree (DA).

[76] The respondents lived in all parts of the country, with the highest percentages coming from the U.S. South (31.1%) and Midwest (26.1%), and a substantial percentage of participants residing in the Northeast (23.8%) and the Western region of the U.S. (17.0%).

that could be deemed working or middle class.[77,78] In terms of spirituality, the respondents were split nearly evenly between those who subscribed to an organized religion and those who were atheist, agnostic, or unaffiliated with any religion.[79]

In the end, more than half of the respondents in the quantitative survey agreed with each cultural value statement we pulled from the qualitative study. Based on that research, we concluded that the values identified were culturally significant for a majority of the Queer population and that those identified values were indeed cultural values for the LGBTQ+ community.

---

[77] Fifty percent of the respondents indicated that their income bracket was $50k or less, 17.7% indicated their income was between $50k–75k, and 12.2% stated their income was between $75k–100k.

[78] Although one's income bracket is important in determining one's level of financial security, "income bracket" should be distinguished from one's income class, which factors in educational attainment and future earnings.

[79] In terms of spirituality or religiosity, the participants in the quantitative study identified as Christian (30.8%), Jewish (5.5%), Mulim (5.0%), Buddhist (2.6%), other (10.8%), atheist/agnostic (21%), and spiritually unaffiliated (24.0%).

CHAPTER 6

LGBTQ+ Cultural Values

As stated previously, the research study on Queer values had two main components. In the first phase of the research, I interviewed leaders in the LGBTQ+ community to glean what they perceived to be LGBTQ+ cultural values. In the second part of the research, I created a survey to determine if a nationally-representative sample of the Queer community agreed that those identified values were central to how they lived as LGBTQ+ people. For each of the values recognized in the qualitative study, a majority of respondents in the quantitative study concurred that those values resonated with them as members of the LGBTQ+ community. Overall, 15 themes emerged:

- Equity
- Diversity/Inclusion
- Community
- Creativity
- Pride
- Self-realization
- Sex positivity
- Gender fluidity
- Nonconformity
- Agency
- Perceptiveness
- Freedom
- Nurture/care
- Resilience
- Zest

In the course of the research, it became apparent that each was a cultural value that resonated with the LGBTQ+ community and had universal application. This chapter outlines each of these values in greater detail and with greater context.

EQUITY

As a concept, equity pinpoints a concern for fairness and justice and speaks to the need to dismantle systems of hierarchy, privilege, and oppression. Given that it is still an oppressed and persecuted group, the LGBTQ+ community cannot afford to take civil or human rights for granted or treat them as negligible issues. Equity is critically important to LGBTQ+ people because of the social and political struggles they have endured. One historian and curator elaborated on the LGBTQ+ political consciousness that informs how LGBTQ+ people respond to inequity and injustice:

> Occupying the liminal, marginal position has influenced me in the most difficult ways possible. I think it's kind of hard to occupy those spaces without getting a sense of the world at large as a predominantly hostile place where one's right to simply exist is constantly being challenged. It has affected my worldview, for sure. I think I don't take for granted any of the achievements

of the gay community and the direction of inclusivity and of de-stigmatization in our culture. I kind of tend to see, especially within the current landscape and our political system, you know, a constant threat that we need to be very vigilant about.[80]

As alluded to by the historian, many of the freedoms that LGBTQ+ people now enjoy have resulted from hard-fought victories, which have caused LGBTQ+ people to remain in a constant state of vigilance. Further, those same freedoms are now being threatened and have led many in the community to recommit to social consciousness and activism. In turn, that renewed vigilance has spawned political engagement and a deeper commitment to the cultural value of equity.

As a result, the pursuit of equity has led many in the community to actively campaign for social change. As one prominent political activist noted, the "activist spirit" seems to be so ingrained in the LGBTQ+ community that "most of our communication has been built up [from] being active and vocal around our experiences to protect ourselves from having negative experiences."[81,82] LGBTQ+ people have an irrepressible nature that lends itself to deconstructing patriarchy, challenging racism, and unbraiding the interlocking systems of oppression that surround us all.

As a new generation contends with systemic and societal discrimination in the modern era, we must remember that social advocacy, demonstration, and social justice are part of the LGBTQ+ cultural "calling card." The cultural values of equity should continue to stir a deep awareness of the community's history and predecessors and the venerable tradition of activism in the LGBTQ+ community.

---

[80] J. Davis Brown, personal communication, December 9, 2017.

[81] J. Davis Brown, personal communications, 2017–2018.

[82] The quotes are taken from ethnographic research of the LGBTQ+ community conducted from October 2017 to February 2018. Due to stipulations by the Research Ethics Board, the sources of the quotes are anonymous.

The need for LGBTQ+ people to foster equity in the larger society has created a cultural value that is fervent, enduring, and abiding. That cultural value of equity has led to a greater awareness of equity and greater appreciation of social consciousness and activism.

DIVERSITY AND INCLUSION

In acknowledging how being LGBTQ+ has made them aware of their differences and distinct worldviews, many LGBTQ+ people concurrently express an appreciation of diversity and inclusion on a global scale. Diversity refers to heterogeneity or the representation of different people, groups, or perspectives within a larger sample.[83] The notion of diversity speaks to the idea of difference, whether demographic or philosophical, and LGBTQ+ leaders note how recognizing their own identity has made them more appreciative of the diversity within the community and given them a desire to experience a more culturally diverse spectrum of society. As one educator shared, "[Being] LGBTQ+ has made me more accepting about those that are different than me because I am different than those around me."

While so many archetypes illustrate the diversity within the LGBTQ+ community, there is a recognizable need to engage specific subcultures that have operated at the margins of the Queer community. For example, some leaders in the study talked about their work in supporting racial equity, while others spoke about the need to raise more awareness around other LGBTQ+ marginalized communities like the transgender community. In their work and stewardship, LGBTQ+ leaders and allies recognize the importance of diversity in the LGBTQ+ community. Further, they are seeking

---

[83] Brown, J. (2016). How to Be An Inclusive Leader: Your Role In Creating Cultures of Belonging Where Everyone Can Thrive. Advantage: Charleston, South Carolina.

to build relationships with groups that were marginalized or different from their own identity.

While some leaders exalted the value of diversity within the community, others spoke to the importance of inclusivity among LGBTQ+ people. Inclusion is the process of creating belonging for groups within a community.[84] A number of leaders talked about their efforts to welcome others or the steps that were taken to make them feel included in the community. Whether immersed in social groups, spiritual gatherings, or recreational activities, many leaders spoke explicitly about their efforts to create a "container" for people to be themselves, especially for those who come from sub-pockets of the LGBTQ+ community. As one community member mentioned who works as an advocate for LGBTQ+ seniors, "I've never fit in… So when you meet someone that's vastly different from the societal norm, you [try to] be supportive of them."

That is not to say that the community is perfect in its attempts to build inclusion. For far too many, the welcoming attitude of the community belies an enduring perception that the LGBTQ+ community has become synonymous with being a cisgender white male. Yet, despite these challenges, there was widespread agreement in the study that the community still strives to be welcoming to all people, despite its imperfections with respect to inclusion. In fact, one LGBTQ+ youth counselor reiterated that while the community sometimes falls short in this respect, at its core, it strives to make space for different people. Although the LGBTQ+ community does not have a perfect record with respect to diversity and inclusion, those cultural values appear to be as important as ever. Through its messaging and iconography in symbols like the Pride Flag, the LGBTQ+ community "sees itself, or wants to imagine itself as accepting of cultural diversity." As one minister noted: "There is an intuitive sense that having different 'flavors' around you is good:

---

[84] *Id.*

It's good for life, it's good for society, it's good for fun, and it's good for experiencing new things." Diversity and inclusion are important values for the community as a whole.

COMMUNITY

Sharing an identity has created an instant bond and sense of community among LGBTQ+ people, and the value of community is held in great reverence by Queer people, whether by a) maintaining connections with friends or loved ones, or b) fostering community and expanding one's circle of confidants and associates. In order to sustain community, literally and figuratively, LGBTQ+ participants in the study stressed the importance of developing strong interpersonal connections, which meant going beyond the pale of social conventions and social graces. As one community leader offered, "I find that [the LGBTQ+ community] is a community that tends to take care of one another, advocate for one another to the best of their capacities, and demonstrate allyship for one another."

While some described the sense of community among LGBTQ+ people in terms of allyship, others expressed their connection to LGBTQ+ people in more esoteric terms. As one interviewee shared, being in the community makes one feel like less of an individual and more like a small part of something bigger. Other interviewees expressed a connection that almost seemed boundless and spiritual as they talked about the idea of shared stories and shared experiences. According to those interviewed, when meeting another LGBTQ+ person, there's a feeling that here too is somebody on the same path with similar struggles and similar goals of self-realization and self-emancipation. As one person shared, "Although we are all different, there's an unshakable feeling that we are still strongly connected."

As a result, the sense of connection in the LGBTQ+ community can feel very much like family. Given that some LGBTQ+ people are estranged from their biological families, many LGBTQ+ leaders expressed a strong desire to forge communities in the absence of those family system structures that heterosexual or cisgender people take for granted. Without the support of their biological family, LGBTQ+ people may cultivate a "chosen family" where there is strong loyalty and undying support that reflects a deep sense of community.

In order to maintain connection and a sense of family, there are multiple ways in which community can be fostered, whether through a) empathy, b) vulnerability, c) being welcoming, d) being playful, or e) engaging in community service. In maintaining that "heart connection," many participants spoke about the importance of emotional transparency. When there is vulnerability, ease, and openness with others, it helps to spark closeness, intimacy, and friendship and makes it easy to relax and connect with people. For other interviewees, creating community meant being welcoming or showcasing a friendly demeanor to others. Other study participants fostered community by being playful and using humor in social interactions to help build connections and forge new relationships. Still, other study participants made connections and developed kinship by assisting others or engaging in community service. As one millennial leader explained: "As I was coming out, I definitely felt more invested in my community and invested in expanding my network and relationships. What this meant was… [acting] in service of the community."

As a result of these social norms, LGBTQ+ people shared how they could be open with others "without the fear of being judged," a nod to how vulnerability fostered community among Queer people. With an inviting sense of rapport and a willingness to acknowledge the humanity of people in their respective circles, LGBTQ+ people have managed to create a sense of community that contributes mightily to the cultural fabric of the Queer community. By fostering connection, showing empathy and vulnerability, showcasing welcoming behavior, exhibiting playfulness, and participating in community service, the idea of *community* is central to the experience of LGBTQ+ people.

CREATIVITY

As multiple interviewees reflected on the LGBTQ+ impact on the arts, *creativity* also surfaced as a salient LGBTQ+ cultural value. Through their creativity, LGBTQ+ people appear to not only have the ability to inspire others, but to establish a creative and distinctive footprint in the world that has made it colorful and unique. The creativity shepherded by LGBTQ+ people has produced a unique ecosystem whereby LGBTQ+ people have curated events that show splendor, experiences that demonstrate imagination, and neighborhoods that possess a special charm and ebullience. Further, the study participants believed that Queer people showcase creativity through an adept sense of flair, or the added stylishness, panache, or originality that LGBTQ+ people apply to everything from dress and dance to literature, film, and poetry.

Although creativity relates to artistic abilities, the study participants highlighted that creativity also speaks to the ability to innovate and engineer a new product, idea, or process. This ingenuity is how LGBTQ+ people routinely build or reshape something from scratch by rethinking purpose, functionality, and presentation. As one interviewee stated: "LGBTQ+ sensibility lends itself to new ways of thinking, not just about relationships, but how we do business, how we create, or how we get a message across." Creativity among LGBTQ+ people has led to innovative developments in fields as disparate as musicianship and medical science. Many interviewees saluted LGBTQ+ people as "innovators who are able to see beyond the trend" and be transcendent in multiple facets of human life, no matter if the field is cuisine, art, fashion, theater, or language.

Further, as several leaders noted, LGBTQ+ people have had to be creative, not only in terms of their social advancement and artistic expression, but also as a means of survival and self-preservation. By recognizing one's talents and potential, creativity has helped LGBTQ+ people challenge gender norms, create a new persona, and facilitate healing. A number of Queer leaders testified to how creativity helped them see their inner beauty.

Moreover, other interviewees discussed how creativity served as a cultural guidepost in their coming out process. As one gamer revealed, he sensed he was Queer since he had an affinity for poetry and arts that other boys did not. Other leaders explained that they recognized they were LGBTQ+ partly because of their creative inclinations and that as they became more settled into their identity, they embraced their creativity more. For some LGBTQ+ people, creativity not only gained increasing importance once they came out, but as they became fully integrated into their community. In that vein, creativity also serves as a personal innovation that helps LGBTQ+ people reclaim parts of their identity, share who they are with the world, and find agency and freedom to navigate society. Creativity has a liberating component that helps LGBTQ+ people accept who they are.

For study participants, creativity touched multiple facets of their lives and reminded them that their personal sensibilities had a distinctive artistic touch that mirrored the sensibilities of their peers. By exhibiting creativity, exploring creative endeavors, exhibiting flair, and channeling imagination and innovation, LGBTQ+ people have left an indelible impression and have proved that creativity is a fundamental cultural value.

PRIDE

Not surprisingly, *pride* materialized as one of the major themes of the study. During the study, pride was described in various ways, but primarily as the unflinching recognition of who we are. In other words, pride signifies paying tribute to one's LGBTQ+ identity.

In hearing stories from the interviewees, a consistent viewpoint emerged: the need to live openly and honestly. As one designer shared, the need for honesty becomes even more important in a society where people are posturing or constantly hiding in order to fit in. Honesty not only creates emotional safety but sets the moral example for being truthful, honest, and "real." Contrary to what some may think, pride is not always born out of an exuberant desire to celebrate one's cultural identity. At its most basic level, pride showcases the ethical choice to be forthright in who we are. When my beloved Aunt Margaret (the first family elder to support me when I told my family I was gay) asked me why I decided to come out, my simple answer was: "To tell the truth of who I am." Pride symbolizes the LGBTQ+ cultural norm of sincerity and is the pinnacle of an individual's journey to embrace who they are.

While pride has an individual dimension to it, participants in the study also appreciated the pride they saw exhibited by others. While some valued how their friends "stood tall" and inspired pride, others appreciated how public figures, such as Martina Navratilova, the tennis icon who dominated the field of women's tennis in the 1980s, resolved to be open about their sexuality. For some interviewees, showing pride and living openly as Queer was doubly important, given the level of repression that still dominates the LGBTQ+ community. In addition, seeing public and community figures talk so openly about their lives has permitted other LGBTQ+ people to be more candid about their lives and identities, paving the way for them to discover their sense of pride in being LGBTQ+.

Of course, in modern terms, pride is not just a personal sensibility, but a community event that resembles a public festival or a liberatory bonfire of epic proportions. Further, most leaders talked about the fanfare of Pride events and how wonderful it is to see people celebrating who they are in such a joyous manner. As one ally and healthcare consultant even noted, Pride has taught a lot of communities that celebrating who you are at your very core is a great thing: "I've always loved that word 'Pride' and felt jealous that LGBTQ+ [people] have coined it because it's such a good term! We ought to be proud, and pride is a good thing." Regardless of where the events take place around the world, Pride events are wonderful examples of how the cultural value of pride is honored within the LGBTQ+ community.

Despite the celebratory aspect, pride also surfaced as a way in which community members could commemorate and honor the historical struggles of the past. Similarly, some interviewees invoked pride as they talked about the sacrifice of others who came before them or as they paid tribute to the community's ancestors like Jose Sarria, a non-binary person who was the first LGBTQ+ person to run openly for public office in the United States. Paying homage to the community and its history is also a way of manifesting the cultural value of pride.

In addition to the collective nature of pride described by some leaders in the study, pride can also have a less ostentatious aspect. Sometimes, pride is shown simply by living life according to one's truth and conviction. The cultural value of pride is expressed every day by "everyday" people showing personal integrity and leading audacious lives.

For so many LGBTQ+ people, it seems that pride and personal integrity are the culmination of a long process of self-discovery, internal acceptance, and external validation. Whether exhibited as a personal affirmation, an annual observance, a fitting tribute to the past, an unbridled street fair, or a glorious party extended to every LGBTQ+ person in the world, *pride* begins with each LGBTQ+ person celebrating themselves. It is a recognizable cultural value among the LGBTQ+ community.

SELF-REALIZATION

Self-realization, or the process by which a person realizes their full potential as a human being,[85] appeared to be a preeminent theme

---

[85] Holmes, E. (2004). *This thing called you*. New York, NY: Penguin Books.

among the LGBTQ+ people interviewed for the study. Many of the leaders we talked to expressed support for the idea of self-realization in terms of healing, maintaining self-awareness, coming out, generating self-acceptance, and adopting a growth mindset.

Appreciatively, a community organizer opined that being an LGBTQ+ person "has given me the best opportunity to seek out and explore my complications." Furthermore, by beginning the long and sometimes arduous process of recognizing one's identity, multiple leaders also saw their identity formation as an opportune time for healing and restoring one's emotional and psychological health. In other words, LGBTQ+ people understand that they can't realize their full potential without taking the first important step of recognizing who they are.

Although self-awareness is a critical component in learning and accepting one's self, many LGBTQ+ leaders conceded that self-awareness is not a linear process. It can take considerable time or an elaborate "trial and error" process to clarify one's views, opinions, and feelings about oneself or the world. One of our study participants was an amateur athlete who used a trip abroad to test his boundaries and learn more about who he was. While traveling through 30 different countries on his own, he showcased various aspects of himself in different locations. When he would meet up with people he knew from time to time on his travels, it would serve as a metric to see how much he had grown and how far he had come. If he wanted to showcase his flamboyance at one hostel, he would. If he didn't want to present that way in another location, he wouldn't. In the process, he was vetting traits he wanted to be a part of his life and shedding those that no longer served him. His story illustrates the dynamic process of facilitating greater awareness and is an insightful account of self-realization.

And yet, there is no better symbolic representation of self-realization for Queer people than coming out or the process by which LGBTQ+ people self-identify as LGBTQ+ to themselves and the world. By coming out, people declare that they want to be their authentic selves to live a life of greater fulfillment, which is what self-realization is supposed to facilitate. On one hand, "coming out" sets expectations for others as to how they should regard you and understand you. On the other hand, "coming out" raises one's expectations for life and self-discovery and gives each LGBTQ+ individual the means to realize who they are. Coming out has helped LGBTQ+ people integrate all parts of their existence and manifest the part of themselves that they had only imagined previously.

As the leaders and allies shared personal stories of maturation, it was clear that they were manifesting a growth orientation or an intentional mindset towards personal development. For some, a growth mindset includes learning from past experiences and constantly testing one's limits. Not surprisingly, an LGBTQ+ teacher I spoke to talked about the importance of having provocateurs in our network to spur growth. As they believed, growth is a dynamic process in which one uses external opportunities—and perhaps personal invitations from those in our network—to try new things and evolve. Adopting a growth mindset and committing to self-mastery is another dimension of directing one's development.

All in all, self-realization, whether through healing, greater self-awareness, self-acceptance, or personal growth, is an important cultural experience for LGBTQ+ people. As a result, self-realization stands out as a critical cultural value for LGBTQ+ community members.

SEX POSITIVITY

Sex positivity describes a healthy and positive regard for sexuality and sexual expression. Even though multiple parties in the study discussed sexuality, what was notable were the leaders and allies' high regard for sex. As one LGBTQ+ leader said very plainly, in a tone reminiscent of the 1990s anthem "Let's Talk About Sex" by pioneering hip-hop group Salt-N-Pepa: "It's okay to talk about it, and it's okay to have sex. It's okay to indulge bodily desires. It's okay to explore that side of a person. That's part of being a human." Although sex positivity means different things to different people, it is important to recognize that sex positivity does not degrade or exalt sex; it simply treats sex as a normal and healthy part of the human experience.[86] In our study, LGBTQ+ leaders depicted a cultural value where the LGBTQ+ community supports the frank and positive conceptualization of sexuality.

Adopting a sex-positive attitude, however, also means letting go of sexual guilt and repression. During our interviews, a number of participants talked about the journey they undertook to reclaim joy in their sexual experience. One leader recounted how they had to remember that sex is not like cleaning a sewer: it's supposed to be fun and arousing and exhilarating. Yet, because of their upbringing, sex had initially been viewed as something that was obligatory, boring, sinister, or predictable. However, like many participants, once they reimagined sexual concepts such as sensuality, sexuality, coquetry, and homoeroticism, they were able to appreciate sexuality and sensuality in a brand-new way. Although some were quick to reiterate that sexuality was a relatively small part of their persona, they also reiterated that sexuality is a fundamental part of the human experience. As some asserted, many people enjoy sex, and the LGBTQ+ community is certainly no different than its heterosexual or cisgender counterparts in having an affinity or inclination for sex. The only difference is that many LGBTQ+ norms don't treat sex as unhealthy or taboo.

Further, LGBTQ+ leaders described sexuality and sensuality in a balanced way, combining elements such as eroticism and assertiveness with others such as gentility or vulnerability. Others also highlighted how sexuality from the LGBTQ+ perspective could avoid the gender binaries and roles that inhibit full connection with

---

[86] Johansson, Warren. (1990). Sex Negative, Sex Positive. In W. R. Dynes (Ed.)., *Encyclopedia of Homosexuality* (pp. 1182–1183). New York, NY: Garland.

another person. The transcendent quality of sex and physical attraction allows people to subvert gender binaries in order to have a more exquisite human experience.

Further, sexual positivity not only refers to one's attitudes about sexuality and sensuality, but one's ability to talk openly about sexuality, pleasure, and intimacy. In the context of dating, romance, and marriage, a number of interviewees lauded the ability of LGBTQ+ people to talk openly and honestly about their sexuality, as opposed to what they believed to be the heteronormative practice of shrouding sexuality in secrecy, shame, and negativity. In their minds, sexuality is a way to express emotion, build connection, and honor one's natural desire. Openly talking about sex helps to normalize healthy sexual behavior, healthy sexual exploration, and safe sexual discovery. Many of the leaders believed the LGBTQ+ community has helped liberate conversations around sexuality from the nests of traditional ideology and religious dogma and placed them in a forum whereby self-empowered people can normalize having intimate conversations and clear expectations about what feels right for their bodies and what feels appropriate in their amorous interactions.

As we know, sexuality manifests in a multitude of forms, and our study participants shared wide-ranging viewpoints regarding sexual acts and behavior, sexual socialization, sex and the concept of gender, and the norms around discussing and expressing sexuality. Overall, it appears that LBGTQ+ community members have a healthy attitude towards sexuality. While there is no one standard way in which the LGBTQ+ community intuits or engages in sexuality, *sex positivity* is a strong cultural value for the LGBTQ+ community.

GENDER FLUIDITY

In all of the interviews, there was no greater example of how LGBTQ+ people challenge social conventions than when it came to gender norms or *gender fluidity*. Interviewees were comfortable in rejecting rigid gender norms in terms of their presentation, sensibilities, and worldview, and what emerged from the conversations were themes of gender nonconformity, spirituality, femininity, and Queerness.

In revisiting their childhood experiences and earliest concepts of gender, a number of interviewees shared how gender fluidity or gender nonconformity gave them the freedom to be different. One leader remembered the relief he felt when he realized he could be his own person without having to follow one of the traditional male archetypes of being a jock or a nerd. Others talked about the freedom to not be seen as "delicate" or "lady-like" and to pursue hobbies and activities that fit their natural interests. Within the community, the value of gender fluidity recognizes that each person has multiple ways of expressing themselves, as opposed to the limited or restricted ways that society has imposed.

The human experience, as some would argue, derives its beauty from masculine and feminine norms, despite the body into which one was born. One Christian minister even went a step further and described gender fluidity as part of the spiritual journey that all people go through:

> I think there's a duality in regards to us as human beings, just like the Divine has a dual [identity]: a feminine and masculine energy within them. I think that we as human beings are spiritual creatures living in a human existence. We have both masculine and feminine aspects of ourselves... we all have it within us, both the masculine and feminine side.

The minister believed that balancing feminine and masculine energy was an existential proposition that LGBTQ+ people—and all people—have to mediate in order to live peacefully in this world. Instead of seeing masculinity and femininity as dual opposites, the minister saw those two dimensions as complimentary parts of a whole.

Yet, others argued that presenting gender in dualistic terms was still an antiquated way of thinking. Based on their perspectives, each of us operates along a three-dimensional spectrum that incorporates gender, gender expression, and gender identity in a way that includes more than just masculine or feminine sensibilities. In their eyes, gender operates not just in an either/or framework but beyond what we currently conceive as male or female. If one consistent theme emerged from this discussion on gender fluidity, it was the idea that current language and norms are insufficient to capture the complexity of gender. LGBTQ+ people seem particularly adept at interrogating how gender is socially constructed in order to resist the harmful patriarchal and cisgender norms in society.

At the same time, honoring gender fluidity means celebrating all aspects of gender, including the feminine, and many of the LGBTQ+ leaders discussed their open embrace of feminine energy and leadership. And while others expressed appreciation for masculine sensibilities, what nearly everyone communicated was the satisfaction they felt in not having to choose: not having to decide between two supposed ends of the gender spectrum and not having to select a pre-determined label to describe who they are. Femininity was not seen as a lesser quantity, and masculinity was not seen as some disposable entity. Gender fluidity creates space for people to be "both," "and," and or "neither", and to redefine gender in an inclusive way.

From a macro level, gender fluidity creates more expansive thinking that frees people from linear, outdated, or traditional thinking. As multiple interviewees alluded to, LGBTQ+ norms dispense with the idea of universal rules. Instead of operating by binary thinking, everyone should have the ability to step "outside the box" and design their life in a way that best represents them. As a result, gender fluidity creates a mindset that also encourages intellectual innovation and cognitive flexibility. According to the respondents in the study,

LGBTQ+ people are skilled and determined to break the proverbial boxes that they believe keep our society confined.

As such, the concept of gender fluidity was a rich and fertile topic of discussion that touched on ideas related to gender nonconformity, spirituality, femininity, and Queerness, with leaders and allies seeing gender in a nontraditional way. To the study participants, gender was not a designation to be viewed as fixed or immutable, but a phenomenon to be regarded as multidimensional and evolving. Further, in order to entertain and recognize the fluidity and constructivist nature of gender, LGBTQ+ people also philosophically reject rigid thinking that disavows new ways of analyzing ourselves and the world around us. Accordingly, *gender fluidity* emerged as a cultural value within the LGBTQ+ community.

NON-CONFORMITY

Non-conformity, or the desire to challenge existing norms and traditions, also emerged as another LGBTQ+ cultural value. Generally speaking, while participants in the study resisted any norms, customs, or values that idealized cis-heteronormativity, they also showed a general aversion to any prescribed rules for living one's life. As a community adviser shared, "I appreciate not being normal" or forced to conform. In thinking about their cultural journey, LGBTQ+ people in the study believed being once deemed social outcasts accorded them a special status: it gave them a unique worldview and a way to avoid the debilitating pressure to be like everyone else. As the executive director of a non-profit explained, non-conformity subverts the "stilted adherence to institutional norms that I find really oppressive." In other words, being LGBTQ+ represents a free-spiritedness that is exciting, edgy, and authentic, whereas being a cis-identified heterosexual represents something stodgy, formulaic, and repressive. Another interviewee agreed and suggested that being LGBTQ+ reflected unconventionality at its best.

In that vein, a few leaders in the study spoke candidly about their attempts to be less conformist. In one of the more frank anecdotes from the study, a university administrator talked about the pressures he faced from his family and friends:

> My mom would be like… "I can't wait until you have babies, and you'll be bringing them around…" And I remember distinctly being disgusted by that statement. I was like grossed out… And to this day, I have a response of it being like a breeding-hamster-gross thing. Yet, in heterosexual society, that's what the norm is, and that's supposed to make you feel good. And I'm like eww… It felt base to me.

In his statement, the administrator rejected not only traditional ideas around sex and identity but also the societal and gender norms around family, marriage, and child-rearing. Many leaders saw cis-heterosexuality as a constellation of values that created an ethos about how family and society were supposed to function, and many of them repudiated any attempt to be indoctrinated into a set and rudimentary life. Non-conformity emerged as a cultural staple in defining one's Queerness and overcoming a set of norms that seemed best suited for a more traditional era.

As a result, a number of leaders saluted LGBTQ+ icons such as Grace Jones, David Bowie, and Prince for challenging the status quo. Even though Prince and David Bowie certainly pushed boundaries on dress, appearance, and musical style, one LGBTQ+ leader appreciated Grace Jones's "willingness to be bold, to be strange, to be unique, and still very much an African woman." The artists referenced by the study participants were irreverent by modern-day standards, and the interviewees in the study respected, admired, and emulated those larger-than-life figures who pursued their craft in an unorthodox way.

In acknowledging the cultural value of non-conformity, we learned that LGBTQ+ people are not just contrarians, but are open to the diverse levels of expression that free thinking can produce. Whether in philosophy, art, politics, or social behavior, study participants appreciated the ingenuity that originality inspires. Although expressed in different ways, non-conformity implicates the positive aspects of individual sensibility, the evolution of existing norms, and the beauty of being different. For these reasons, *non-conformity* became a salient theme and identifiable cultural value for the LGBTQ+ community.

AGENCY

One of the things admired most in the study was the ability of LGBTQ+ people to use *agency*, or personal power, to achieve their desired outcome. For some, the notion of agency spoke to the talent of LGBTQ+ people to wield their influence to create safety for themselves. For others, agency was used as a means of self-preservation, and yet for others, agency was a way to unleash their individuality. However, no matter the circumstance, agency in this study meant empowerment or the ability to direct one's life and temper one's environment—a key value for LGBTQ+ people.

For some, agency meant controlling their own personal narrative of who they were. For others, agency meant reclaiming their story. In the case of one historian, agency meant reclaiming aspects of their sexuality that were previously overwhelmed by shame and stigma as part of their cultural upbringing. Another study participant suggested that LGBTQ+ people approach agency with the mindset of wanting to create precision in how they convey themselves to the world, with the hope of not being further misunderstood or ostracized as they have been, by and large, for most of history. For others, agency meant using certain interpersonal skills to command respect in an environment. Through the force of their personality, gender and sexual minorities may use agency to assert themselves when seeking to be visible or connect with others.

While agency has significance in the individual domain, it has also manifested itself in the collective sphere as LGBTQ+ people have secured political capital to fight discrimination. As several leaders joked, if LGBTQ+ people know nothing else, it's the ability to mobilize and fight oppression. As many of the leaders and allies talked about their level of activism, what was evident was their desire to achieve justice and fair treatment. One LGBTQ+ politician explained how the collective choice to fight back against discrimination was an easy one. Either LGBTQ+ people could submit, or they could become active and vocal and say, "Look, we're here, and we're Queer, and we're tired of you beating us up." As one public speaker summed it up:

> You know... whether it be ACT UP... or drag queens at Stonewall... or heteronormative gay couples, whatever it is, we are present, and I think, like any group that fights for its own rights, we make the world better by fighting for our homes and our sense of visibility.

At the same time, the leaders and allies reiterated that agency can be expressed in many different ways, like "the power of charisma... [the] power of personality... [the] power of analysis." Additionally, as one IT professional noted from her work with LGBTQ+ tech entrepreneurs, younger generations of LGBTQ+ people use agency differently. They may feel more empowered than older generations of Queer folk to seek out integrated venues or patronize mainstream organizations to connect, network, and develop personal and professional contacts. That is not to suggest LGBTQ+ people in the 1970s, 80s, or 90s were not empowered; indeed, by the example of organizations such as the Gay Liberation Front, Daughters of Bilitis, the Combahee River Collective, ACT UP, and many others,

LGBTQ+ people have always had agency to some degree. However, with increasing social acceptance in future years, newer generations of LGBTQ+ people had options that were not available to their predecessors. As such, having personal agency in more recent decades meant making different choices, whether voting for LGBTQ+ presidential candidates, instituting company boycotts, or using celebrity testimonials to gain support.

Despite the generational differences, various groups within the LGBTQ+ community continue to learn from each other and organize together to exhibit empowerment. On the individual scale, as they have for decades, LGBTQ+ people continue to use their grit and determination to lay claim to their place in the world. Relying on the cultural value of agency, LGBTQ+ people continue to muster the strength and the fortitude to assert their independence, design their own lives, honor their identity, and fight for the rights of others. The LGBTQ+ example and journey have always been synonymous with agency.

PERCEPTIVENESS

Another value invoked during the interviews was the value of *perceptiveness*, which I defined as insight or the ability to understand things at a high level. Multiple interviewees described how this quality had become a prized attribute or trait among community members. For some leaders and allies in the study, perceptiveness meant being discerning or having a deep understanding of phenomena around you; for others, being perceptive meant being discerning and having the ability to understand ideas or assess one's environment properly. Both activities require a high degree of perceptiveness and reflect how the leaders and allies in the study saw LGBTQ+ people engage their friends and navigate their environment.

As was revealed in the study, one's level of perceptivity is sharpened by virtue of being LGBTQ+. As one interviewee stated, "I wouldn't have come to view the world as I do if I had been straight. I think I'm very analytical [because as a Queer person]... you're just forced to be." Other LGBTQ+ leaders agreed and pinpointed how their "minority status" gives them a critical lens by which to observe and critique the world around them. Due to their social status and their historical experience of living life culturally on the fringes of society, LGBTQ+ people have a unique ability to observe society from an outsider's perspective. As a result, LGBTQ+ people have fostered the ability to analyze global society while retaining the consciousness to see the system for what it is. Mezirow spoke to the transformational quality that results when a person becomes aware of the filter or epistemological framework in which they live,[87] and leaders in the study stressed the need to question the normative frameworks in which we operate. To illustrate this point, one political leader attributed his ability to adopt this transformational mindset to being LGBTQ+, which already gave him the unique position to see society critically and discerningly.

Further, the inclination of LGBTQ+ people to flout traditional gender norms helps illuminate how society caters to certain demographics and can create a parallel reality. Queer people can see and often negotiate multiple realities. As one community volunteer indicated during the study: "I think living between genders gives you a unique perspective. It allows you to be a bridge between the two primary parts of society." The duality that LGBTQ+ people possess gives them insight into socially-constructed norms that they would not have otherwise. It allows LGBTQ+ people to be socially conscious and social commentators in a discerning and thoughtful way.

Within the Queer community, perceptiveness is also displayed in the interpersonal context. Some experienced perceptiveness as depth—a supreme form of insight—and underlined the tendency for LGBTQ+ people to show great wisdom. A number of allies

---

[87] Kegan, R. (2000). What "form" informs? A constructive-developmental approach to transformational learning. In: J. Mezirow & Assoc. *Learning as transformation*. San Francisco, CA: Jossey-Bass.

credited the community and their circle of Queer friends for being reflective, exercising empathy, and promoting thoughtful dialogue on a regular basis. One Pride organizer celebrated her Queer friends for their ability to show depth, withhold judgment, show reason, possess a balanced perspective, and talk on levels she felt she could not do with many of her straight counterparts. Other participants in the study heralded the ability of Queer people to go beyond superficialities, have open and honest conversations, and talk about life and love in all of their varied dimensions.

Further, discernment has a practical use as a way of maintaining safety in foreign environments. At times, the perceptivity may be immediate; in other situations, perceptivity may come from a methodical mental process. That is not to say that LGBTQ+ people are intrinsically smarter than others. Like any tool, one's sense of discernment becomes sharper the more it's used, and as social minorities, LGBTQ+ people are forced to use discernment routinely to ensure their safety and maintain protection. Our unique social circumstances as social outsiders can give us critical insight as we scan and negotiate our surroundings to determine who is an ally, what environments are welcoming, and which situations are advantageous to our well-being. As a result, our perceptivity and situational awareness have become finely-tuned and highly developed to the point where it has become a normal customary practice.

Naturally, a number of leaders in the study also spoke about discernment in recognizing or identifying other LGBTQ+ people. Some members spoke about the vaulted concept of "gaydar" and "queer vision," or the uncanny way of recognizing members of the LGBTQ+ community when they detect a person who doesn't fit gender norms or gender expectations. If a person is non-confirming, eager, friendly, or even flirtatious, LGBTQ+ people might surmise that a new friend, associate, or acquaintance is also LGBTQ+. Without stereotyping and profiling, LGBTQ+ people use subtle social cues to identify other community members. Although the process seems mysterious, the leaders helped illuminate the percipient skill that makes it easier for them to find community. Given that nonverbal communication accounts for more than 50% of all communication[88] and that communication, verbal or not, always possesses cultural cues and signifiers,[89] perhaps it is not surprising that LGBTQ+ people rely so heavily on perceptivity when they meet other people. LGBTQ+ people use social cues, creative observation, and colorful ways to identify each other and foster community development.

Perceptiveness appears to be a cultural value that LGBTQ+ people exhibit. It can manifest itself in one of two ways: as deep insight or as radiating discernment as people assess their environment. In either case, those skills appear to be derived from a cultural value of perceptiveness in which LGBTQ+ people are observant, notice details, show mental acuity, and remain sensitive to their surroundings. Although most human beings arguably use perceptiveness to some degree, it appears to be more than a mental by-product for LGBTQ+ people; it is a preeminent LGBTQ+ cultural value according to this cohort of leaders and allies. Based on the perceptions and experiences of Queer people and allies in this study, it is evident that *perceptiveness* is a powerful tool for LGBTQ+ people to build relationships, foster community, preserve their safety, and engage the world in a more thoughtful and analytical way.

FREEDOM

As a community still politically and socially persecuted, the ability to live freely remains a cherished notion, and *freedom* is an important cultural value for LGBTQ+ people. In the context of the study,

---

[88] Mehrabian, A. (1972). *Nonverbal Communication*. New Brunswick: Aldine Transaction.

[89] Bernstein, R. (2017, March 28). 7 Cultural Differences in Nonverbal Communication. Retrieved from https://online.pointpark.edu/business/cultural-differences-in-nonverbal-communication/

I defined freedom as the ability to live without limitation or restriction. The theme was further explored under the subtopics of liberation and uninhibitedness.

For some study participants, the easiest way to intuit freedom was in the guise of liberation, which suggests freedom from oppressive norms perpetrated by family units, governments, or religious institutions. As such, LGBTQ+ people may seek freedom from disapproving families that reject who they are by moving to areas where they can fully be themselves. Cities like Berlin, San Francisco, Johannesburg, Taipei, and Medellín have become LGBTQ+ meccas by providing safety, refuge, and freedom for community members.

In other instances, freedom was the condition or sensibility that LGBTQ+ people wanted to provide for others politically, socially, and economically. While sharing his admiration for LGBTQ+ leaders who work on the frontlines, one seasoned military veteran spoke of how proud and ecstatic he was to see activists working so publicly to give other LGBTQ+ people the freedom they deserve.

Moreover, freedom was also defined as uninhibitedness or the desire to live life without restraint. Several activists in the study revered the sensibility of LGBTQ+ people to live their lives openly, whether in terms of their sexuality, family structure, or their unapologetic approach to activism. As an under-represented group, LGBTQ+ people have the freedom to operate on the margins within society and eschew norms that can feel predictable, traditional, and burdensome. As one social worker described his LGBTQ+ experience:

> I feel like there's more freedom to... to be yourself, whatever that
> may be. You're free to be single, you're free to be in an open rela-
> tionship, you're free to have a partner, you're free to not have kids
> if you don't want to. And I know that we're all technically free to
> do those things, but with straight people, it's different, because
> society has certain expectations that they have to fulfill.

Without the weight of those societal expectations, LGBTQ+ people can live freely and comfortably as self-determinative people.

Freedom is an esteemed cultural value in the LGBTQ+ community in several key ways. Firstly, the community aspires to be free from social, political, and religious persecution. Secondly, LGBTQ+ people seek freedom in positivist terms to live life in a way that suits their aspirations. Thirdly, LGBTQ+ people seek to promote liberation for freedom-seeking people everywhere, including other sexual and gender minorities who continue to face discrimination, bias, and reprisals in their local communities. Freedom is a value that LGBTQ+ people support individually and in the aggregate. The notion of *freedom* feels very libertarian, but in the community context, it is also connected to previously discussed themes of equity, diversity, and inclusion.

NURTURE/CARE

The next salient theme that emerged from the data was the idea of *nurture* and *care*, or the act of showing care, concern, and compassion for others. In the study, the value of nurture fell into two general categories: care for people and nurture for the community. Digging a little bit deeper, the ways in which LGBTQ+ people were said to provide care were multi-faceted. At times, nurture/care may be exhibited in thoughtful communication, while in other situations compassion may be shown by caring for the marginalized. As LGBTQ+ leaders discussed the norm of nurture/care, they observed how LGBTQ+ people liked to be easy, affectionate, and playful with each other. They also noticed how LGBTQ+ people might go out of their way to be service-oriented, gracious with their time and energy, and mindful in their interactions, all of which serve as cornerstones of a nurturing or caring mindset.

From a professional standpoint, some leaders and allies theorized that LGBTQ+ people sought caretaking vocations or industries to channel their nurturing sensibilities. Outside of the workplace, other leaders highlighted how the caring nature of LGBTQ+ people extends to parties and community events, where as a host, the focus is to ensure that everybody is comfortable and is going to have a good time.

And yet, the value of nurture/care extends not only to festive occasions but difficult times as well. As one Buddhist leader in the study emphasized, LGBTQ+ people are also adept at providing support to one another during sickness, various rites of passage, family isolation, and financial hardship. LGBTQ+ people seem to take great pride in assisting others and providing care to those most vulnerable within the larger community.

Naturally, the question arises: where does this nurturing spirit of LGBTQ+ people come from? While some suggested that LGBTQ+ people care because of their respect for "feminine energy," others theorized that LGBTQ+ people had developed a sense of nurture and care because of our historical journey in which we had to fend for ourselves and be self-sufficient. Still, others identified the coming out experience and the attendant recognition of one's marginalized status as playing a huge role in wanting to care for others. Speaking from experience, one leader disclosed that their capacity for kindness, nurture, and care increased once they came out and realized the depths of their suffering. As one immigrant-rights advocate indicated, "I became much more accepting of human foibles [and] people who are less fortunate once I identified as Queer." In sum, LGBTQ+ people have developed a great capacity for care as they have become more aware of their identity and the world around them.

As a result, we see from the study the ability of Queer people to relate to the humanity of others. From the edges of social marginalization, where we as a community have experienced a disproportionate amount of despair and death, LGBTQ+ people want to provide others with what they have been denied socially: love, support, and care. And as LGBTQ+ people have become more accustomed to receiving aid, assurance, and encouragement, it has also become easier for community members to extend that love to others and give help where help is needed.

As generations of Queer people have cared for the community and those around us, that value of nurture/care reflects how we aspire to interact with the world. LGBTQ+ people value kindness and aspire to support whoever needs it, sometimes without any regard for themselves. It is at both times a deep desire and a palpable Queer sensibility to live, love, and bring positive energy into the world in order to bridge the gaps that separate us as people. No matter the circumstance or the recipient, the community ethos is one of living with kindness, offering support, and providing compassion. The perception among a majority of participants in this study is that LGBTQ+ people have a deep and abiding capacity for caring for others, and the value of *nurture/care* appears to be a cultural trademark of the LGBTQ+ community.

RESILIENCE

When discussing the community's mettle, some LGBTQ+ leaders and allies invoked the theme of grit, or the toughness used to overcome problematic situations. As we delved deeper, we discovered that the study participants had an affinity for mental and emotional toughness, and as a result, we identified *resilience* as an LGBTQ+ community value.

Resilience is described as fortitude in the face of adversity. It manifested itself in the many stories where leaders talked about their journeys and how they navigated difficult times. Whether being dissuaded from certain life goals because of their identity or being persecuted for simply coming out, LGBTQ+ people have shown defiance or open resistance to certain norms, beliefs, or behaviors. One psychotherapist in the study hailed what he called the "F—you" mentality of the community and how that form of resilience was something they emulated as they dealt with hardships and unforgiving circumstances. Using their strength to be assertive, unapologetic, and resilient, LGBTQ+ people have refused to be victimized and have become particularly adept at using negative circumstances as a proving ground for their greatness.

For many of the people we spoke to, resilience seems like a natural way of life for Queer folk. The strength, grit, and resilience that Queer people have channeled from one another have helped LGBTQ+ people survive during periods of repression and social strife, especially as the community was ravaged by the AIDS epidemic or assaulted by new waves of conservative legislation. Unable to rely on social benevolence or the slow march of progressive social causes, LGBTQ+ people have been able to withstand the persistent challenges they have faced from a hostile society by constantly channeling resilience.

As we were reminded, "it takes courage to come out and go against the norm," and the courageous spirit referenced in the study is no different than the resilient fervor shown by LGBTQ+ icons such as Sylvia Rivera, Dell Martin, Phyllis Lyon, Bayard Rustin, or Harvey Milk. Those figures were exemplars of courage and leadership who showed fearlessness in making things happen, and their legacy illustrates how resilience has deep roots within the community.

LGBTQ+ people possess the inner strength to be transcendent and go beyond the limits imposed by society. As a result, *resilience* emerged as an LGBTQ+ cultural value in the study and continues to be wielded in order to inspire and sustain the future progress of the LGBTQ+ community and future generations to come.

ZEST

Another LGBTQ+ cultural value is that of *zest* or living life to the fullest. In considering what it means to be Queer, several leaders relished the hunger, exuberance, and desire for life that Queer people possess. Although the community is not the first to contend with oppression, according to the study's interviewees, LGBTQ+ people manage to overcome that struggle with unyielding joy and a collective festive spirit. LGBTQ+ leaders and allies took pride in how the community can transmute life's thorns into positivity and turn their social stigma into joie de vivre.

Not surprisingly, the hunger for life and positivity has also led Queer people to seek a greater quality of life or to live at its highest level. Moreover, the search for refinement has created a greater appreciation for the arts, aesthetics, and adventure. Additionally, the cultural value of zest also leads LGBTQ+ people to appreciate beauty and aesthetics, whether that includes "well-apportioned living and work environments" or the customary LGBTQ+ pride parades with their rich colors, splash, and infectious energy, as some suggested. Separately, other LGBTQ+ leaders talked about how the Queer community brings vibrancy to the world and helps revitalize communities and neighborhoods through retailing, artisanal trades, and beautification.

Based on those factors, LGBTQ+ people seem to have a higher regard for fun than the average individual, a quality that the study's allies seemed to appreciate more than the leaders themselves. As one painter and artist expressed their admiration, "LGBTQ+ people seem to have a great capacity for fun and laughter with the attitude of 'I'm not trying to be anything different than what I am.'" And while the forms of our cultural exuberance may vary, what a number of leaders admired is how Queer people have the endearing ability to turn the pedestrian into something fanciful or the mundane into something exciting. The community's knack for vitality, adventure, and wellness is the very essence of *zest*. It demonstrates an LGBTQ+ cultural value that endears us to the world and makes the globe a more invigorating place.

CHAPTER 7

Meta-Themes

The 15 values experienced by LBGTQ+ leaders and allies can be further categorized into nine meta-themes: justice, authenticity, verve, resilience, sex positivity, perceptiveness, interconnectedness, gender fluidity, and creativity. These meta-themes help organize each of the 15 values articulated in the study and lay the foundation for understanding how LGBTQ+ values have a strong leadership compass.

Justice, or a sturdy belief in fairness and a genuine concern for people, encapsulates many values like diversity, inclusion, and equity. The importance of equality for all people, regardless of their culture, is emphasized. There is a responsibility to further justice in the world by using one's power or agency to advocate for the disenfranchised on the macro level and by using social awareness to practice inclusion with associates, friends, and community members on the micro level. Each of those primary themes spoke to the desire of LGBTQ+ people to promote fairness and *justice* for all people in society.

Authenticity, or the complete and open embrace of who one is, emerged as a very important meta-theme. As the study participants talked about the importance of freedom, it was in the context of LGBTQ+ people living life without needing to cover up any aspect of their identity. As the participants spoke about non-conformity, they alluded to the desire of LGBTQ+ people to shed any social labels or traditional norms that would suppress who they are. Moreover, as the participants shared experiences of when LGBTQ+ people were unfiltered, they referenced gender fluidity on numerous occasions. Overall, the study showed that LGBTQ+ people revel in being honest about who they are and that *authenticity* is an essential part of the cultural experience for members of the LGBTQ+ community.

Verve was another meta-theme for LGBTQ+ people. It can be described as the confluence of vigor, spirit, and enthusiasm. As the interviewees described the creativity, zest, and pride that Queer people possess, it was apparent that they were describing an ethos that predominates in the community. Verve symbolizes the positivity, exuberance, and joy that Queer people express in creative pursuits, day-to-day living, and the gratifying celebration of their identity. Relatedly LGBTQ+ people have demonstrated how a growth mindset creates more fulfillment and excitement in their lives. *Zest*, pride, and self-realization are all examples of a passionate approach to life.

Interconnectedness, or the idea of being emotionally, mentally, and spiritually connected to others, also emerged as a larger meta-theme. It is important for Queer people to be connected to other members of the larger LGBTQ+ community, to the historical icons who fought fearlessly for LGBTQ+ rights in the past, and to the people they encounter in their daily lives. The notion of interconnectedness was not only relational but emotional and described how LGBTQ+ people felt psychologically connectd to a larger community of Queer people that exist all over the world. Further, the study participants noted how LGBTQ+ people foster interconnectedness by providing holistic nurture, care, and support to others who might genuinely need it, regardless of whether they come from the same subculture or not. According to the leaders and allies in the study,

LGBTQ+ people maintain an abiding belief in the *interconnectedness* of all people and seek kinship with people both inside and outside the community.

While several meta-themes describe some of the original values more expansively than the original list of values mentioned in Chapter 2 (e.g., justice, authenticity, verve, and interconnectedness), five of the meta-themes are consistent with the values identified in the study (e.g., resilience, sex positivity, perceptiveness, gender fluidity, and creativity). In the case of *resilience*, not only do LGBTQ+ people show an incredible amount of grit, but they also exhibit a great deal of strength in overcoming obstacles and social barriers. In terms of *sex positivity*, the allies and leaders in the study stated that LGBTQ+ people maintain a healthy and positive attitude towards sexuality in all of its different forms. In highlighting *perceptiveness*, LGBTQ+ people were thought to possess incredible insight that makes them good social observers, systems thinkers, and relational experts. With respect to *gender fluidity*, LGBTQ+ people respect both masculine and feminine energy and reject the binary thinking that comes with traditional gender norms. Finally, when it comes to *creativity*, the LGBTQ+ community not only evinces a penchant for artistic expression, but a strong inclination for innovative thought that imagines new possibilities and new ways of being.

On balance, these nine meta-themes—justice, authenticity, verve, resilience, sex positivity, perceptiveness, interconnectedness, gender fluidity, and creativity—encompass the patterns witnessed in the data and summarize the primary cultural values that were identified for LGBTQ+ people. When properly contextualized, these meta-themes constitute the core of LGBTQ+ wisdom and Queer cultural genius™. As an example, in the leadership context, sex positivity speaks to somatic awareness and gender fluidity highlights the importance of non-binary thinking, as discussed in later chapters. These leadership competencies constitute the core and the very foundation of transformational leadership.

For the leaders who participated in this study, their journeys reflected self-realization and a deep awareness of themselves as LGBTQ+ people. For the allies who participated in this study, their stories reflected great humility and an abiding concern for a community that they have come to call their own.

Ironically, a few respondents challenged the idea that an actual LGBTQ+ culture exists—much less a cohesive and identifiable one—even as they talked about their experiences in collectivist terms. For some of the leaders in the study, there were many aspects of their lived experience that they had never considered explicitly in connection with other Queer people. Yet, many other leaders recognized the commonalities they shared with other community members, even if they had not thought explicitly about those values or themes for quite some time. Each theme contained various elements and dimensions. By articulating different facets of each theme, the participants provided a comprehensive review of how each theme showcased the cultural values of the community. Despite the different interpretations, what stood out from the data was how a majority of the participants invoked each theme almost uniformly. In turn, the quantitative study reinforced the importance of each value to the community at-large.

Yet, as we think about cultural values, it is important not to confuse the existence of values with the specific way in which divergent members of the community might express them. For example, as more people lament the supposed "extinction" of the gay community, as was suggested in a *New York Times* column,[90] it is important to remember that while values may be more enduring, the most visible aspects of the culture and the espoused values related to the culture may change. Edgar Schein likened culture to the human

---

[90] Bruni, F. (2018, April 28). The extinction of gay Identity. *The New York Times*. Retrieved from https://www.nytimes.com/2018/04/28/opinion/the-extinction-of-gay-identity.html

body. He noted that while the core elements of culture (e.g., like our bones, skin, or organs) are relatively stable, the superficial elements of culture (i.e., things people use to adorn the body, such as jewelry and clothing) may change depending on social interactions.[91] For example, some LGBTQ+ people may be just as passionate about social justice in 2018 as Queer people were in 1980, but they may choose a different way to be "political."

As such, millennial LGBTQ+ people may demonstrate the value of social justice by influencing the electoral process and developing more LGBTQ+ political leaders through organizations like the Victory Fund or the National Gay and Lesbian Task Force. For other generational cohorts within the community, the pathway for honoring social justice may be engaging in civil disobedience, which proved effective for Queer activist groups such as ACT UP or Queer Nation. When we think of the value of interconnectedness, a segment of the community may interpret that value differently as well. Whereas a group of lesbian women in Indianapolis may display interconnectedness by connecting with other lesbian women online, transgender women in San Francisco may find community by visiting an old "dive" bar in the Transgender District. Both sets of people adhere to the same cultural values; they just express them differently. The difference in cultural artifacts ("chat rooms" vs. "a bar in a gay neighborhood") or even a slight philosophical variation in espoused values (e.g., "we should elect leaders who look like us" vs. "we should take to the streets") would not necessarily suggest that values are divergent among LGBTQ+ people. Instead, it could be entirely plausible that certain cultural values may endure, albeit with distinct social features or within a different social context where norms dictate new or different behavior.[92]

---

[91] Schein, E. (2017). *Organizational culture and leadership* (5th ed.). Hoboken, New Jersey: Wiley & Sons, Inc.

[92] *Id.*

That being said, cultural values represent the glue that binds people together. The metathemes provide a composite or profile of the LGBTQ+ community that is reinforced by its own lens and supported by its own narrative. The opportunity before us is to tell the story of who we are in a full and rich way that humanizes Queer people and provides the proper platform to deploy our cultural genius and share our leadership capacity with the rest of the global communtiy.

LGBTQ+ LEADERSHIP: THE VALUE OF QUEER FOLK

With a healthy amount of curiosity, careful analysis, compassion, and cultural intelligence, we can not only better understand the lives, culture, and souls of LGBTQ+ people, but we should also be able to recognize the value that LGBTQ+ people bring to society overall. The values, norms, and lived experiences of LGBTQ+ people are instructive for all, especially leaders who want to grow, evolve, and create transformational cultures. Focusing on the nine meta-themes: 1) justice, 2) authenticity, 3) verve, 4) resilience, 5) sex positivity, 6) perceptiveness, 7) interconnectedness, 8) gender fluidity, and 9) creativity, LGBTQ+ people can serve as role models for emerging, aspiring, and seasoned leaders who care about people, the planet, peace, prosperity, and community partnership. The Queer (LGBTQ+) leadership competencies are:

- Justice
- Authenticity
- Verve
- Resilience
- Somatic Awareness

- Perceptiveness
- Interconnectedness
- Non-binary Thinking
- Creativity

CHAPTER 8

Justice and LGBTQ+ Leadership

After the #MeToo and Black Lives Matter movements, it may seem hard to remember a time when Americans weren't as keenly aware of social justice and social activism as they are now. Fifty years after the American Civil Rights Movement, the world appears more galvanized and primed to talk about social justice than it has been in a generation. As a result, many organizations are engaging in social justice marketing, volunteerism, philanthropic campaigns, culture change efforts, and DEIB (diversity, equity, inclusion, and belonging) initiatives to respond to customer and employee pressure to be more socially responsible. In fact, the *Harvard Business Review* proclaimed that the business world is entering the "age of corporate social justice" as more and more companies realize that a social justice bent correlates to increased profitability.[93] Fortunately, LGBTQ+ leaders and employees possess a cultural perspective that

---

[93] Zheng, L. (2020, January). We're entering the age of corporate social justice. *Harvard Business Review.* https://hbr.org/2020/06/were-entering-the-age-of-corporate-social-justice

can help organizations sustain this seemingly newfound interest in social justice and transform the underlying support for said initiatives from money-driven campaigns to human-centered organizational movements.

UNDERSTANDING WHAT "ACTIVISM" IS

When we think of activism, it is tempting to think of it as the collage of activities in which we engage other people to initiate social change. In other words, the central idea of activism for some is the idea that people with fervent political beliefs become activists because they want to change other people's minds or to illuminate how people from under-represented communities are being treated. The premise of activism, as socially constructed, is that we must educate and inspire others as we seek greater equity in the world at large.

Yet, in considering activism, we must also think about our own "activation." In other words, we as employees and leaders must also become activated in our consciousness in order to become the leaders the world needs. What this means is threefold: Firstly, it requires us to elevate our thoughts and place them in a higher plane. If there is one good thing that came from the COVID-19 pandemic (which, admittedly, is hard to identify, given that millions of people have died as a result of it), it is the notion that each of us had to re-evaluate who we were. As a society, we appear to have been rethinking our collective priorities, having been stripped of our 12-hour workdays, our reflexive consumerism, our privileged ability to travel, and our ability to distract ourselves from the unrelenting question of who we are trying to be. Activism forces us to look in the mirror and ask ourselves: "Am I really ok with the world as it currently exists? How have I contributed to the world as it exists? And most importantly, what does the world's condition say about who I am?" Activists must constantly entertain the question: Who am I choosing to be right now? And if you, like millions of people across the world, want to be better and do better, then you have to dedicate yourself to curiosity, growth orientation, and reflection as you raise your consciousness.

As we change our mindset, we must recognize that our reality is inextricably connected to the experience of others. As a global citizen, I cannot witness the suffering of others without realizing that the conditions that keep others in bondage also serve to keep me in bondage as well. For example, while many whites might rail against the racism that racial minorities face across the globe, it must also be understood that perpetuating racism—whether wittingly or unwittingly—has also desecrated the humanity of white people as well. You can't maintain a system that debases the humanity of another without also minimizing your own humanity and diminishing your capacity for love, grace, and compassion. Similarly, when we think about activism, we cannot just focus on helping or "saving" others. We must realize that activism is necessary to save ourselves from the doldrums of complacency, apathy, and mindless living.

Not only does activism require an awakening of sorts, but it also requires intentional behavior. Activism must go beyond pithy posts on social media or simply "liking" a politically-charged statement online; it must tangibly effect (not a typo) a meaningful and positive outcome. To borrow a metaphor, we have to get our hands "dirty" in this messy thing called society if we want social dynamics to improve. Accordingly, activism must go beyond the cozy confines of the armchair or the keyboard; it must find its way into the public sphere.

Activism doesn't necessarily mean that we need to take to the streets or act with the machinations of a political operative or a community organizer. Instead, activism should compel us to take strategic action designed to lead to a particular outcome. As individuals, we can write letters to our elected officials, talk to neighbors about a discrete issue, or even run for public office. As leaders within organizations, we can donate to social causes, lend social capital to public initiatives, or use our mantle to create equity to counteract the systemic bias that exists elsewhere in society.

LGBTQ+ ACTIVISM "UP CLOSE"

Only after personal activation has taken place is it possible to advocate for equity in a way that supersedes superficiality. Proudly, the LGBTQ+ community has a long, storied, and persistent history of activism dating back to the turn of the 20th Century. We've seen organizations that have inspired the Queer activist legacy such as the following: the Society for Human Rights in 1924, the first gay rights organization in the United States; COC Nederlands, a Dutch LGBTQ+ group founded in 1946; the Daughters of Bilitis, which was the first organization in the U.S. dedicated to lesbian rights; and Germany's Bund fur Menschenrechte (Union for the Rights of Men), which was the first mainstream LGBTQ+ Organization in 1946 that was open to women. LGBTQ+ activism has also spawned groups such as the Combahee River Collective in 1974 and ACT UP, as well as groups worldwide such as GALCK (the Gay and Lesbian Coalition of Kenya), Pink Dot SG in Singapore, and Iguales in Chile. Courageous figures like Alexya Salvador, Marsha P. Johnson, Harvey Milk, and Arsham Parsi (the Harriet Tubman of LGBTQ+ activism) have transformed the world by being unapologetic about their commitment to Queer causes. LGBTQ+ activists like Bayard Rustin and Urvashi Vaid have also co-led social justice movements that were not exclusively or predominantly LGBTQ+-focused. In addition, thousands of faceless and nameless activists have lent their voice and blood to the struggle without ever having the privilege to be known as household names or to be talked about in historical discussions.

Activism and social justice are core values of the LGBTQ+ community because its members continue to face discrimination, abuse, and repression in every part of the world. It wasn't until the 1994 case of *Toonen v. Australia* that discrimination based on sexual orientation was held as a violation of international human rights law.[94] As of this writing, 71 countries still criminalize homosexuality ("Homosexuality: The Countries Where It Is Illegal to Be Gay," BBC, 2021), while 37 countries have, in effect, made it criminal to be transgender.[95] What's more, according to the International Lesbian & Gay Association (ILGA), only 25 countries in the world have passed legislation making it easy for transgender people to change their gender legally.[96] These statistics highlight a precarious predicament, especially given the rise of anti-LGBTQ+ legislation in places like the U.S., Hungary, and Poland. Furthermore, in jurisdictions like Florida where it is illegal to discuss sexual orientation and gender identity under the "Don't Say Gay" bill passed in February 2022, it seems like it is "open season" against the LGBTQ+ community. There were 300+ anti-LGBTQ+ bills introduced in 2022 alone.[97] These realities exist against the backdrop of unprecedented violence against transgender and gender nonconforming people from 2017–2021.[98]

---

[94] Angelo, P. J. & Bocci, D. (2021, January 29). The Changing Landscape of Global LGBTQ+ Rights. *The Council on Foreign Relations.* https://www.cfr.org/article/changing-landscape-global-lgbtq-rights

[95] Wareham, J. (2020, September 30). New Report Shows Where It's Illegal To Be Transgender in 2020. *Forbes.* https://www.forbes.com/sites/jamiewareham/2020/09/30/this-is-where-its-illegal-to-be-transgender-in-2020/?sh=58550f8e5748

[96] Chiam, Z., Duffy, S., González Gil, M., Goodwin, L., Mpemba Patel, N. T. (2019). Trans Legal Mapping Report: Recognition before the law (3rd ed.). *International Lesbian & Gay Association.* https://ilga.org/downloads/ILGA_World_Trans_Legal_Mapping_Report_2019_EN.pdf

[97] Human Rights Campaign Fund. (2022, November 22). United Against Hate™—Fighting Back on State Legislative Attacks On LGBTQ+ People. Retrieved from https://www.hrc.org/campaigns/the-state-legislative-attack-on-lgbtq-people

[98] Human Rights Campaign Fund. (2021, November 17). *Marking the Deadliest Year on Record, Human Rights Campaign Announces Release of Annual Report on Violence Against Transgender and Gender Non-Conforming People* [Press Release]. Retrieved from https://www.hrc.org/press-releases/marking-the-

I am not arguing the moral superiority of LGBTQ+ people. It is well understood that the LGBTQ+ penchant for social justice and activism is inherently tied to its global struggle for acceptance and equality. However, given that the LGBTQ+ community extends into every corner of the world and includes people from every social demographic, it stands to reason that LGBTQ+ people are more likely than their heterosexual or cisgender counterparts to be invested in social justice and activism on a broader scale. LGBTQ+ people have held prominent roles in major social movements. For example, Bayard Rustin, an out gay man, was the Senior Adviser to Dr. King and the architect of the 1963 March on Washington for Jobs and Freedom. In the early 20th century, three women involved in same-sex relationships—Jane Addams, Sophonisba Breckenridge, and Anna Howard Shaw—led the National American Suffrage Association, the nation's largest feminist organization. Additionally, few seem to recognize that the Black Lives Matter movement was started by three Queer women of color who would ignite the most important social movement of the modern era. These examples show that LGBTQ+ people have served in the vanguard of movements of multiple social groups, not just those representing LGBTQ+ interests.

Further, even when we consider racial equity, as an example, studies show that members of the LGBTQ+ community have more progressive racial attitudes than their heterosexual, cisgender counterparts in terms of their morals and understanding of white privilege (Cooperative Congressional Election Survey, 2016).[99] While there is certainly bias and discrimination within the LGBTQ+ community, it is important to note that, culturally speaking,

---

deadliest-year-on-record-hrc-releases-report-on-violence-against-transgender-and-gender-non-conforming-people

[99] Ansolabehere, S., Schafner, B. F. (2017). "CCES Common Content, 2016." [Data set]. Cooperative Congressional Election Survey. https://doi.org/10.7910/DVN/GDF6Z0

LGBTQ+ people care about social justice and activism to the extent that lends itself to inclusive leadership. As a result, organizations and community cohorts would do well to emulate the values of the LGBTQ+ community and support social justice, advocacy, and activism—not only from a marketing or political standpoint, but from a humanist perspective as well.

LESSONS IN LGBTQ+ LEADERSHIP: JUSTICE

In supporting activism, I would offer the following recommendations to senior leaders within any organization, system, or movement:

1) **Think about why you are doing what you are doing.** I'll never forget meeting the executive director of a prominent political organization and asking her: "Why is it important for you to support racial equity?" She first glared at me as though I had made an indecent proposal. Then, she stumbled through an answer that was something less than poetic. In a word, she couldn't really answer the question and suggested that my question was irrelevant.

   Yet, I can assure you: the question of **why** is quite germane in the interest of supporting equity and social justice. If a leader can't thoughtfully articulate why they are committed to a cause or offer a careful recitation of the issue(s), then any ensuing action will be misguided. As a result, organizational support will wane, and the leaders within the organization will be seen as empty mouthpieces for a cause they don't really support.

   Instead, be clear about your "North Star" or the underlying motivation for your organization's social justice platform. Then, research the issues and take every opportunity to listen, learn, and examine different viewpoints. Understanding your motivation as a leader will make it easier to garner support, inspire collective action, and deliver results.

2) **Don't forget the human imperative.** Far too many organizations get involved with social movements only when it starts to impact their bottom line. This Machiavellian approach has been spurred on by political pressure from the public that companies do more to support social justice. For example, in a 2020 study of 1,000 U.S. consumers, respondents indicated that they

wanted brands to take positions on social issues, suggesting that those companies that refused to support social positions could lose market share.[100]

However, an equity mindset is difficult to sustain without the necessary buy-in from leaders, and buy-in requires a head, heart, and hands approach. While many senior leaders are eager to recognize the intangible benefits of social awareness and are even more eager to do "something" in the name of expediency, they often forget to connect with their humanity. A genuine desire to improve the human condition and support freedom and justice for all should be at the root of any activism.

3) **Be proactive.** In 2020, my typical intake calls with a prospective client went something like this:

Prospective Client:	We have never done anything related to social justice and equity, and we're starting to get pushback from our employees.
Me:	So, in short… You've been around for ___ years and are just now focusing on social justice?
Prospective Client:	Yes.
Me:	Why are you focusing on social justice and equity now?
Prospective Client:	Because of all of the polarization we're seeing in the country. Can you help us create a strategy or game plan in the next week?

---

[100] "Brands should take a stand on a social issue that is important to their customers." (2020, August 17). YouGov. https://yougov.co.uk/topics/resources/articles-reports/2020/08/17/brands-should-take-stand-social-issue-important-th

While I am confident in who I am as a change agent, I assure you, I am no magician. Typically, these organizations reached out to me only after being called out for being slow-footed and clumsy in responding to a specific social issue. As a result, they took a reactionary stance that left them playing catch-up after enacting half-hearted measures that were only designed to appease their constituents instead of generating actions that showed true fidelity to social justice. When organizations are reactionary, they often act recklessly and haphazardly.

Yet, it behooves organizations to support social awareness and promote social activism given the communities in which they reside and given the communities which their employees represent. When companies invest in social justice to support their employees and connect with their customer base, the net result is that employees will believe they are part of a community that cares about more than just products and services. Instead, they realize that the organization wants to help improve the planet.

That is not to suggest that companies need to prognosticate or try to predict the whims of social change. It just means that the next time you think about social justice, it should not be the *first* time you think about it. Listen to your employees. Connect the dots to understand their social and cultural narratives. Develop greater global awareness so that you can proactively support social causes that directly impact your community. Finally, invest in measures that will help create meaningful change over an extended period of time.

4) **Take substantive measures to advocate for social causes.** If you are a senior leader or in charge of public relations and marketing, do not let words define your activism. Make sure that your actions are aligned with a coherent strategy and evoke well-defined goals and outcomes, both in the short-term and long-term.

5) **Be genuine in your efforts.** Employees and customers can easily see through half-hearted attempts at social advocacy. Among the LGBTQ+ community, opportunistic attempts at marketing are called "pride washing" or "pink washing." Pride washing or pink washing is the practice of using LGBTQ+ iconography and symbols to pander to the LGBTQ+ community. Additionally, pride or pink washing occurs when organizations use marketing during LGBTQ+ Pride Month[101] to distract from negative organizational practices, behaviors, and policies that actually harm the community during the rest of the calendar year. In other ethnic communities, this type of marketing may be referred to as "Black washing" or "woke washing." It is designed to manipulate the consumer/employee into thinking that the company is progressive when in fact, it is not.

While at times this practice may be deceptive, it can also simply be disingenuous: the by-product of ill-conceived attempts to be socially relevant during times of social discord. Examples of superficial marketing abound: if you sponsor a float in the annual Pride Parade but have taken no measures to groom the next generation of LGBTQ+ leaders, you are engaging in pride washing and disavowing social justice. If you support National Coming Out Day but fail to sponsor an LGBTQ+ employee resource group, you are not evincing a substantive measure of social responsibility. If you have no "out" LGBTQ+ members in senior leadership ranks, your commitment to social justice may be suspect at best. Finally, if you donate to campaigns to fund LGBTQ+ hostile legislation like the "Don't Say Gay" bill but market extensively to the LGBTQ+ community to advertise movies and television programming, your efforts will be seen

---

[101] LGBTQ+ Pride Month typically takes place in June of each year depending on the location. In the global south, LGBTQ+ Pride celebrations take place at different times to take advantage of seasonal weather.

as insincere. And rest assured, LGBTQ+ people will certainly take notice.

Symbolism is important; it can provide meaning and guidance when leaders are faced with an improbable task or journey. But symbolism can't override substance. Make sure you pair your symbolic gestures with substantive actions that show the full breadth of your commitment to a social cause.

6) **Remember: Social advocacy extends within the organization as well.** Equity, social justice, and corporate social responsibility are enduring values that require heartfelt commitment. But companies must make sure that their social advocacy also directly impacts the stakeholders inside the company. For example, if you create a company holiday for Juneteenth but fail to take corrective action when your employees are being micro-aggressed, then your strategy is imbalanced and too externally focused. Keep in mind that nearly half of LGBTQ+ employees are closeted,[102] and far too many companies and social organizations maintain a public brand that preaches social justice and DEIB without making any real strategic commitment to supporting equity work. Promises and words must be paired with tangible results that tangibly but positively impact your employees and stakeholders. The best ambassadors for your organization are those who work for you daily. Employees with positive work experiences will spread the word that your company is an "employer of choice." They will tell their friends, family, and neighbors that yours is an organization of social integrity.

An organization that supports the equity principle internally is just as socially responsible as an organization that engages in

[102] Catalyst. (2017, May 30). Lesbian, Gay, Bisexual and Transgender workplace issues. Retrieved from http://www.catalyst.org/knowledge/lesbian-gay-bisexual-transgender-workplace-issues.

philanthropy externally. The difference is that the company that first and foremost provides psychological safety for its employees is more in alignment with what true corporate social responsibility entails.

Indeed, it is unfortunate when leaders rail against social inequities while presiding over an organization that is stratified, dysfunctional, and exclusive. This dynamic not only plagues traditional or homogeneous companies but more progressive organizations as well. In fact, I have partnered with a number of progressive organizations that were surprisingly "progressive" in name only. If you want to commit to social justice and advocacy, then a socially-minded mantra and mindset should extend doubly to your workforce as well.

7) **Honor the fact that all movements are intersectional.** Do not fool yourself into thinking that social issues are isolated; all movements are intersectional. For example, you cannot say "Black Lives Matter" but then ignore the needs and concerns of Black Transgender youth. The two positions are cognitively and socially inconsistent. Bias in one diversity dimension creates a slippery slope for showing bias in another. Being impassioned about equity in one area does not preclude you from being biased in another diversity area if for no other reason than our confidence in one area of social justice may lead to overconfidence in another.[103] We must remember that racism, sexism, heterosexism, classism, cisgenderism, ableism, and religious fanaticism all serve to reinforce each other. Each of us is layered and diverse, with multiple identities, and the issues we face as a society are complex and belie a simple analysis that should prevent us from

---

[103] West RF, Meserve RJ, Stanovich KE. Cognitive sophistication does not attenuate the bias blind spot. J Pers Soc Psychol. 2012;103:506–19. https://doi.org/10.1037/a0028857

championing some equity issues while sitting on the sidelines for others.

Further, given the fact that our current generation of young leaders (Generation Z, or those born after 1996) is said to be the most diverse ever, it may be dangerous to "pick and choose" which J.E.D.I. (justice, equity, diversity, and inclusion) issues to focus on first. Even for homogenous populations, the lived experiences of Gen Zers as a heterogeneous cohort would suggest that more and more people care about social justice, regardless if they belong to a group that is directly targeted or impacted. For example, let's say your best friend growing up was Filipino or your sister identifies as a lesbian, or perhaps your co-worker is Muslim and disabled: the likelihood that you would be invested in social justice is probably still high, even if you grew up in a different era or in homogenous confines. With the shifting demographics and mindset of new generations, employers cannot afford to be single-minded in deciding which social justice causes deserve their support.

8) **Measure impact.** As you take action, it's important to gauge whether your actions have had their intended impact. Leaders and organizations can sometimes adopt "feel good" measures that do little to increase equity for under-represented populations. In addition, leaders can sometimes be conditioned to be omniscient, foregoing the opportunities to solicit input from those around them.

Instead of following the "lone wolf" model whereby leaders make decisions on their own, it is recommended that you check in with those around you to design effective strategies and measure impact. Failing to seek input from marginalized communities can come across as patronizing or ego-driven. Likewise, failing to account for impact can lead to measures that are hollow gestures instead of concrete solutions. As a senior leader, make sure that what you do is a collective endeavor that drives positive results at every level within the organization.

9) **And get at it again.** Given the nature of our society, the need for social justice is ubiquitous. It will never be completely addressed or resolved. And if bias is seemingly managed effectively on one front, it stands to reason that bias will rear itself again in new and unique ways as emerging groups challenge existing norms, mores, and customs on a different front. Leaders must employ a growth mindset and resolve themselves to be consistent as they push their organizations to be agents of change and advocates of justice. As you think about a growth mindset, ask yourself: How do I handle mistakes? More specifically:

1. Do I show myself compassion?
2. Do I see them as lessons and learning opportunities?
3. Do I use them to help me gain knowledge?
4. Do I make space at the right time to see their value?

Or do you focus on failure? More specifically:

1. Do I dismiss feedback?
2. Do I stay in my comfort zone?
3. Do I show frustration and give up when I experience discomfort?
4. Do I adopt a fatalistic approach? (i.e., "This was never going to work anyway because (fill in the blank)").

The morale of your employees depends on you making an effort. As you incorporate a "justice" lens into your leadership, adopting a growth mindset will help you align with the moral compass of building an imperfect but awakened world.

CHAPTER 9

Authenticity & LGBTQ+ Leadership

To be or not to be authentic… that is the question. The word authentic has been used in a number of corporate-y ways, not the least of which is the emerging field of authentic leadership that preaches the need to be genuine. Yet, the topic of authenticity has never enjoyed the same level of relevance or prestige in academic or professional circles that it has enjoyed in urban circles or among the school of hard knocks. But as people started to make the connection that they couldn't be their "best self" if they couldn't at some level be their authentic, cultural "self," they realized that their timidity, repression, and conformity was a disservice to themselves, the community, the organization, and the world. The LGBTQ+ community has helped to reframe the importance of being authentic in the world, and as we examine this trendy notion of authenticity, we can also see how authenticity has deep and considerable implications for transformational leadership.

HOW AUTHENTICITY BEGAN

Long before I remember the word "authenticity" being used in boardrooms and corporate training, the idea of being authentic and "keeping it real" was a rallying cry for millions of disaffected Gen Xers and Millennials. Many of these folks were BIPOC and were fatigued with the idea of putting on "false airs" for the establishment. The concept of authenticity was both an aspiration and a fait accompli, especially for racial minorities whose skin tone made their difference obvious and for minoritized communities that never had any delusions that who they were would be acceptable to the mainstream. Authenticity is also what spawned social movements like the Black Power movement when white supremacy was no longer being tolerated. Authenticity was the very foundation of artistic movements and gifted us with art forms such as beat poetry and hip-hop because of their unabashed nature. As an example, at its very essence, hip-hop doesn't care what you think of it because its purpose was to provide unflinching social narratives and biting social commentary, which is why the culture has had such global appeal for the last 40 years. From a counter-cultural perspective, authenticity has been relevant for emerging communities for the last half-century. And as minoritized communities gain more social and political power, authenticity has not only been the anthem but the lifeline that has kept their consciousness alive and kept their communities together.

AUTHENTICITY AS AN LGBTQ+ CULTURAL STAPLE

Accordingly, the call for authenticity is a rather ubiquitous one, one that is no less important for LGBTQ+ people. Arguably more than any other cultural group, authenticity comes at a premium for the LGBTQ+ community because we do not have the privilege of growing up in any national culture that is LGBTQ+ and trans-affirming. There is no country in which the culture, by default, is based on

LGBTQ+ sensibilities. Further, there is no Global homeland (maybe with the exception of San Francisco) where the LGBTQ+ community has not had to fight from a marginalized position. As a result, our culture is lovingly preoccupied with authenticity because for us to not be authentic is to not exist at all. It harkens back to the 1987 LGBTQ+ slogan "Silence = Death," which recognized that silencing our voices and thus downplaying authenticity would prove fatal to the prospect of LGBTQ+ hegemony and LGBTQ+ rights. Pride celebrations were born from the need for people to be authentic to who they are. In celebratory and ritualistic fora, towns, cities, and countries all around the world, LGBTQ+ people gather faithfully every year to celebrate their culture, regardless of what the outside world may say. It is not the only example of a culture celebrating authenticity on record, but it ranks among the most splendid displays of authenticity we see.

Yet, authenticity is not just related to pride and other communal celebrations such as the Trans Day of Remembrance or National Coming Out Day. On the individual level, authenticity can show up in a dozen discreet ways as we honor our unique sensibilities, and no single act can showcase one's authenticity more than coming out.

Coming out is the cultural metaphor used to describe the instance or situation when an LGBTQ+ person shares their identity with the outside world. Originating in the early 20th century, the phrase *coming out* was compared to a debutante's entrance to a social ball.[104] Just as a young woman was making her introduction to society, the LGBTQ+ person who decided to "come out" was said to be making their entrée into the "homosexual community." The coming out process may have been initiated by a sexual encounter, interpersonal experience, personal revelation, or simply one's journey into self-acceptance.

---

[104] Chauncey, George. (1994). "Gay New York: Gender, Urban culture, and the Making of the Gay Male World, 1890–1940." New York City, NY: Basic Books.

After the Stonewall Rebellion in 1969, "coming out" became more political and represented the rebuke of a system of oppression. Accordingly, coming out was a repudiation of the shame, guilt, and repression synonymous with hiding one's identity. Also, in order to build visibility and political power, "coming out" became part of the rallying cry for many LGBTQ+ activists in the late 1970s and 1980s as they sought to seize the newfound visibility and clout of the LGBTQ+ community. In a speech celebrating the defeat of Proposition 6, a 1978 California ballot measure that would have prevented LGBTQ+ people from serving openly in the state's public schools, Harvey Milk implored LGBTQ+ people to come out en masse:

> Every gay person must come out. As difficult as it is, you must tell your immediate family. You must tell your relatives. You must tell your friends if indeed they are your friends. You must tell the people you work with. You must tell the people in the stores you shop in. Once they realize that we are indeed their children, that we are indeed everywhere, every myth, every lie, every innuendo will be destroyed once and all. And once you do, you will feel so much better.[105]

With this inspirational statement, Milk recognized the importance of coming out and the value of living authentically.[106]

Coming out is not signified by a single act or moment in one's life, nor does it exclusively relate to sexual orientation. Additionally,

---

[105] Epstein, Rob. "What Harvey Milk Tells Us About Proposition 8." HuffPost. December 22, 2008.

[106] As inspirational as this statement is, it was made with an element of social privilege. Not everyone has the freedom to come out without fear of reprisal or death. Not everyone has an intersectional identity that insulates them from the more insidious aspects of bias. Nonetheless, Milk's statements recognized the importance of coming out and the value of living authentically.

coming out is a non-linear process by which a person becomes aware of their gender identity, same-sex attraction, gender expression, and non-heteronormative sensibilities. As an LGBTQ+ person recognizes their own cognitive and cultural dissonance with the world around them and peels back the layers of traditional norms in which they have been submerged, they begin to gradually accept who they are in successive stages. Since the modern world has been ill-equipped to describe, much less honor, the three-dimensional world where gender, sexuality, and identity intersect, coming out is a ceaseless journey of excavating one's truth, discovering new ways of being, and refining one's self-image.

Simultaneously, coming out is also the repetitive act of notifying people that your identity contradicts traditional norms. Over the course of a lifetime, an LGBTQ+ person will come out numerous times as they interact with extended relatives, family, associates, co-workers, or members of the community at-large. I first came out in 1995, and even today, I still find myself coming out to people all the time: the random man who expects me to objectify a woman passing by, the maître d who assumes my colleague is my girlfriend, or the sweet church lady who asks me when I'm going to settle down and find a nice woman. In those instances, while being met with various states of horror, surprise, or confusion once I divulge my identity, I have had to challenge the assumption that I was heterosexual or heteronormative.

One of the more poignant examples occurred during my first year in law school. When I was a first-year student at the University of Virginia School of Law, I remember it was "diversity week" in my Constitutional Law class, which meant that every searing diversity topic imaginable seemed to take front stage during those five days. In short order, we covered topics such as affirmative action, abortion, privacy, and sodomy, and students from marginalized backgrounds had the unenviable task of having their freedom and livelihood discussed nonchalantly by a largely white, cisgender, male, and upper-middle-class assemblage of students. When we got to the issue of LGBTQ+ rights, there were the predictable groans from classmates who thought the issue was over-blown, to put it mildly. As we discussed hostile LGBTQ+ legal precedent like *Bowers v. Hardwick* and *Romer v. Evans*, I tried as hard as I could to be restrained until it became unbearable. Then, realizing no reinforcements were coming (although there were other LGBTQ+ people, albeit closeted, in the class), I argued that LGBTQ+ people constituted a discreet minority and that our experiences were comparable—not similar—to those of other marginalized groups. The professor entertained my comments but quickly returned our collective attention to the dicta, or the nonmaterial commentary offered by the judges in a case articulated by the Supreme Court Justices.

After class, one of my African American classmates approached me with a pensive look on his face and said:

"Do you understand why LGBTQ+ people are always trying to compare their struggle to ours? I mean… I don't get it."

As you can imagine, the question was one of the most ironic questions I had ever been asked. There I was, in what was supposed to be a moment of racial solidarity, having to explain to a fellow African American the importance of LGBTQ+ rights. As I answered his question, I looked him dead in the eye and made the most intentional use of the pronouns "we" and "us" that I have ever made in my life:

Well… the reason *we* LGBTQ+ people sometimes speak of *us* Black people or Black experiences to highlight our journey is because *we* want to reason by analogy. The experiences of the two communities are not similar but analogous, and in a country that has a twisted obsession with race, it can be hard for LGBTQ+ people to create space for dialogue on gender and sexuality. In many intersectional ways, the communities are not separate and distinct but one and the same. And as a result, we have to find ways for all marginalized groups to have their voices heard and be supportive of each other.

As my words sunk in, my peer did the customary heteronormative stutter, where he politely stumbled through his words and tried to mask his astonishment. Unfortunately, he left our conversation seeming more perturbed than he did when he initiated it. We stayed collegial during law school, but the story underscores how easy it is in this society for people to assume that friends, neighbors, and classmates possess the same heteronormative identities as anyone else. As an LGBTQ+ person living in an unequal society, there is a constant need to reframe, re-explain, and re-establish who we are to avoid being submerged in an unrelenting sea of heteronormative and cisgender expectations. When friends asked me why I came out, I told them it wasn't about making a statement as much as it was about not being swallowed whole by a world that would dare to make me something other than who I am. There would be time for statements later; when I came out, I just needed to survive mentally, emotionally, and spiritually.

As one can imagine, coming out is not a process that is accepted with universal praise, and with each subgroup within the LGBTQ+ community, the experience is nuanced and different. When LGBTQ+ people come out, their declaration can be met with the following phrases:

1. "You're just going through a phrase."
2. "You have to pick a 'side.'"
3. "You're confused."
4. "It's not a real identity."
5. "You need more male/female role models in your life."
6. "You haven't met the right person."
7. "You're too young to think you're trans."

And yet, despite the torrent of negative feedback, it takes deep conviction and dogged determination to reveal to the world who you are. The revelatory power that comes with coming out allows LGBTQ+ people visibility in the guise of illumination, truth in the name of power, and authenticity as a means to liberation.

As it stands, this community of people—LGBTQ+, BIPOC, and otherwise—who have become accustomed to living openly outside of work, is not keen on the idea of operating sheepishly at work. The new generation of leaders, who have been groomed and influenced by the unapologetic generations before them, wants to be more open and unguarded as they seek to accelerate their careers and embellish their positions of influence.

AUTHENTICITY IS APPEALING TO EVERYONE

Apparently, people have taken notice, as the desire for authentic leadership has become more mainstream. More people realize that the traditional norms related to leadership and professionalism are outdated and restrictive. The historic norms around leadership have been built on militaristic, individualistic, and hierarchical themes that do not appeal to today's generation. It is not an accident that authentic leadership now seems to have more cache. As more cultural communities like the LGBTQ+ community have overcome social barriers and gained more prominence, the less attractive the norms of yesteryear seem to be.

THE IMPACT OF BEING INAUTHENTIC

More than simply wanting to be boisterous or unrestrained, today's generations of leaders want to leverage their cultural sensibilities in the service of their organizations. They see opportunities to tap into new and underserved markets. They see opportunities to recruit and retain more talent from underrepresented communities that have simply not had the opportunities that others have had. They understand that the world is diverse and that their organizations should mirror or compliment that diversity. They want to be their best selves.

Yet, in a seminal study conducted by Deloitte of 3,129 employees at 220 *Fortune 500* Companies, It was reported that 61% of employees cover or hide at least one axis of their identity at work.[107] Covering, or the practice of people with marginalized identities masking those identities to preserve some sense of safety, is a concept first coined by sociologist Erving Goffman in his book *Stigma*.[108] Taking the concept one step further, legal scholar Kenji Yoshino said that covering occurs in several ways: 1) how we present, 2) what we advocate for, 3) who we associate with, and 4) what groups we affiliate with. When the results from that same Deloitte study were analyzed further, it was revealed that 83% of LGBTQ+ people, 79% of Black people, and 66% of women reported covering.

Not being authentic costs organizations time and money and causes leaders to be disengaged or disinterested. Statistics show that employee disengagement costs the U.S. economy anywhere from $319–398 billion per year and the world economy $8.1 trillion a year.[109,110]

SELF-ACTUALIZATION

Yet, the push for authenticity shouldn't just be based on social advocacy or business expediency. It also reflects the deeper desire

---

[107] Yoshino, Kenji & Deloitte University (2016). "Uncovering Talent: A New Model of Inclusion."

[108] Goffman, Erving. (1963). *Stigma: notes on the management of spoiled identity.* Englewood Cliff, N.J.: Prentice-Hall.

[109] Adkins, Amy. "Only 35% of U.S. Managers Are Engaged in Their Jobs." Gallup. April 2, 2015.

[110] Spanjart, Jasper. "Engagement issues: Europe has the least engaged employees in the world." Totalent. August 16, 2021.

humans have to be self-actualized or to fully realize their potential. Maslow described self-actualized people as those who are doing all they are capable of.[111] It is hard to imagine an individual attaining their full potential without being able to identify themselves in a way that gives voice to their full *being-ness*. Self-actualization is not just about achievement in the material sense, but a full acknowledgment of the internal self. Before we can perform acts or deeds or build long lists of achievements, we must first have confidence that we can achieve that goal. Before we have confidence, we must have the consciousness or the awareness that such a thing—whatever the endeavor is—is a possibility. And before we have the consciousness or awareness that things are possible, we must also be aware of our purpose in acting as a catalyst to make that *thing* a reality. And before we know our purpose, we must come to understand who we are and what our place is in this world. The ability and freedom to identify the self—apart from all the other realities and identities that exist—is how we stay rooted to deal with this thing we call life. It allows us to stand our ground when our demons and insecurities tear at the fabric of who we are. Self-actualization is what helps LGBTQ+ people withstand being blown apart by a world that would seek to remake them in its own prejudicial image.

When people achieve self-actualization, they become immovable; they become stalwarts capable of directing fate and shining their light. When leaders become self-actualized and aligned with their purpose and power, they gain self-mastery or freedom from negative impulses which could derail their lives. In the organizational context, self-mastery could mean the ability to lead versus the propensity to shrink in the face of adversity. Self-mastery could mean forging your path as opposed to following in someone

---

[111] Maslow, Abraham (1943). "A Theory of Human Motivation." *Psychological Review* (50), pp. 370–396.

else's footsteps. Self-mastery could mean the difference between cultivating a creative culture or reinforcing a listless culture where your employees are not self-actualized.

When leaders possess self-mastery and are fully self-actualized, they exhibit certain characteristics. Leaders with a high degree of self-mastery honor the following:

1) They recognize their values. Leaders who exhibit self-mastery understand what their values are. They use their values to be authentic, play to their strengths, and fully align with their larger purpose. They also use their values as guideposts for action and as gateways for high living. Finally, they repeatedly see their values as gracious invitations to be their unique selves.

2) They minimize distractions. Leaders who engage in self-mastery minimize internal and external distractions that may push them away from their desired objectives. They are not immune from doubts or insecurities, but have developed well-honed strategies for managing and avoiding self-sabotage. They solicit meaningful feedback from others, when necessary, but do not let other people drive their vision or dictate their self-worth.

3) They understand their limitations. Leaders who show self-mastery have a healthy and realistic sense of their talents and capabilities. In addition, they know how to stretch themselves in order to grow and evolve, but they do not embellish or over-estimate what they can do. They take pride in who they are and relish what they can do, knowing that their particular skills and talents have great value in the world. Instead of trying to be all things to all people, leaders who exhibit self-mastery rest in the comfort that who they are is enough without over-compensating or extending themselves beyond measure.

4) They exhibit wellness. Leaders who possess self-mastery understand their power is not inexhaustible. They take time to refuel and recharge so they can operate from a wellspring of health, enthusiasm, and inner joy. They create harmony in their environments and seek balance within themselves in order to maintain the necessary energy level to serve the world. In addition, they prioritize their health and consistently safeguard their mental, emotional, social, spiritual, and physical well-being.

5) They wield their power in a healthy way. At the appropriate time and in the appropriate context, leaders who engage in self-mastery use their power to inspire and influence others to produce tangible outcomes. They are unafraid to exact control and understand that the source of one's power comes from an internal place. They possess the clear-headed ability to visualize the social and political landscape but they are not victims of their condition. In addition, they pair compassion with competence. They understand their words and thoughts must be matched with actions and deeds to make material changes in the outside world.

6) They promote equity. A leader who exhibits self-mastery disavows the notion of "power over" in favor of the idea of "power with." They understand that mastery of self does not come at the expense of others because the "self" only exists because of the support, love, and care provided by other human beings who themselves are on related but dissimilar paths. Leaders with self-mastery remove obstacles and barriers and share their power to help others liberate themselves. Leaders who demonstrate self-mastery understand the structural, political, social, and symbolic considerations of our world and strategically work to build movements, coalesce power, and lead equitably with others.

7) They honor their commitments and live faithfully in the realm of truth and integrity. They keep their obligations and act and speak from a place of deep moral conviction. Each day, they re-commit themselves to being the best person they can be while also being mindful of their "shadow side" or the places where they need to grow. They recognize when they have not acted with integrity and always seek to reconnect with the parts of themselves that have never been compromised or disturbed. In addition, they seek truth not because they are infallible, but because truth and honesty are where they are most comfortable.

LGBTQ+ PROFILES IN SELF-MASTERY

As one contemplates the components of self-mastery, one can do no better than to study the profile of one of the most gifted and dedicated public servants of the 20th century: U.S. congresswoman Barbara Jordan. Jordan was a civil rights leader and a U.S. congresswoman from the state of Texas. She was also a modest but esteemed member of the LGBTQ+ community. Having grown up poor in Houston, Jordan decided early on that she wanted to be involved in government and politics. Gifted with words, Jordan graduated from Phyllis Wheatley High School in Houston in 1952 and received her B.A. from Texas Southern University in 1956. In 1959, Jordan obtained her law degree from Boston University and became a member of both the Texas and Massachusetts Bar during the same year before returning to Houston to practice law in 1960.[112] She excelled at debate and worked on John F. Kennedy's presidential campaign before seeking public office in Texas. Jordan tried unsuccessfully on two occasions to run for the Texas House of Representatives. In 1966, Jordan won her bid for the Texas Senate and became the first African American state senator in the U.S. since 1883 and the first Black woman ever to hold a seat in the Texas chamber. Upon her installment, the other state senators (all white, cisgender, and male) received Jordan coolly. Still, Jordan adopted a workmanlike attitude and pushed through bills outlawing discrimination in business contracts, establishing a minimum wage, and creating the state's Equal Opportunity Commission. In 1972, Jordan's peers elected her to the position of president pro tempore of the Texas Senate, which had

---

[112] "Barbara Jordan Chairline" *History, Art & Archies of the United State House of Representatives.* https://history.house.gov/People/Detail/16031

the responsibility of presiding over the legislative body and acting as governor if the governor and lieutenant governor were out of state. Jordan fulfilled that ceremonial role on June 10, 1972, becoming the first Black chief executive in the history of the United States.

Later that same year, Jordan was elected to the U.S. House of Representatives, along with Andrew Jackson Young Jr. of Georgia, becoming the first two African Americans in the 20th Century to be elected to Congress from the Deep South. In response to criticism from her challenger, Jordan's political pragmatism took the front stage: "I'll only be one of 435. But the 434 will know I'm there."[113] Jordan won with 81% of the vote in the general election, and in the next two election cycles, Jordan captured 85% of the general vote. Jordan understood the limitations of the system in which she worked but managed to sponsor 70 congressional bills[114] during her tenure in Congress, all of which sought to aid marginalized and underprivileged communities.

Jordan understood how to work with Congress's "power levers" to support her constituents. She also never allowed herself to become so invested with any group that it would impinge on her ability to operate within the institutional framework of the U.S. government. Jordan stood in solidarity with her Black and women colleagues, but she acted with a singular mind, spoke with a singular voice, and acted with a singular purpose. Jordan was an unapologetic human rights activist, a sharp tactician, and brilliant influencer.

As an energetic and gifted speaker, Jordan became nationally recognized for her speech during President Richard Nixon's impeachment trial in 1974. Before a nationally televised audience, Jordan said: "My faith in the Constitution is whole; it is complete; it is total."

---

[113] "Barbara Jordan Chairline" *History, Art & Archies of the United State House of Representatives.* https://history.house.gov/People/Detail/16031

[114] "Barbara Jordan Chairline" *History, Art & Archies of the United State House of Representatives.* https://history.house.gov/People/Detail/16031

In one of her most compelling statements, Jordan argued that if her fellow judiciary committee members did not find the evidence compelling enough to convict President Nixon, perhaps "the 18th Century Constitution should be abandoned to a 20th Century shredder."[115]

However, Jordan's impact went far beyond her oratory. In the aftermath of the Vietnam War and the Nixon Impeachment, she acted as the conscience of the nation. She opposed Gerald Ford's nomination for vice president due to his meager record on civil rights. She also sponsored provisions in 1975 that would expand the scope of the Voting Rights Act of 1965 to include Asian Americans, Latino Americans, and Native Americans.[116] In addition, she campaigned vigorously for Democratic presidential candidate Jimmy Carter and, in 1976, became the first African American and woman keynote speaker at the Democratic National Convention.

Though warned against bringing female companions on the campaign trail in the early years of her political career, Jordan never shied away from her communities, both Black and LGBTQ+. She was proud, if not boastful, about her relationship with her long-term partner Nancy Earl.[117] In 1978, citing her internal compass, which dictated that she move "away from demands that are all-consuming," she left public office. Afterwards, she was appointed as the Lyndon Johnson Chair in National Policy at the LBJ School of Public Affairs at the University of Texas in Austin where she taught until the 1990s.[118] Jordan was a beloved figure and threw parties for her

---

[115] Quotations from Jordan and Hearon, "Barbara Jordan: A Self-Portrait: 10–11." 7 January 1979, *Washington Post Magazine*, 6–11.

[116] "Barbara Jordan Chairline" *History, Art & Archies of the United State House of Representatives*. https://history.house.gov/People/Detail/16031

[117] Werder, Corrine. "Queer Women History Forgot: Barbara Jordan." 15 March 2017, *GOMAG*. http://gomag.com/article/queer-women-history-forgot-barbara-jordan/

[118] "Barbara Jordan Chairline" *History, Art & Archies of the United State House of Representatives*. https://history.house.gov/People/Detail/16031

students every semester. Jordan died in 1996, and upon hearing of her death, the editors of the *New York Times* wrote: "No landmark legislation bears her name. Yet few lawmakers left a more profound and positive impression on this nation than Barbara Jordan."[119]

In short, Barbara epitomized self-mastery. She understood the instructive value of her principles and used those values to exercise her power to further equity. She understood the limitations of her office but did not let the limitations imposed on her prevent her from doing the work of honoring her constituents. Jordan was savvy and bullish, compassionate and visionary, genuine and uncompromising. She recognized the importance of wellness and heralded the unending need for truth and integrity. Jordan remained authentic to the core, like so many nameless and voiceless LGBTQ+ people across the generations and throughout the world. What made Barbara Jordan an icon was her single-minded determination to use her humble beginnings to create a more perfect world.

Consciously or not, LGBTQ+ people seek to bring more freedom and beauty to the world by challenging the barriers that rob us of our humanity. I remember once being in a barbershop, overhearing two barbers making fun of a non-binary patron. When the patron left, I turned to the barbers and said, "Don't make fun of what you don't understand. That LGBTQ+ person who walks down the street in their 'queer' way makes it easier for you to exist in this world. They make the freedoms you take for granted possible." The authenticity and self-actualization that LGBTQ+ people model make it easier for everyone to be themselves and operate from a place of strength, courage, and wisdom. Barbara Jordan's example of self-realization is consistent with a long line of LGBTQ+ leaders who have demonstrated incredible self mastery in order to liberate themselves and uplift the community, whether it's Cecilia Chung (a trans Asian-American woman who has led a long and distinguished

---

[119] "Barbara Jordan's Ideals," 19 January 1996, *New York Times*, A28.

career supporting civil rights),[120] Audrey Lorde (the brilliant writer, poet, and essayist who became the premier thought leader in shaping discourse around racism, queerness, and feminism),[121] Binvananga Wainaina (the award-winning Kenyan gay rights activist who was dubbed as one of the most influential writers in the world),[122] Claudia Lopez (the journalist, anti-corruption activist, and mayor of Bogotá, Colombia),[123] or Manvendra Singh Gohil (the openly gay Indian prince who runs a charity dedicated to HIV/AIDS education and prevention).[124] If today's leaders operate with the self-mastery of LGBTQ+ people, they will inspire others to overcome self-doubt, break free of their self-imposed limits, and faithfully attend to their personal growth. They will serve as examples for all leaders—particularly in today's educational, financial, governmental, medical, industrial, and professional organizations—on how to foster authentic and empowered leadership.

Authenticity is the unyielding need for the soul to express itself fully. Much more than narcissism or the ego-driven need to be the center of attention, authenticity is the means by which all human beings get to display their unique talents and sensibilities to the world. For the LGBTQ+ community, authenticity is not only a personal revelation but a collective liberation from the oppression forces

---

[120] "About Cecilia Chung." http://www.ceciliachung.com/bio Retrieved 2022-08-14.

[121] Lorde, Geraldine Audre. (1984). *Sister Outsider: Essays and Speeches.* Berkeley, CA: Crossing Press.

[122] Flood, Allison. (2019, May 19). "Binyavanga Wainaina, Kenyan author and gay rights activist, dies aged 48." *The Guardian.* https://www.theguardian.com/books/2019/may/22/binyavanga-wainaina-kenyan-author-and-gay-rights-activist-dies-aged-48

[123] Claudia López: Colombia's capital elects gay woman as mayor. (2019, October 28). *BBC News.* https://www.bbc.com/news/world-latin-america-50205591

[124] Bullock, Andrew. (2022, June 20). "Pride and Prejudice: Indian royal Manvendra Singh Gohil on being the world's first openly gay prince." *Tattler.* https://www.tatler.com/article/prince-manvendra-singh-gohil-gay-indian-royal-interview

that bind us. Whether it is celebrated annually as Pride or performed courageously as "truth-telling," authenticity comes from our desire to step out of the shadows and let go of the masks that hide our most vulnerable selves. Authenticity is the first step we take when we choose to seek our full potential.

Yet, it is one thing to discuss authenticity; it is another to practice and embrace it. Authenticity is not just an academic exercise; it must be borne out in our words and how we live. LGBTQ+ identity, by its mere presence and definition, has always been at the center of this social initiative. Through its struggle, pain, and emancipation, the LGBTQ+ community has always strived to live out loud, even if social realities forced us to be strategic and savvy when we wanted to be unguarded or unabashed. Historically, LGBTQ+ people knew that authenticity was never just about being authentic; it was about self-actualization or the fulfillment of the promise to be fully expressed... no matter the layers to be uncovered, no matter the cost.

As we persist in the journey to self-actualization—one that is repeating and never-ending—we as human beings will be asked to do several things: 1) to recognize our best self, 2) to visualize our highest contribution to society, and 3) to make that vision and life a reality. In the process, we will be encouraged to embrace ourselves over and over again. As leaders, we will be called to nurture our talents as well as to heal our frailties. We will be invited to be emergent and maximize our potential, since leaders cannot lead others if they cannot lead themselves.

Accordingly, authenticity and self-actualization require self mastery. Self mastery doesn't mean perfection. It doesn't mean you won't make mistakes. Instead, it means showing discipline so that when we make mistakes (as we inevitably will), we will have the means and wherewithal to regain our footing and begin anew. It means creating a practice where we aspire to be our best every day. LGBTQ+ people have shown the world how to start this process in earnest. And yet, it is up to each and every one of us to figure out how to complete the journey in our own unique, imperfect, and beautiful way.

LESSONS IN LGBTQ+ LEADERSHIP: AUTHENTICITY

1) **Ask yourself: What does authenticity mean to me?** Visualize who you would be if you were operating as your "best self." Write a short story describing how your day would unfold if you were your best self.

2) **Be curious about yourself.** What personal values support you in being your most authentic self?

3) **Explicitly identify your values.** Values are the DNA of who you are. There are several ways to explore what your values are:

   a. If you are unsure what they are, identify five people you respect and admire. They can be current icons or historical figures. They can be people you know or people with whom you have no relationship. They can work in any industry or capacity. Identify the characteristics they embody. List no more than five to seven such attributes.

   b. Next, ask people who you trust what they admire about you. Then, based on what they share, create a short list of about five to seven characteristics.

   c. Combine your two lists and scour the larger list for words that resonate with you. These are "energy" words and are likely indicators of what *values* are most important to you.

   d. Ask yourself how to use or incorporate your values more explicitly into your leadership practice.

4) **Perform a workplace assessment.** As you think about your workplace experience, ask yourself: In what context am I being the most authentic? In what context am I being the least authentic? Are there people or circumstances that help or hinder me in being my best self? Be specific.

5) **What self-care strategies can you adopt to help you be your most authentic self when you feel discomfort or anxiety?** Identify at least three.

6) **What role models do you have that embody a healthy sense of authenticity?** What practices do they emulate that you can incorporate into your leadership practice?

7) **Assess your leadership brand.** What are the values that have helped formulate your leadership brand? Why? Are they consistent with the values you would embody when you're being your best self? Are you creating the type of impact you want to have? Ask friends or colleagues how they experience you as a leader, and take note of where your leadership brand converges or diverges from the type of leader you would choose to be.

8) **Review the competencies for self mastery.** On a scale of 1 to 5, rate your level of proficiency or success based on each competency (5-high, 3-medium, 1-low). In what competencies are you most proficient? In what areas are you underdeveloped?

9) **Review the areas of self-mastery that are underdeveloped.** Choose no more than two. What strategies can you take to exhibit greater self mastery? Be specific.

10) **Write a personal note of what you love most about yourself.** Post this note in a conspicuous place so it can serve as a daily reminder of your beauty, charm, and power.

CHAPTER 10

Verve & LGBTQ+ Leadership

Verve is one of those leadership qualities that can be easily misunderstood. Whether you call it flair, panache, or "flava" (as we say in the African American community), verve can give the impression that leaders must be exceedingly charismatic or act like a jester of sorts. In other instances, leaders may believe they must mimic some high-profile thought leader to make an impact. I remember joining a business development group that a popular business consultant led. Let's call him Tom (that sounds consultant-like) and everyone thought they had to act like Tom to be popular. Members of the business group borrowed Tom's jokes; some borrowed his colloquialisms and nomenclature. Others tried to take on Tom's personality to disastrous results. Subsequently, people missed the biggest lesson in business development: You must play to your unique strengths if you want to succeed.

With verve, the goal is not to become some mini-version of someone else, but to accentuate your personality and leadership style in such a way that it magnetizes people to you. When leaders can be themselves and act authentically, it makes them more relatable;

when leaders show vulnerability, people know they can trust that whatever they see is genuine.

Verve is not an extension of something fake or external; it must come from the reservoir of who you are. What makes you who you are is your values, or the ideas and life principles that are most important to you. Values are the DNA of who you are, and I imagine if we were to reduce each person down to their core elements, your values would separate you from every other person on the planet. Of course, people can share values, but how we order our values and how we *express* our values signals who we are apart from the other eight billion people on this rock.

Once you are clear on your values, you can take the extra step of determining how to incorporate those values into your leadership practice. In short, this is where you get to apply your individuality and your unique sensibilities. That does not mean you have to be extravagant or grandiose; it just means you have to honor who you are and not try to be like the "Toms" in the world, as great as Toms are.

LGBTQ+ FLAIR

LGBTQ+ people have a particular penchant for owning style and flair. If you have spent time in an LGBTQ+ environment, you can see the diverse array of styles within a room. One of the many things I appreciate about the community and its members is our ability to forge our own style and unabashedly "own" who we are. After overcoming decades of hardship and oppression, LGBTQ+ people have an unflappable ability to take control of who we are and be unapologetic for it.

I remember an incident with one of my siblings that illustrates how LGBTQ+ people experience flair. I was scheduled to perform spoken word poetry one evening as part of a cabaret show in Kansas City. My brother and Mom were in town, and as usual, I wanted to wear something bold and energetic when I stepped on stage. I decided to go to my favorite clothing store in Kansas City to pick out a shirt for the evening. The store imported most of its merchandise from Europe, and most of its clientele was gay. My brother asked to come along as he wanted to spruce up his attire as well.

Once we got to the store, my brother and I parted ways, separated by the racks of colorful clothes lining the retail space. As I circled around with a few selections on my arm, I looked up and saw my brother talking to one of the store attendants at the rear of the store. While I couldn't hear the actual words of their conversation, I could tell that my brother was a bit frustrated and agitated. Eventually, I made my way to the back of the store to see if I could help.

As I approached them, I asked my brother: "You good? What's going on?" Looking slightly exasperated, he said, "I just want a *plain* black shirt, and they don't seem to have any." I then looked at the attendant, who seemed equally frustrated and puzzled, and asked: "You don't have anything in black?"

The attendant looked at me and said, "Well, we do… umm… I showed him these three shirts, but he didn't seem to like them."

Each shirt was *technically* black. The base color was black, at least. But the shirts also had "loud" design patterns on them. I thought they were stylish, but then I thought, what do I know? I was bold but certainly not ostentatious like Liberace. While my brother and I had similar tastes, he often referred to my fashion taste as "expressive." So, I said to my brother: "What's wrong with these shirts? They all look nice. What's the problem?"

My brother looked at me with a sense of betrayal and said with emphasis: "I just want a *plain* black shirt. I don't want dots and squiggly lines and stars and stuff. Why is that so hard?!" Realizing what he meant, I pulled the attendant aside and said, "I think I know the problem."

The attendant:	"We have a few more shirts I could try. Would that help?"
Me:	"Maybe, but I should tell you one thing: He's not gay... He's straight."
Attendant:	(laughing) "Oh! Now I get it!"

And with that, the attendant found exactly what my LGBTQ+-affirming, straightforward, straight-dressing, "non-expressive" brother was looking for: a very plain black shirt. Problem solved. The attendant and I bonded over that incident because, in that intercultural exchange, it wasn't the language that was the barrier. Instead, there were different cultural sensibilities at play, and while being LGBTQ+ doesn't make one a *fashionista*, the community does value flair, verve, creativity, and personality.

VERVE FROM A LEADERSHIP PERSPECTIVE

Despite my natural inclination towards verve and flair, after reading so much about authentic leadership and verve as a young professional, I quickly became worn out with those concepts because these words appeared everywhere and seemed to be over-hyped, over-generalized, and overly simplistic. Many commentators failed to recognize that before you can showcase your personality and flair, you also need to have the "safety" to be authentic. Amy Edmundson revolutionized the field of leadership development by coining the phrase *psychological safety*, which refers to the level of interpersonal risk-taking sanctioned within a particular environment. It is easy to preach authenticity if you work in a homogenous environment and are part of the majority. However, if you are a woman, a person of of color, a person who is differently-abled, or LGBTQ+, it is a very different calculation altogether to be authentic, as it were.

And yet, the fact that the LGBTQ+ community could be so possessed of originality is remarkable given the tide of anti-LGBTQ+

sentiment that still flourishes in the world. The question then arises: How are LGBTQ+ people able to display such noble audacity in the face of such hatred? Surely some of it comes from resignation or the realization that someone will take issue with you for breathing as a member of an underrepresented group, so you may as well be yourself. Fortunately, when you overcome that type of adversity, you can develop a certain indifference to biased opinions.

But in the business world, you can't necessarily be immune to feedback and critique, especially when you're tasked with being responsive to the needs of clients or internal partners. So, how then should the modern leader think about verve in the context of providing good leadership? The answer is simple: Being your *unique* self allows you to integrate your distinctive edge and sensibility with your work self in order to inspire people and deliver high quality results. To be sure, bringing your unique self doesn't mean presenting your irascible self if that part of your personality is not endearing or effective for a particular occasion. It doesn't mean bringing your Sunday morning self when your hair is scruffy, your breath has a little "kick," and you've slept in until 11 a.m. It doesn't mean bringing your Friday night self when you're being festive, feisty, and probably more irreverent than usual. Instead, verve (and by implication, flair) means bringing that part of you that people love and want to be around. It means bringing that "weird," colorful, and fanciful part of you so that you can leave your special imprint in the world. Whereas authenticity is about having the courage to be forthright, verve is about possessing the insight to know what makes you an original. It means harvesting the personal and cultural viewpoints that allow you to engage the world in an idiosyncratic (but effective) way.

When anchored in their culture, LGBTQ+ people can invoke their personal gifts and cultural genius™ to improve their communities and organizations. Based on this cultural example, modern leaders should look for concrete ways to leverage their verve in order to transform their workplace culture.

THE ATTITUDINAL ASPECT OF VERVE

To be sure, verve starts with one's disposition. When people bring enthusiasm and passion to everyday life, it creates an infectious attitude that permeates the entire environment.[125] Enthusiasm is zeal, passion, and interest. We demonstrate enthusiasm when we smile, show encouragement, display positive body language, and envision positive outcomes.

As we will discuss, developing healthy enthusiasm in the leadership context is important. First, being enthusiastic means bringing energy to what you do. It will be difficult to maintain enthusiasm if we appear lethargic with our words and actions. In sports, we see this all the time. When a player completes a routine play, it may help their team, but it doesn't necessarily uplift their teammates or energize their crowd. However, when a player adds a little "razzle dazzle" and does something extraordinary, it serves as a catalyst to boost performance. In basketball, if a player completes a routine layup, the net result is two points. Yet, if a player like Giannis Antetokounmpo or LeBron James dunks the ball in spectacular fashion, the larger impact is that their teammates are roused to perform at a higher level. Enthusiasm matters not only for the individual but the people who surround them.

The second element of bringing enthusiasm (and thus igniting your verve) is finding joy in what you do. For example, if you work in retail or customer service, focus on the regular customers who make you smile during the day. If you're a consultant, focus on the people whose lives you are helping to make better. If you are an artist, relish the ingenious way you've brought something to life. In all ways, shift your attention and find discreet ways to create joy.

Thirdly, leaders can generate enthusiasm when they stimulate their senses. Find ways to stimulate your body so that you are physiologically

---

[125] Fowler, J. H., & Christakis N. A. Dynamic spread of happiness in a large social network: longitudinal analysis over 20 years in the Framingham Heart Study. BMJ. 2008 Dec 4; 337:a2338. doi:10.1136/bmj.a2338. PMID: 19056788; PMCID: PMC2600606.

led to a place of cheerfulness. Wear special clothing items, such as that favorite sweater that makes you feel comfortable. Spend time in nature if you find that nature soothes you. Eat food that relaxes you and helps you feel satiated. When I want to embellish my mood, I always light candles or get Ethiopian food. Yet, the opportunity is for you to determine your mood energizers. Here are some other common examples:

1. Exercise
2. Sunlight
3. Music
4. Making art
5. Excursions (art galleries, museums, day trips, etc.)
6. Physical contact (e.g., hugs)
7. Electronic "holidays" (avoiding social media)

Stimulating your senses creates more of the hormone dopamine, which increases the amount of pleasure we feel. So, when we feel better in our bodies, it stands to reason that enthusiasm is a likely by-product.

Finally, leaders who want to generate verve and enthusiasm should surround themselves with other people who show enthusiasm. When we seek company with those who maintain good spirits and high positivity, we can create a zone around us that bolsters our efforts to be enthusiastic when the circumstances dictate.

With any of the aforementioned suggestions, we can create the necessary mindset to build our enthusiasm and bring verve to the zone around us.

POSITIVE PSYCHOLOGY

Some may feel that emotional energy generates itself organically when, in fact, emotional energy is influenced mightily by an individual's decision to change their outlook and perception of the events around them.

For example, in a study conducted by researchers Scott & Barnes,[126] they discovered that those who intentionally cultivate a positive mood or positive effect to support the labor with which they have been tasked generally experience a happier mood. If we go beyond the superficial measure of simply putting on a "happy face" and try to change our mindset, we can elevate our energy and change the feelings we have about our experience. We can transform our mood and rewire our brains through any number of personal wellness rituals, whether it is showing gratitude for what we have, mentally going to our "happy place," or focusing on the simple things that give us joy.

As much as I am an optimist and a believer in positive energy, I once had my beliefs tested in a very improbable way during "laughing yoga." It wasn't the yoga that your mindfulness teacher might be used to, but instead, the accumulation of a number of exercises (including different breathing techniques and movements) that was meant to promote intentional laughter. At first, it was bizarre: I looked around the venue at the room full of cackling strangers and thought: "What have I gotten myself into? Is this a joke?" (No pun intended). But as time wore on, it worked. When I listened to the instructors and gave myself permission to participate, I found myself laughing uncontrollably. My mood became more lighthearted, and I connected with participants who, just minutes prior, I thought were high on drugs. When I set the intention and took the appropriate action steps, I felt happier in a genuine way.

In fact, shifting one's attitude to impact one's experience is largely built on the scientific field of positive psychology, which is dedicated to helping people focus on positive events and experiences in life to support their wellbeing. Positive psychology is not a "Pollyanna" way of dismissing real world concerns or ignoring existing structural

---

[126] Scott B. A., & Barnes C. M. (2011). A multilevel investigation of emotional labor, affect, withdrawal, and gender. *Academy of Management Journal, 54*, 116–136.

inequalities. Instead, it should be viewed as a means of maintaining one's inner peace, even when we are facing stress or anxiety. As one Ukrainian refugee said after she fled with her daughter from her hometown during the Russian invasion in 2022, "Smiling helps us stay alive."[127]

I was reminded of this lesson during my last job as an employee in corporate America when I worked as a litigation consultant for an insurance company. When I started work, I made small talk, said good morning/evening to my colleagues, cracked jokes, and tried to know one personal detail about everyone in the office. I invited people to ask non-work-related questions and tried to be as collegial as possible. But after months of having a "workplace bully" for a supervisor, I withdrew and saw the job as just a job. I stopped joking and making small talk and largely kept to myself.

One day, my work "wife" Judy pulled me aside and said, "What's going on with you? You're not acting like yourself." I told Judy that I was demoralized and didn't enjoy working there anymore. Judy sympathized and then told me something I will never forget:

> Joel… Don't ever underestimate the impact you have on people. If you don't know it, people get a lot from you… I get a lot from you… Just your presence and smile and demeanor light this place up. When you are not being yourself, we all feel it. I appreciate what you bring here. Don't let these folks and their [expletive removed] rob you of your joy.

Judy reminded me of an important lesson: no matter who we are, people are always watching us. They are always taking cues from our behavior. Regardless of whether we are aware of it or not, our energy

---

[127] Interview by Sara Sidner with "Margarita," a Mother of two and Ukrainian refugee. CNN Newsroom with Fredericka Whitfield, Interview with Broadcast. March 5, 2022. 8:54a.m. PST.

can light up a room or darken a corner. From then on, I never forgot the influential power we all have. In silent and deeply profound ways, our neighbors, friends, and colleagues look to us for strength, courage, and motivation. The verve that we bring (or don't) can mean the difference between a lively workplace/community gathering or a job/neighborhood dynamic we want to get away from desperately.

The idea of positive interpersonal influence is supported by new fields in psychology and emerging research in metaphysics and neuroscience. According to the HeartMath Institute in California, the heart is believed to have greater electromagnetic power than the brain. It is also believed that the heart's signal can affect another person's brainwaves, with heart-brain synchronization occurring between two people when they interact. Further, new science shows that the heart can transmit electromagnetic information to another person's brain nearby (within five feet).[128] Put differently, the nervous system acts as an antenna that is attuned to the feelings, emotions, and vibrations of people around us. Think it's odd? Have you ever been around a stranger or new friend with whom you immediately felt kinship? Have you ever met someone and immediately been repelled by their energy? If you have, then you've experienced a phenomenon that has seemingly defied logic or scientific explanation. The idea of aura, or an energy field extending beyond the physical person, has long been a theory in spiritual circles. Although the research on the heart-brain connection goes beyond the scope of this book, this research indicates verve could be even more important than previously imagined in interpersonal situations, given the scientific implications. In other words, one's disposition, level of verve, and propensity towards enthusiasm can sway one's peers and transform one's environment.

As such, attitude is verve's "secret sauce" and a cornerstone of effective leadership. While flair is part of verve, leaders who show

---

[128] HeartMath Institute. https://www.heartmath.org/articles-of-the-heart/science-of-the-heart/the-energetic-heart-is-unfolding/

excitement and enthusiasm can initiate a transformation for themselves and their organizations.

Further, verve is the energy we bring to our environment when we are our most inventive and peculiar selves. Metaphorically speaking, verve is the frosting on the cake, the streak of color in our hair, or the bedazzled jewelry around our neck. It is the colorful, unusual, unconventional, or unorthodox element that we use in serving humanity.

Verve is not just personality, but also creativity. When we innovate and create new ways of doing things, re-engineer existing processes, or re-imagine ways in which we partner with our peers, we bring our originality and ingenuity to the world. When we step outside of our "comfort zone," we can usher our unique, superhuman talents to do unthinkable things in our homes, communities, and workplaces.

Yet, verve is not only about one's special talents, but the attitude we each bring to the world around us. Even the most unadventurous or conformist person can bring flair just by having an enthusiastic and positive attitude that inspires people. In that sense, flair is the emotional energy we bring to our work to create attitudinal shifts and positive engagement with people in our sphere.

As we think about verve and leadership, it is important to remember what this exercise is truly about. In essence, we are being asked to see our beauty and to revel in it. Each of us is endowed with unique skills, energy, spirit, and capability that can transform our respective organizations and the spaces we occupy. If the LGBTQ+ community, a group that continues to face stigma globally, can have the collective wherewithal to enliven the world, then perhaps each of us can find the opportunity to use verve and invigorate our environments and energize the people we engage with every day.

As we become more aware of the cultural genius™ of the LGBTQ+ community, I offer the following recommendations for any leader looking to tap into verve and remake their leadership model.

LESSONS IN LGBTQ+ LEADERSHIP: VERVE

1) **Love yourself.** Point. Period. Done. Place notes around your living/workspace to remind you of your greatness. Ask people to send you messages about why they appreciate you. Place those notes in a folder for days when you feel unsure of yourself. Use those words to bring you back to yourself. When you love yourself, you create space for your light (i.e., persona) to shine through.

2) **Honor your creativity.** Just because you do not have an independent career as an artist does not mean you are not creative. Any person, professional, or leader is creative if their craft finds some form of expression. Your creativity may not be sanctioned or recognized by official critics. It may not generate a sizable income. It may even experience such significant lapses such that you have to reacquaint yourself with your artistry in the frantic moments you need it the most. Despite those circumstances, you should still view yourself as creative if it aligns with who you believe yourself to be. Take inventory of how you are creative in small and grandiose ways, regardless of what external validation you may have received.

3) **Don't worship sacred cows.** With care and savvy, question sacred norms and traditions and ask: Are the customary practices effective? Who are those traditions serving? Is there a way to accomplish the stated objectives in a new or novel way to create an even greater impact? If the answer is affirmative, use your insight and ingenuity to innovate existing practices within your organization.

4) **Mine and mind your values.** Take time to re-discover and re-familiarize yourself with your values. Find ways to incorporate your values more explicitly into your leadership practice and your unique thumbprint into the orbit of the organization.

5) **Create psychological safety.** Create an environment of cultural safety for yourself and others to showcase their personality and bring their "unconventional self" to light. Be comfortable, take bold measures to "stretch" yourself, and reveal some of your natural personality.

6) **Take risks.** Ask yourself: Are the risks I am sensing in revealing more of myself coming from my external environment or my internal mind? Are the threats I am feeling perceived or real? Lean into your discomfort and test the environment for ways in which you can show verve without jeopardizing your career or credibility.

7) **Don't be "Tom."** With apologies to anyone named "Tom," don't expend your energy and personal capital by trying to be someone else. No matter how dynamic a person may be, the true currency of verve lies in your ability to be yourself. No matter how hard you try, you will never be able to replicate someone else. You are the light that the world needs. And, despite how unoriginal you may think you are, please know there is something distinctive about you that separates you from the crowd, even if that feature is your ability to get work done or be impeccable with your word. Your talent or gift does not have to be extravagant. Verve is a relative term, and the most important aspect of verve is finding that sweet spot and wonderful place where you can add your imprimatur to a project, organization, or a movement. Appreciate your differences and use your appealing quality ("je ne sais quoi") to make a difference in the world.

8) **Give people space to imagine creativity in their own way.** Give people license and permission to be creative in ways that take advantage of their talents. Create flexibility to meet organizational standards in ways that support ingenuity, artistry, flair, and independent thought.

9) **Mind over matter.** When you do not feel strong or up to a task you are being asked to perform, find the inner reserves to shift your energy. Make the decision to generate positive thoughts. A positive mindset can be the energetic disinfectant to help you operate enthusiastically and lead with verve.

CHAPTER 11

Resilience & LGBTQ+ Leadership

It's fair to say that LGBTQ+ people know something about resilience. In my estimation, resilience is the ability to recover in the face of hardship or difficulty. Under circumstances that should be fairly recognizable, LGBTQ+ people have faced seemingly insurmountable difficulty trying to be themselves. Remarkably, between 2018 and 2022, there were nearly 400 trans-hostile bills introduced across the United States.[129] The fallacy would be assuming that discrimination, bias, and hostility against LGBTQ+ people existed in yesteryear. Unfortunately, the animus and systemic hostility against LGBTQ+ people remain a clear and present danger.

But to be sure, our modern society has posed challenges for all of us. To put it mildly, the 2020s have had a very ominous beginning.

---

[129] Branigin, A., & Kirkpatrick, N. (2022, October 14). Anti-trans laws are on the rise. Here's a look at where—and what kind. The Washington Post. https://www.washingtonpost.com/lifestyle/2022/10/14/anti-trans-bills/

Not only do LGBTQ+ people face new measures to rob them of their livelihood, but all citizens are facing serious challenges that threaten our existence. Whether it is climate change, the COVID-19 pandemic, displacement and immigration, poverty, war in Eastern Europe, or right-wing extremism, our world appears to be at a cross-roads as it contemplates how to deal with these existential threats.

What should we make of this world? How shall we classify it? And is it fair to characterize the world we live in as any more unsta-ble than it was 50 years ago? Much of the world's population has had instability due to colonialism, imperialism, and enslavement. As oppressed people, LGBTQ+ people are no strangers to flux, insta-bility, and survivalism. If, in laboring with global variability, main-stream populations have earned a bachelor's degree, marginalized communities like the LGBTQ+ community have earned their doc-torate degree.

That being said, 10 years ago, social scientists started describing the world we live in as a V.U.C.A. world. Now, before anyone starts thinking that V.U.C.A. is an under-reported pandemic, V.U.C.A. refers to the increasing volatility, uncertainty, complexity, and ambi-guity that characterizes the modern world. To clarify what each of these themes means, let's review each one in turn.

Volatility refers to the increase in internecine conflicts across the globe. If you have been awake during the last 20 years, you recognize evidence of the increased volatility in places like the United States. The country has struggled to reconcile its traditional past with the idea of a more egalitarian future. I don't think it's a stretch to say that the U.S. in particular is going through a civil war as it contends with competing ideas about what it means to be an American.

Uncertainty refers to the lack of predictability about social norms and outcomes. The COVID-19 epidemic is probably the best example of a social phenomenon in which it's been hard to predict what the future will hold or what the enduring social trends will be. Several years ago, I had never heard of an N95 mask except for use during the California wildfire season. Now, masks are part of our daily wardrobe, and one's vaccination status is a regular part of everyday conversation. I remember medical experts hoping that COVID-19 could be corralled within a year. Now, we have endured successive years of the pandemic with serious disruptions as to how we socialize, conduct business, interpret the news, and manage our health. We also are faced with the fallout from climate change as parts of the world experience extreme weather resulting in water shortages, severe temperatures, ecological destruction, and human displacement. Overall, we are now in an era where we are less able to predict what the world will look like than at any other time in human history.

Complexity refers to the number of variables we must account for in order to live, work, and commune with others successfully. If we think about the workplace, we must realize that we live in a global marketplace with business partners and clientele worldwide. There isn't now (nor was there ever) a universal way to conduct business, lead, make decisions, facilitate teamwork, generate new ideas, or communicate. In fact, all of these dynamics have become increasingly nuanced based on the cultural differences we can find in any social ecosystem. If we examine the United States, we have 50 little "kingdoms" or states with their own cultural norms and values. If we delve deeper, we recognize that within each of those states, hundreds of towns and municipalities have their own unique heritage. Further, within those towns, cities, boroughs, and hamlets lie numerous communities, each defined by dozens of diversity identifiers, including sex, gender, race, spirituality/religion, socio-economics, class, gender identity, sexual orientation, and age. All of those cultural differences come to bear in our organizations, and each of those differences adds complexity to how we interact and do business.

Finally, *ambiguity* refers to the lack of clarity in achieving a result. As we think about securing clarity to meet a key objective, it is helpful to categorize the two types of challenges that most leaders face. In his book *The Practice of Adaptive Leadership*, Heifetz[130] describes the two types of challenges in our world: technical challenges and adaptive challenges. Technical challenges are challenges to which we already have a solution. They are easy to identify, and with the right bit of ingenuity and know-how, they can be solved by people possessing the right expertise. For example, a technical challenge in an organization may be determining how to streamline payroll or how to conduct a business meeting when you have partners on several continents. These are challenges that are fairly salient and fixable if leaders apply solutions that are readily available.

Conversely, adaptive challenges are those that have no prescribed remedy. There is no clear course of action, and adaptive challenges typically require leaders to use their ingenuity to achieve a feat that has not been previously accomplished. Alternatively, adaptive challenges may have been resolved, but in ways that may be ill-suited for a particular time, organization, or community.

THE LGBTQ+ COMMUNITY AND V.U.C.A.

In the V.U.C.A. world in which we live, it is important to understand the need for resilience among today's leaders. The LGBTQ+ community has been particularly adept at managing V.U.C.A. based on its cultural journey. To further examine LGBTQ+ resilience, let's contextualize resilience within the LGBTQ+ cultural experience.

OVERCOMING VOLATILITY

LGBTQ+ people have to overcome volatility in a world that is hostile to LGBTQ+ sensibilities. Naturally, some may point to the fact that

---

[130] Heifetz, R. A., Linksy, M., & Grashow, A. (2009). *The practice of adaptive leadership*. Cambridge, MA: Harvard Business Review Press.

LGBTQ+ people are enjoying more acceptance than ever before. In the U.S., for example, a 2021 GLAAD study showed that 81% of non-LGBTQ+ people expect that nonbinary and transgender people will become a more familiar part of life just as gay and lesbian people have.[131] And yet, despite the shift in public attitudes towards gender minorities, in 2021 alone, over 100 legislative bills were introduced in the U.S. to restrict the rights of trans women, people, and youth in healthcare, education, and sports.[132] As another example of LGBTQ+ hostile legislation, the governor of Texas directed the Texas Department of Family Health and Human Services to classify gender transformational care for adolescent teenagers as child abuse. The directive called for parents who support their children in receiving such treatments to be investigated, and it imposed penalities on any teachers, administrators, doctors or nurses who fail to report such cases to the authorities.[133]

Moreover, when we employ a global perspective, the narrative is fairly consistent. A 2019 Yale School of Public Health study estimated that 83% of the world's sexual minorities keep their orientation hidden from all or most people in their lives. Based on research conducted in 28 countries in Europe, the researchers used a statistical model and created a structural stigma index that estimated the level of LGBTQ+ bias for every country in the world.[134] Based on

---

[131] Accelerating Acceptance 2021. Gay and Lesbian Alliance Against Defamation. https://www.glaad.org/publications/accelerating-acceptance-2021

[132] Accelerating Acceptance 2021. Gay and Lesbian Alliance Against Defamation. https://www.glaad.org/publications/accelerating-acceptance-2021

[133] Bouranova, Alene (2022). Explaining the latest Texas Anti-Transgender Directive. BU Today. https://www.bu.edu/articles/2022/latest-texas-anti-transgender-directive-explained/

[134] Pachankis J. E., Bränström, R. (2019) How many sexual minorities are hidden? Projecting the size of the global closet with implications for policy and public health. PLoS ONE 14(6): e0218084. https://doi.org/10.1371/journal.pone.0218084

that modeling, the world is very volatile and precarious when it comes to LGBTQ+ inclusion.

NEGOTIATING UNCERTAINTY

The volatility that LGBTQ+ people face leads to uncertainty about what people and organizations to trust, when to come out (if at all), and whether the world will support their dreams and ambitions. Discrimination makes life unpredictable, as do elections, court decisions, pandemics, and social unrest. The world in 2022 looked much different than in 2017, and despite what cable news shows will tell you, no one knows what life will look like from minute to minute. Yet, if the past is any indication, what we do know is that LGBTQ+ people are much more likely to be impacted by any unpredictability due to lingering systemic inequalities.[135] As a result, LGBTQ+ people must use their powers of discernment and adaptability to overcome bias, prejudice, and social hostility.

LGBTQ+ people have a particularly unique relationship with the uncertainty that has been under-reported in light of recent world events. Although COVID-19 killed nearly 6.5 million people worldwide at the time of publication, the pandemic is not the first that some of us have experienced; we would do well to remember the LGBTQ+ community has contended with the HIV/AIDS epidemic during the last quarter of the 20th century. While HIV/AIDS has been designated a chronic and not fatal disease, it may be easy for non-LGBTQ+ people to forget the horrors that LGBTQ+ people faced during that period. Although strict medical protocols were established during the early days of the AIDS epidemic, people were not able to get regularly

---

[135] As an example, COVID-19 has disproportionately affected LGBTQ+ people in terms of employment. Edelstein, Michelle. "LGBTQ+ People Experience Higher Unemployment as a Result of COVID-19, Impacting Health." Rutgers University. https://www.rutgers.edu/news/LGBTQ+-people-experience-higher-unemployment-result-COVID-19-impacting-health

tested because there were limited options. No single treatment was available, and the public played a waiting game as they witnessed unprecedented death. As one survivor noted, it seemed like people were disappearing every day: "It was the bank teller at your bank who wasn't there one day. It was your favorite bartender. It was the guy who did your hair. They just stopped being there."[136]

In contrast to how most victims of COVID-19 have been treated, LGBTQ+ people who contracted HIV/AIDS were stigmatized: they were kicked out of their homes, fired from their jobs, or disowned by their families. Politicians debated instituting a Gay Quarantine, and HIV/AIDS was labeled as the "Gay Plague." LGBTQ+ people were blamed for the disease, and as Dr. Dana Rosenfeld, a well-known British epidemiologist, noted, HIV/AIDS decimated the Baby Boomer population that identified as "gay." In fact, it is estimated that 1 out of 10 gay male Baby Boomers died from HIV/AIDS by 1995.[137] Moreover, 324,029 men and women in the U.S. died of HIV/AIDS alone from 1987–1998, after a U.S. President could barely mutter the words HIV/AIDS.[138] The HIV and AIDS pandemic produced a lot of uncertainty for the LGBTQ+ community for nearly 30 years.

With the community facing grave uncertainty and unimaginable loss and grief, LGBTQ+ people had to find ways to recreate support systems that were no longer available. In the 1980s and 1990s, African American and Latino Queer communities used ballroom culture to provide solace, safety, and support for LGBTQ+

---

[136] Brammer, John P. "Three decades later, men who survived the 'gay plague' speak out." NBC News. December 1, 2017. https://www.nbcnews.com/feature/nbc-out/three-decades-later-men-who-survived-gay-plague-speak-out-n825621

[137] Rosenfeld, Dana. "The AIDS epidemic's lasting impact on gay men." The British Academy. February 19, 2018. https://www.thebritishacademy.ac.uk/blog/aids-epidemic-lasting-impact-gay-men/

[138] Rosenfeld, Dana. "The AIDS epidemic's lasting impact on gay men." The British Academy. February 19, 2018. https://www.thebritishacademy.ac.uk/blog/aids-epidemic-lasting-impact-gay-men/

youth who were ostracized and kicked out of their homes by their biological family. Houses were led by elders or adopted mothers in the community (many of whom were transgender) who helped LGBTQ+ youth mature and become self-actualized.[139,140]

In turn, each family unit or "house" performed in urban ballroom pageants to display their artistic flair, honor their unique cultural sensibilities, and raise money to sustain the household. The pageants were organized by demographic and judge based on different thematic categories, some of which had bodacious names like "Realness," "Butch Queen," or "Runway." Those houses which won the competitions earned prize money as well as the short-term prestige of being crowned artistic savants in the neighborhood.

In between the competitions, the respective "houses" operated much like any household would, where the "house mother" made sure that each member of the family attended to their emotional, educational, and mental needs. Like any family unit, members of the house were responsible for going to school (where applicable), maintaining a clean home, eating regularly, and supporting each of the other family members in their personal growth and development. This "ballroom" subculture turned tragedy into community and created a new social contract, one which treated would-be strangers as kinfolk who were in need of a community to take them in and offer them love and support. The ballroom culture would not have flourished without the resilient edge of Black and Brown Queer people, most of whom were estranged from their own families and forced to remake the idea of "family" in their own image, one that eschewed traditional gender roles and defied traditional family norms related to biology, capitalistic business pursuits, and religious dogma.[141]

---

[139] Livingston, Jennie. Paris Is Burning (1990) (film). Jennie Livingston & Barry Swimar.

[140] Busch, Wolfgang. How Do I Look (2006) (film). Wolfgang Busch.

[141] *Id.*

The community overcame uncertainty by remaking the idea of family and creating stable domestic units.

MANAGING COMPLEXITY

The complexity of the heterosexist and cisgender normative world means that every LGBTQ+ person must circumvent multiple social variables in order to live freely. LGBTQ+ people must deconstruct the web of societal bias, which means constantly deconstructing the interlocking ways in which anti-LGBTQ+ bias perpetuates itself in concert with other forms of oppression, such as white supremacy, patriarchy, and the like. It means LGBTQ+ people have to continually code-switch, evaluate, and reevaluate their circumstances to assess their environment and preserve their safety.

When I was in my second year of law school, I went to the gym to play basketball and blow off some steam. Some of my other classmates were already there, and although I didn't know most of them, most were familiar enough to me to exchange pleasantries and organize a game of five-on-five. Immediately, I had to contend with two competing stereotypes: I was supposed to be good at basketball because I was Black, but I was not supposed to be athletically inclined because I was gay.

Beyond challenging stereotypes, I also had to navigate the various social dynamics at play in just that one recreational outing. I had to consider how to negotiate the bravado and competitive energy that is naturally a part of sports, as well as how to temper any machismo in order to be true to my sensibilities. When the other team got physically aggressive because we were beating them handily, I had to decide how much of my "masculine" energy I would use to protect myself and how much feminine energy I would use to extend grace and compassion to my teammates who felt rattled or were under-performing. Finally, after the exhibition, I wanted to build upon the camaraderie to develop friendships, or at least talk about something other than class. Yet, I didn't want my classmates to think I was hitting on them. I even had to ask myself if it was okay to slap my teammate on the butt for a good play, which is a customary signal of support and solidarity in sports.

Ultimately, I just decided to play the game as I normally would, but that doesn't mean I didn't have to consider each of the variables at various moments during the afternoon. These decisions are made at both a conscious and unconscious level, often instantaneously. Sometimes the process is efficient and orderly; other times, it can feel debilitating. Many times as a marginalized person, you are not aware that these social calculations are taking place because they are an ingrained part of your cultural experience. And just think: this was the mental, emotional, and interpersonal labor I went through to play a meaningless basketball game (although I was on fire that day) and give myself a much-needed distraction. Imagine if my focus was on a job, a doctor's visit, or walking through an area where someone who shares the same gender identity as me was murdered the week before? As a marginalized community, LGBTQ+ people must overcome the minority tax or the additional burden of negotiating social stigma and stereotypes as they perform seemingly innocent tasks in an unequal society. These dynamics add considerable complexity to the lives of sexual and gender minorities in a multicultural society.

DEALING WITH AMBIGUITY

The world creates ambiguity in how LGBTQ+ people can achieve their goals and objectives based on the unpredictable and random nature of bias. Given the vagaries of LGBTQ+ hostility, not to mention an ever-changing world, how LGBTQ+ people connect with their community, advance their careers, and advocate for civil rights will not always be clear.

One of the ways in which this dynamic has been illustrated is in maintaining a sense of community among the LGBTQ+ populace by virtue of LGBTQ+ ghettos, otherwise known as "gayborhoods." Gayborhoods are commercial districts and residential neighborhoods that openly celebrate LGBTQ+ culture. Sociologist Amin Ghaziani states that gayborhoods have four distinct qualities: 1) the geographic center is where LGBTQ+ people come to socialize, 2) a high concentration of LGBTQ+ residents live there, 3) they serve as the commercial center for LGBTQ+ businesses, and 4) they unapologetically salute LGBTQ+ culture and power.[142] Some of the more well-known gayborhoods in the world include the Castro district in San Francisco, Greenwich Village in New York City, the Marais in Paris, and De Waterkant in Cape Town, South Africa.

Over the years, gayborhoods have lost some of their luster. In some instances, gentrification has made it cost-prohibitive to maintain a vibrant community that supports aspiring artists, young people, college students, and low-income workers. As a result, LGBTQ+ people have left some gayborhoods in search of cheaper rent, easier commutes, or the quiet living offered by a more suburban area. In other instances, hetero-assimilation, where non-LGBTQ+ people start to over-populate LGBTQ+ areas due to their entertainment value, changes the cultural milieu of the neighborhoods and makes them less gay-friendly. For example, I used to go to Miami Beach regularly until the "Janes & Joes" and "Hot Mamas & Bros" started to dominate the scene and make it less comfortable for LGBTQ+ people to coexist peacefully.

Lastly, some gayborhoods have become exclusive domains that only cater to gay men. Coming from the file of strange statistics, cities like Los Angeles and San Francisco have zero lesbian bars.[143] Further, some trans people report harassment in bars that cater strictly to gay

---

[142] Dockray, Heather. "Gayborhoods aren't dead. In fact, there are more of them than you think." Mashable. March 12, 2019. https://mashable.com/article/gayborhoods-changing-amin-ghaziani

[143] Marloff, Sarah. "The Rise and Fall of America's Lesbian Bars." Smithsonian Magazine. January 21, 2021. https://www.smithsonianmag.com/travel/rise-and-fall-americas-lesbian-bars-180976801/

men. Given the passé nature of gayborhoods, it is not always clear how LGBTQ+ people can find and nurture a community.

Yet, as Ghaziani asserts, gayborhoods didn't die; they just evolved and function more like archipelagos than traditional urban neighborhoods. For example, lesbians have formed gayborhoods (sorry...I couldn't find a cute lesbian-positive word to apply here) in rural and suburban areas like Silver Spring, Maryland, or Northampton, Massachusetts, where the cost of living may be cheaper. LGBTQ+ communities of color have flocked to Baltimore and Oakland, where BIPOC communities have a greater presence. Finally, transgender people have created districts like San Francisco's Transgender Cultural District, the first district of its kind in the world, to support their community, history, and culture.

Furthermore, the idea of gayborhoods has changed with the advent of online platforms and social apps, creating digital gayborhoods where LGBTQ+ people don't have to live in physical proximity to each other in order to build a sense of community.

While the LGBTQ+ community has shown adaptability and resilience in fostering a sense of family, the ambiguity encountered in maintaining a sense of community is symbolic of the challenges that all of us will face in the society we have now. The idea of sustaining a community lacked a clear-cut solution, and LGBTQ+ members had to adapt their thinking to support their neighborhood vitality.

TYPES OF RESILIENCE

As we make sense of the V.U.C.A. world, resilience should become a more important topic for any of us who want to protect our livelihood. As evidenced by our previous discussion, it is clear that LGBTQ+ people have a great deal of cultural resilience in responding to shifting norms, trends, and dynamics in the V.U.C.A. world. As leaders, we can use the LGBTQ+ example to think about resilience in a practical way.

INTERNAL RESILIENCE

The first type of resilience that a modern leader needs to possess is internal resilence. Internal resilience is when you manage or overcome your negative self-talk in order to lead effectively. In my short existence on Earth, I have yet to meet anyone who has not had to overcome doubt or insecurity in their life. For some of us, insecurity and doubt can come up several times during the day. For example, I experience self-doubt when I'm working out with my trainer and he wants me to do another set of planks. I sometimes experience self-doubt when trying to get home from a remote part of the city, although I have used the NY subway hundreds of times before. I even experienced self-doubt when I initially thought about writing this book seven years ago. For business leaders, anxiety and doubt are no less ubiquitous. A 2020 study in the *Journal of Internal Medicine* estimated that nearly 80% of professionals experience imposter syndrome at some point in their lives.[144]

When we experience "monkey chatter" or the belief that we are unworthy, unlovable, or just too inexperienced to meet the challenges that lie ahead, we have to show resilience in order to not give power to that voice that is telling us to be "small" or to give in to our insecurities. That is not to say our concerns about life are not justified, but there comes the point where we have to decide if we want to remain hostage to the "noise" or honor the truth of who we are and seize upon the opportunity before us. We have to exercise self mastery before we can begin to consider resilience in the outside world.

LGBTQ+ people show resilience as part of their cultural identity pathway. As we examine the LGBTQ+ life cycle, we can see LGBTQ+ people demonstrate resiliency as they move through six different life stages that help them solidify their identity. The Gay

---

[144] Bravata, D. M. et al (2020), "Prevalence, Predictors and Treatment of Imposter Syndrome: A Systematic Review." J. Gen Intern Med.

and Lesbian identity model, which was developed by Vivian Cass, is similar to models developed for other socially minoritized groups, such as the Nigrescence model developed by William E. Cross, Jr., which identified the stages of racial identification. Although the Cassian model did not explicitly include bisexual or transgender people, I'm confident that each stage will also feel familiar for other gender and sexual minorities. According to Cass, gays and lesbians move through six stages as they develop their identities.

In the first phase of the Cass Identity Model, known as "identity confusion," gay and lesbian people realize that they are different without having the necessary language to describe their innermost feelings. In the second stage, called "identity comparison," gays and lesbians start to become more acutely aware of their differences and try to name who they are. In this stage, they may take initial steps to identify themselves or explore the community. In the third and fourth stages, called "identity tolerance" and "identity acceptance," gay and lesbian people become more settled in their identity and begin to affirm who they are. They no longer see their identity as fleeting or peripheral and learn to accept who they are. They develop coping strategies for occupying heteronormative spaces. The fifth stage of the gay and lesbian identity model is "identity pride." It signifies the period when community members embrace who they are and seek to accumulate as much knowledge as possible about what it means to be LGBTQ+. They seek to be around other LGBTQ+ people and aim to immerse themselves in the LGBTQ+ cultural experience. They may also feel animosity towards heterosexuals as they become more aware of the systems that have oppressed them and the community. In the sixth and final stage, called "identity synthesis," gay and lesbian people develop a more holistic cultural perspective in which they hold their gay or lesbian identity in perfect balance with other aspects of their being. They may still be wary of heterosexuals, but they are willing to have a more nuanced view of non-LGBTQ+ people and the world-at-large.

This model is not being used to suggest that LGBTQ+ identity formation is linear or that social stigma does not play a role in how identity is formed and developed. I use this model to highlight aspects of the LGBTQ+ life cycle, which would include various cultural milestones. These cultural landmarks include socially-alienating experiences such as "coming out," having one's first sexual experience, gender dysphoria, connecting with other LGBTQ+ people, or attending one's first Pride, and how those moments and stages require temerity, grit, and courage.

In each stage, LGBTQ+ people have to show tremendous resilience. When you first realize you are LGBTQ+, it takes a lot of strength to love yourself and hold onto who you are. When I came out, I likened the experience to walking through a wind tunnel with a lighted candle. Everything in the world feels like it's trying to snuff you out and extinguish your light: your family, your friends, the community, your God, and the world. To hold onto your identity and keep your spirit lit—to prevent that candle from being blown out—requires a remarkable amount of fortitude and groundedness. It requires faith to listen to that singular voice inside of you who loves you and knows who you are.

As an LGBTQ+ person, once you've sorted through the "muckety-muck" and claimed who you are, your resilience not only helps you hold onto your core convictions and beliefs, it also becomes an act of sheer defiance. You almost dare others to challenge who you are. Your pride becomes your shield. The culture becomes your launching pad. The community becomes your saving grace. And your LGBTQ+ mojo is your gift from the "transcestors" or ancestors that nothing can stop you. You are "steeled." You feel golden. If, at the granular level, you can discover your beauty amidst the torrent of hate and prejudice that tells you you're not worthy to exist, then nothing in the outside world can disturb your inner sense of peace or your inner sense of resolve.

There's a spiritual element to being LGBTQ+ that is understated. The act of self-realization and self-acceptance is another form of being "born again" (as Christians would say), except that when an LGBTQ+ person finally accepts themselves for who they are, it really is like being born for the first time. It is something that non-LGBTQ+ people may take for granted, particularly if you were raised in a world that affirms everything you are. For LGBTQ+ people, the process of self-realization is inverted: you are born physically, but we have to learn to emerge culturally. Without invitation, you must take the intentional steps to be who you are. And when you do that, you manifest a power you will never relinquish. You deeply understand who you are, what your being represents, and what your soul desires: to live as authentically as possible. And you are able to achieve personal clarity just by virtue of your cultural journey. Although spawned by humble notions, the internal resilience that LGBTQ+ people have to exhibit just to be themselves is remarkable and extraordinary.

EXTERNAL RESILIENCE

Whereas internal resilience is supported by a sense of spirituality, an enduring faith, and a perfect knowledge of who you are, external resilience for LGBTQ+ people feels more strategic. External resilience is how we respond to the external dynamics in our life. External resilience may be necessary when we're dealing with negative psycho-social (affecting interpersonal dynamics), psychological (affecting emotional or mental health), or psychosomatic (affecting the body) stimuli in the environment.

On most days, I leave the house feeling pretty upbeat or positive. I like to assume the same about others. But as we all know, there's a big world out there with millions of other people just like ourselves pursuing their agenda, and at times, stuff happens. Perhaps we hit traffic on the way to work or get that email that throws the day's schedule into chaos. Maybe we read about some tragedy in the news? Or maybe it's just as simple as leaving the house without an umbrella and suddenly finding yourself in the middle of a downpour, with a new hairdo, slick shoes, and all?

In addition to the normal challenges we face in the modern world, LGBTQ+ people encounter additional challenges and "inconveniences" that necessitate external resilience. For example, external resilience may be needed when someone uses the term "sexual preference" or refers to transgender people as "transgenders," thus invalidating the cultural experience. External resilience may be needed if some well-meaning stranger tells you, it's a "shame" that you're lesbian and living a life of sin. And other times, external resilience may be necessary when you're working at your job and you find yourself being micro-aggressed. Regardless of whether you are LGBTQ+ or not, the question for any of us is how to shake off negative energy and reset, refocus, and give ourselves the space to act in our best interests.

For LGBTQ+ people, resilience is so ingrained in us that many may take it for granted or find it negligible. Because resilience is so fundamental to our cultural experience, many of us have forgotten to see our resilience as a "superpower" or leadership trait, but it is. The ability to overcome hardship and sustain the effort, focus, and determination in the face of insurmountable odds is a beautiful dimension of our culture that is instructive for everyone. If we look at some of the key milestones in LGBTQ+ culture, we will realize that resilience is a cornerstone of the LGBTQ+ experience.

LGBTQ+ CODE-SWITCHING

One of the strategies that LGBTQ+ people use to display external resilience is code-switching. Code-switching is when a member of a marginalized group uses certain language or modifies their behavior or presentation to adapt to a hostile environment. Code-switching could be as elementary as suppressing aspects of one's personality or using vernacular that is only familiar to one's community or in-group. For example, when I clerked for a law firm in my first year of law school, I wore dress shirts in colors other than the snow white, cloud white, and off-white shades that were implicitly approved. One day, I wore a pastel pink dress shirt in the office (with the complimentary tie and gray slacks, of course), and a partner said to me: "It takes a secure man to wear a pink shirt." I replied, "I think it takes a stylish man to pull it off." But despite my retort, the message was clear. On days when I met with clients, I stayed away from the more colorful colors in the rainbow and wore gray and blue colors until I didn't care about office politics anymore. I conformed to the unofficial dress code to curry favor with the senior attorneys in the office.

Of course, code-switching happens in other contexts, such as when gay men and lesbian women pose as opposite-sex couples to conceal their identity from anti-LGBTQ+ neighbors and interlopers. In China and Taiwan, for example, tongzhi (gay men) and lalas (lesbian women) have been known to partner or cohabitate to resist familial pressure to marry someone of the opposite sex.[145] In some situations, the tongzhi and lalas marry because their "spouses" act as permissive allies who allow them to have same-sex relationships secretly under the cover of marriage. Those marriages are called cooperative marriages because of the secretive pact the tongzhi and lalas instigate to maintain some semblance of freedom and personal integrity.

In other contexts, code-switching has been used to help LGBTQ+ people identify sexual partners and partake in sexual fetishes. For example, in the 1970s, gay men in urban areas created an elaborate code whereby they would signal to each other their sexual preferences by wearing certain color handkerchiefs in

---

[145] Wang, Stephanie Yingyi. When Tongzhi Marry: Experiments of Cooperative Marriage between Lalas and Gay Men in Urban China. Journal of Feminist Studies: Vol. 45, No. 1 (2019), p.p. 13–35. https://doi.org/10.15767/feministstudies.45.1.0013

different back pockets of their jeans.[146] A handkerchief on the left indicated a more dominant role, while a handkerchief on the right indicated a more permissive role. In inventive ways, LGBTQ+ people created a code-switching scheme so that words and conversation in a mainstream (or even hostile) environment wouldn't be necessary.

At times, transgender people also code-switch if they are in cisgender environments. In a blog post entitled "Gender from the Trenches," which amplifies the voices of transgender people, one transgender woman spoke of the need to code-switch after she transitioned. As a transgender woman, she felt the need to speak softer, talk at a higher pitch, take shorter steps, or "swish" to avoid getting "clocked" or detected among a trans-hostile crowd.[147] Her code-switching continued until she felt safer and more confident in who she was and more empowered as a member of the community.

At other times, code-switching doesn't involve clothing or behavior but language. Dating back to World War II, members of the LGBTQ+ community used to refer to each other as "friends of Dorothy," a reference to the character Dorothy in the "Wizard of Oz." Dorothy resonated with members of the LGBTQ+ community because she found herself on a wondrous adventure to find herself. As such, the phrase "friend of Dorothy" became an example of LGBTQ+ folk language and part of the lexicon LGBTQ+ people used when interacting with unsuspecting non-LGBTQ+ people.[148]

---

[146] Villareal, Daniel. "We're Loving the Push to Revive the Hanky Code for a New Queer Community." Hornet. August 20, 2021. https://hornet.com/stories/new-hanky-code/

[147] "Code-Switching By Gender." Gender From the Trenches. https://medium.com/gender-from-the-trenches/code-switching-by-gender-a611ee212fd9

[148] Deutsch, James. "Are You a Friend of Dorothy? Folk Speech of the LGBT Community." Folklife Magazine. Smithsonian Center for Folklife & Cultural Heritage. October 25, 2016. https://folklife.si.edu/talkstory/2016/are-you-a-friend-of-dorothy-folk-speech-of-the-lgbt-community

Code-switching has become a necessary tool of resistance in order for LGBTQ+ people to ensure safety and to resist compulsive heterosexuality and gender rigidity; it has served Queer people well when non-LGBTQ+ people reflexively evangelize and flaunt their sexuality and gender norms without even the slightest idea that those norms may be offensive to the person to whom they are speaking. The behavior is designed to compel the Queer person to partake in the behavior or language. When that invitation is resisted, the reaction is one of surprise, amusement, befuddlement, or downright anger. I can't remember how many times I've been asked to objectify a woman in near vicinity because a heterosexual, cisgender man thought I was part of the "club." When I have objected, the response has been intense. But as I've gotten older and our community has become more visible, I've engaged in less code-switching and taken certain liberties where perhaps I wouldn't have done so before.

THE RESILIENCE OF LGBTQ+ PEOPLE

LGBTQ+ people are ardent and steadfast examples of resilience. Whether it's the V.U.C.A. world we live in now or the historical circumstances of the 20th century, LGBTQ+ people have shown resilience by being resistant and refusing to let others tell them who they are. However, resistance can take many forms. With the customary resilience that this community has been known for, LGBTQ+ people have shown the fortitude and moxie to manage internal doubt and external pressure to move the community forward. For each LGBTQ+ person, the form of resilience is a personal choice designed to simply help them move honorably from one moment in life to the next with as much dignity as they can possibly muster. When faced with peril, LGBTQ+ people demonstrate savvy, situational awareness, strategic thinking, and lively adaptability that should be the envy of any leader who wants to be more resilient in the beautiful but ever-shifting world in which we live.

LESSONS IN LGBTQ+ LEADERSHIP: RESILIENCE

1) **What aspects of LGBTQ+ resilience do you admire the most?** What LGBTQ+ stories of resilience, either from this chapter or from your knowledge of LGBTQ+ life, culture, and history, have inspired you? How can you use these stories as motivation or insight for overcoming professional challenges in your own personal or professional life?

2) **What are some examples of resilience you've shown in your own life?** What did you do personally to sustain your sense of resilience? What can you do to invoke that same energy today in your personal or professional life?

3) **Think about the V.U.C.A. model: What situations in your professional life have you found hard to adapt to?** What is volatile, uncertain, complex, or ambiguous?

4) **What could you do to shift your thinking?** What if the problem is not really a problem? How could you see the "problem" differently?

5) **What solutions could you employ to deal with the problems you identified in question #3?** How could you adapt your current leadership approach to the dilemmas before you?

6) **What impairs your ability to be resilient?** What thoughts or limiting beliefs do you want to mitigate in order to best your best self?

7) **What could you do to cultivate adaptive thinking on a regular basis?** What rituals do you want to use to help you get "unstuck" and think more creatively?

CHAPTER 12

Somatic Awareness & LGBTQ+ Leadership

As stated previously, sex positivity is one of the core cultural values that members of the Queer community hold. When we think about the term "sex positivity," the word that will naturally stand out is "sex," and many leaders will understandably want to steer clear of any mention of sex, particularly as it pertains to their organizations and the modern workplace.

With that being said, let's avoid making this discussion a typical lightning rod moment that overshadows any dialogue about the cultural gifts of LGBTQ+ people. With this topic, like any other, it would be helpful to be more investigative. When we talk about sex positivity, are we strictly talking about sex, or are we acknowledging a part of the human experience that can inform how we process information about our well-being? Are we discussing libidinous acts, or are we examining interpersonal dynamics and how managing those dynamics can create more inclusion in the workplace? In this chapter, we are focusing on the latter considerations and the opportunities for leaders to grow and positively impact the environments in which they sit.

As an initial matter, we have to restate what sex positivity is. While, in its simplest terms, sex positivity is the positive regard for sexuality and sexual expression, it can also be posited as honoring holistic information and somatic awareness. In thinking about holistic wellness, listening to the information that our body gives us allows us to adopt healthy practices for long-term health. Our body gives us information daily that helps inform us whether our actions support our physical, emotional, and mental well-being.

Secondly, sex positivity could be framed as the recognition that sexuality can be balanced in healthy ways to allow for positive and safe interactions in the workplace. Given the prevalence of sexual harassment that women (and men) are subjected to daily, a healthy and frank discussion about sexuality could quell some bad behavior in the workplace and help leaders embody greater emotional intelligence. Leaders can grow in recognizing somatic health and in being mindful of sexual energies that can impact interpersonal relationships.

HOLISTIC WELL-BEING

Having coached senior leaders for 15 years, the one issue I've seen plaguing leaders consistently is their reticence to honor their bodies and take better care of their physical health. Groomed in the "old school" leadership tradition of irregular eating, sitting for hours on end, and working until twilight, exhibiting poor physical health has almost become a badge of honor among today's organizational leaders. With nearly everyone I have coached, the issue of physical well-being has impacted some aspect of their job performance, family dynamics, and overall welfare. Yet, those leaders who prioritize their health and wellness are at a greater advantage than those who do not. According to the Center for Creative Leadership, leaders who exercise regularly were rated significantly higher by their bosses, peers, and direct reports on measures related to leadership effectiveness than those who don't.[149]

As a result, it is imperative that today's professionals and leaders develop rituals and habits that support their physical well-being. In the wellness context, a ritual is an intentional practice that is designed to create more personal fulfillment. Our happiness depends on our level of satisfaction in one of four areas: the emotional, mental, spiritual, and physical dimensions of our lives. The emotional aspect refers to our level of joy and whether our level of fulfillment is trending upward or downward. The mental dimension references the level of presence we show when engaging others and tending to our daily responsibilities. The spiritual element speaks to purpose and the level of meaning we derive from our lives. And the physical component refers to our ability to maintain physical vitality.

As we look to develop rituals, we have to first assess our state of well-being in each of the four holistic dimensions. For example, as we look at our emotional well-being, we may ask ourselves: "How much gratitude do we feel throughout the day?" When we examine our mental well-being, we may consider: "How well do I manage distractions during the day?" It is important to understand our current state to craft an effective strategy for improving one's life.

Once you have determined your current state of wellness, then you can design your rituals to address specific areas of concern. When creating rituals, we should always follow the **S.M.A.R.T.** rubric to ensure success:

Specific: Rituals should be detailed enough to address one's needs.

Measurable: They should have progress indicators and metrics to gauge what conditions will achieve success.

---

[149] "A Leader's Best Bet: Exercise," Center for Creative Leadership, 2022.

Achievable: Rituals should be reasonable and attainable and reflect
             a realistic chance of success.
Relevant: They should be related to the particular area of concern.
Time-bound: Rituals should be initiated within a specific time
             frame. They should have a deadline. Otherwise, they
             run the risk of being aspirational in perpetuity.

In addition to following the S.M.A.R.T. rubric, rituals should stretch us to create meaningful change. Our personal lives are organized to maintain the status quo and keep us in a place of complacency, even if these are unhealthy aspects of our lives. As we seek to improve our lives, we must design rituals that help us overcome the inevitable inertia we will face in trying to make substantive change. Like grooves worn into a tire, our brains are wired to support the behaviors and actions we routinely take. However, we know from the field of neuroscience that we can rewire our brains to develop new responses to stimuli in our environment. Neuroplasticity is the ability of brain cells to adapt and facilitate behavioral change.[150] As you work to make sure your new rituals "stick," I would encourage you to take into account the following considerations:

1. Change is hard. Be kind to yourself as you initiate rituals. If you regress, focus on discipline instead of perfectionism.
2. Anticipate the reaction. When we initiate rituals, we have to anticipate that challenges will arise *and* create a plan to overcome them.
3. Find joy in repetition. Find joy in repetition. Find joy in repetition (borrowing from the song written by the badass musical artist Prince). The key to rituals is making them habits. Habits are

---

[150] Bergland, Christopher. "How do neuroplasticity and neurogenesis rewire your brain?" Psychology Today. (2017).

automated, unconscious responses cued by our environment,[151] and when we repeat our rituals consistently, we help to make them habits that underline a new, healthy way of being.

4. Support recovery. Establishing new rituals will test your mental, emotional, spiritual, and physical fortitude. Set aside time for rest and recuperation, so your new rituals don't become burdensome.

5. Share your goals with others who can support you in maintaining your rituals.

6. Find an accountability partner who challenges you in healthy ways to commit to the goals you've set.

7. Create a reward system that incentivizes certain behavior. For example, when writing this book, I set daily writing goals that, if achieved, meant that I could participate in some social activity.

By following these activities, you can rewire your brain and create lasting rituals that improve your holistic health.

SOMATIC AWARENESS

Somatic awareness is not just about exercise and physical vigor. It also refers to the ability to recognize the emotions, stressors, and energy we hold in our body, giving us insight into our overall state of being. In Western societies and due to Western colonialism and religious precepts, we have been taught that the mind is the sole province of intelligence while the body falls victim to sordid urges and desires.[152]

---

[151] Mazar, A., & Wood, W. (2018, November 9). Defining Habit in Psychology. https://doi.org/10.31234/osf.io/kbpmy

[152] *Catechism of the Catholic Church* (2nd ed.). *Libreria Editrice Vaticana.* 2019. *Paragraph 2351.*

Aristotle, however, argued that the soul derives vitality from the body. In his investigation of the nature of human existence in 350 B.C., Aristotle wrote in *De Anima* that the "soul is the actuality of a body that has life" (412b5–6).[153] In other words, one's life has credence because the body possesses energy and intelligence essential to leading a fulfilled life.

It seems like Aristotle was on to something. When we can tap into the intelligence that our body provides us, it can help us lead more empowered lives and give us insight into our mental, emotional, and spiritual well-being. At times, that intel may come in the form of uncomfortable sensations. At other times, that information may come from energetic feelings and positive sensations. In either case, the data is neither good nor bad; it simply provides a compass as guidance for how to better live our lives.

Many years ago, I worked in-house for an insurance company that handled commercial defect litigation claims. The work was not exactly life-affirming, but the job allowed me to move to the Bay Area. At first, I was excited about the work: it was with a reputable company, I liked my colleagues, and I used my analytical brain in ways that only a lawyer can. I kept those things in mind daily as I made the 45-minute commute from San Francisco to the far reaches of the East Bay suburbs.

However, a funny thing happened: I started to pay attention to my body in between my daily hip-hop and R&B serenades to my fellow commuters as I zipped down Interstate 580. In the morning, as I got further away from home and closer to work, I noticed a pit in my stomach and tightness in my chest. I felt a part of my life force slipping away, and because I didn't fully appreciate the cues, I assumed the sensations were due to me trying to navigate Bay Area traffic or overcome a rough night of sleep. I spent months in this state of dysphoria until I noticed that those symptoms instantly

---

[153] Aristotle. (1994). *Aristotle's "De Anima."* Leiden; New York: E.J. Brill.

disappeared as soon as I drove—or rather "raced"—back to San Francisco. In the afternoon, once I "punched the clock" and headed for the door, I felt a wave of relief that I didn't feel during standard business hours. When I finally took some quiet moments and started to reflect, I realized my body was trying to tell me something. The knots I felt in my stomach as I drove to work were symptoms of dread; I didn't like my job, and I really didn't care for my supervisor, who had a Napoleonic complex like none I had ever seen. The relief I felt when my workday ended was my body telling me that I needed to find another job, a realization that I shared with a stranger at a bar wearing a Santa hat when I finally resigned in December of that year.

Our bodies give us information all of the time: about the dispirited jobs we hold, the long-term locales in which we've been living, the family dynamics that we dislike but have become accustomed to, the person we've been dating but are on the fence about, or the outsized friendship circle in which we've outstayed our welcome. *Dis-ease* in the mind leads to *disease* in the body, which can manifest as discomfort, pain, or stress and could be indicative of distress, stagnation, or imbalance in our lives. When our bodies give us information, we have an opportunity to use and apply that information in service of our greater good.

Somatic awareness is not just relevant in uncomfortable situations, but also in affirmative situations as well. When I lived in the Bay Area full-time, I was attracted to the landscape, the accessibility of nature, the creative and spiritual energy, and the entrepreneurial bent of the region. I loved that the LGBTQ+ community was so visible and that snow was only something I saw on newscasts coming from the East. But every time I came back to New York City, I felt a different energy than I experienced in "Da Bay." When I stayed with my circle of friends in NYC, I felt a warmth and aliveness in my body that I didn't feel elsewhere. Even my family said I sounded, looked, and walked differently. As my sister-in-law said, "You wear New York well." At some point, I made the leap to live in New York for half the year, and almost immediately, I felt this extra bounce when I walked the streets of Alphabet City, Bed-Stuy, or Harlem during my favorite jaunts in the city. I felt invigorated, and my body told me that I had made the right decision. Ever since then, I have been proud to call San Francisco and New York home (Oakland & Paris...I see you :)).

Some may call it intuition. Some may call it a "sixth sense." A certain favorite superhero of mine referred to it as "Spidey sense" and similarly, the gift that the LGBTQ+ community provides to the world is the recognition that our bodies are not just primal or carnal; they possess knowledge that is instructive for our lives and self-actualization. Whatever you name it, being open to somatic awareness allows us to be more present with the truth of who we are. Perhaps so many people may view this form of intelligence as something mystical, magical, or other-worldly because we have been socialized to focus on cognitive intelligence while downplaying or dismissing the intelligence that comes from other parts of our being. Despite the cultural and historical norms that mitigate against it, somatic awareness is a great way for leaders to really enhance their self-awareness.

HEALTHY SEXUALITY AND THE ENDURING PROBLEM OF SEXUAL HARASSMENT

Of course, no discussion of somatic awareness can happen without acknowledging the sexual energy and the sexual nature of the human experience. However, when unhealthy attitudes toward sexuality mix with professional dictates, the results have been harmful and problematic. According to the Equal Employment Opportunity Commission in the United States, 6,500 sexual harassment claims were filed in the 2020 fiscal year.[154] But not surprisingly, the number

---

[154] Hentze, Iris, and Tyus, Rebecca. (2021). "Sexual harassment in the Workplace." National Conference of State Legislatures. https://www.ncsl.org/research/labor-and-employment/sexual-harassment-in-the-workplace.aspx

of sexual claims filed does not tell the entire story. Consider the following statistics:

1. 38% of women experience sexual harassment in the workplace[155]
2. Over 70% of women harassed at work don't file a complaint[156]
3. 68% of LGBT workers have experienced harassment at work[157]
4. 81% of women and 43% of men have experienced some form of sexual harassment in their lifetime, according to the non-profit organization Stop Street Harassment, which is dedicated to ending gender-based street harassment worldwide[158]
5. 1 in 7 women and 1 in 17 men have switched jobs due to sexual harassment[159]

To put it mildly, these numbers are alarming, especially when you consider these two factoids:

[155] Chatterjee, Rhitu. (2018). "A new survey finds 81 percent of women have experienced sexual harassment." NPR. https://www.npr.org/sections/thetwo-way/2018/02/21/587671849/a-new-survey-finds-eighty-percent-of-women-have-experienced-sexual-harassment

[156] Clark, Maria. (2021). "70+ Sexual Harassment in the Workplace Statistics." https://etactics.com/blog/sexual-harassment-in-the-workplace-statistics

[157] "Sexual harassment of LGBT people in the workplace." (2019). Trades Union Congress. https://www.tuc.org.uk/sites/default/files/LGBT_Sexual_Harassment_Report_0.pdf

[158] Chatterjee, Rhitu. (2018). "A new survey finds 81 percent of women have experienced sexual harassment." NPR. https://www.npr.org/sections/thetwo-way/2018/02/21/587671849/a-new-survey-finds-eighty-percent-of-women-have-experienced-sexual-harassment

[159] Kearl, H., Johns, N. E., & Raj, A. (2019). *Measuring #metoo: A national study on sexual harassment and assault.* Available from Stop Street Harassment: http://www.stopstreetharassment.org/wp-content/uploads/2012/08/2019-MeToo-National-Sexual-Harassment-and-Assault-Report.pdf

1. 99% of employees successfully recognize a sexual harassment issue[160]
2. 140 countries have laws prohibiting sexual harassment[161]

Something is not working, to put it bluntly. These statistics beg the question: if sexual harassment is something that more employees recognize and employers discourage, why does the incidence of sexual harassment continue to be so high? In short, because a) those legal protections are not enforced, b) perpetrators are allowed to act with impunity, and c) because, despite the awareness of sexual harassment, some employees may not care about the lives of their victims.

Yet, what if we have been approaching the problem of sexual harassment with wrong thinking? What if, in our efforts to simply repress inappropriate behavior (as most sexual harassment training does), we've neglected to deal with the root causes of sexual harassment? As we learn from the LGBTQ+ community about greater self-awareness, it is also an opportune time to think about how we regard feminine energy and manage sexual attraction if we want to uproot sexual harassment from the workplace firmly.

EMBRACING THE FEMININE

To put it plainly, people don't try to impair something that they believe has value. But as we look at the issue of workplace harassment, it seems obvious that men seek to control, manipulate, and

---

[160] "[Infographic] Workplace Harassment: Understand the Numbers." Team True Office Learning (2019). https://www.trueofficelearning.com/blog/workplace-harassment-understand-the-numbers

[161] Arekapudi, Nisha & Recavarren, Isabel Santagostino. (2020). "Sexual harassment is serious business." World Bank Blogs. https://blogs.worldbank.org/developmenttalk/sexual-harassment-serious-business

harm women because the energy that women possess is seen as threatening.

But, what if we stopped seeing masculine and feminine energy as polar opposites or stopped seeing feminine energy as oppositional in general? How might that shift in thinking create greater gender equity in the world? To re-balance our competing ideas about masculinity/femininity requires us to revisit the norms that created the gender paradigm in the first place. As we know, the norms around gender are socially-constructed, which means that our social interpretation of gender is based on who is in power and who has been marginalized. If we understand this dynamic and the history of the world we live in, then we can recognize one truth: men have to dismantle patriarchy and deconstruct why feminine energy is such a threat to their masculinity and sense of autonomy.

Contrast that mainstream reality with the dynamic in the Queer Community where community members aspire to celebrate both masculine and feminine energies. LGBTQ+ people celebrate gender fluidity, or the norm in which people can acknowledge the value of their masculine and feminine energy without having to choose one over the other. As demonstrated by the LGBTQ+ community, gender fluidity signifies that people can move seamlessly between socially-constructed phenomena and integrate them into their daily lives. As opposed to seeing masculine and feminine energies as seemingly opposing forces, the LGBTQ+ community seeks to hold the masculine and feminine energies as mutually reinforcing.

And while honoring feminine energy is a small measure to undo the centuries-old repression of women and feminine sensibilities, it does begin to help men interrogate their relationship with feminine energy and their adherence to a version of masculine energy that is toxic, abusive, and harmful to women (and also other men) in the workplace. Somatic awareness means that each of us has an opportunity to review how we hold our masculine and feminine energies together. The example set by LGBTQ+ people should help leaders examine their relationship with masculine and feminine energy while dissecting masculine norms in the workplace, uncovering sexist and gender conformist practices, and focusing on ways to create more inclusion in the workplace.

HOLDING SEXUALITY DIFFERENTLY

But even as we acknowledge the tension between masculine norms and feminine energy in the workplace, the issue of sexuality is important in addressing the under-discussed topic of romance in the workplace. To paraphrase urban lingo, "humans are going to human," and people are going to find themselves attracted to each other as employees work longer hours, and the nature of our work creates more touchpoints for employees to engage than ever before. Whether it's through emails, video conferences, face-to-face meetings, work trips, team outings, or leadership retreats, modern professionals are interacting in a myriad of ways that make it hard not to connect and push boundaries.

Dare I say: the challenge in the workplace is not with attraction; the challenge is with how employees handle their attraction. But as long as human resource representatives and legal counsel focus on stopping egregious behavior without dealing with the underlying causes, I fear that far too many people will learn how to repress their behavior without addressing the root cause.

Disagree with me? The numbers speak for themselves. Even today, after the resurgence of the #metoo movement, sexual harassment still affects nearly 1 out of 3 women in the workplace. And although women bear the brunt of sexual harassment in the workplace, we also know that this issue affects people on all ends of the gender spectrum and within all dimensions of the human sexual experience.

By studying the sensibilities of the LGBTQ+ community, society, in general, has to embrace a more robust understanding of what sexuality is in order to engage in it in healthy ways. Discussing sexuality flies in the face of the repressive nature of many societies based on Judeo-Christian teachings, but discussing sexuality in a more candid way could help many leaders avoid the conundra still rampant in many organizations: sexual harassment and sexual politics.

Suppose we taught people (presumably men, but every professional) how to regard their sexuality in a more conscious way. What if we counseled employees on how to recognize attraction, how to manage attraction, and how to diffuse attraction? What if we started to talk about the elephant in the room as opposed to ignoring it and hoping it would go away on its own? In these scenarios, I believe employees would learn how to manage their sexuality healthily to avoid bias, sexual harassment, and romantic aggression. In similar fashion, we tried the "head in the sand" approach when addressing teenage pregnancy by preaching abstinence until marriage and according to public health experts, the campaign was a disaster.[162] There is an African proverb that reads: "You can't resolve what you don't acknowledge." If we want to resolve sexual harassment, we must acknowledge the shortcomings of an approach that focuses on compliance instead of human psychology. Throughout its history and by its norms, the LGBTQ+ community has attempted to talk about sexuality in a freeing, healthy, and liberatory way. That doesn't mean adopting a policy of "live and let live;" it means contextualizing sexuality so employees are better prepared to deal with the tensions and complications that may arise. My fear is that the failure to adopt a more progressive approach will only result in more of the same result, with thousands of women (and men)—regardless of their sexual orientation or gender identity—being harmed and the rest of society losing the benefit of their extraordinary talent.

---

[162] *Abstinence-only Education Is a Failure.* (2017, August 22). Columbia Mailman School of Public Health. https://www.publichealth.columbia.edu/public-health-now/news/abstinence-only-education-failure.

If we focus on the literal translation of sex positivity, we may miss important ideas that can be helpful for leaders as they seek to grow and lead their respective organizations into periods of breakthrough and transformation. Greater somatic awareness can help leaders become more aware of their feelings and needs in order to promote greater mental, emotional, spiritual, and physical health. When we become aware of areas where we're falling short, we can develop effective rituals that lead to greater fulfillment. Somatic awareness can also help us recognize when things in our lives support or hinder our greater good.

Additionally, a nuanced discussion about somatic awareness can help leaders broach the topic of workplace harassment in a much more effective way. The issue of sexuality need not be treated as taboo. We can create a safer workplace for employees at all levels within the organization if we abandoned the compliance model with respect to sexual harassment and adopted a progressive and frank examination of gender dynamics and romantic attraction.

LESSONS IN LGBTQ+ LEADERSHIP: SOMATIC AWARENESS

1) **Take time to be still.** Find some time each day to draw your attention to your body. Being still allows us to be fully present with what is going on inside of us.

2) **Pay attention to the cues in your body.** Concentrate on what you're feeling without judgment. Then, ask yourself if those sensations are tied to specific interactions or engagements.

3) **Do a three-center check-in.** Introduced to me by wonder-coach Tara Quinn, a three-center check-in is a great meditative exercise to help raise your level of somatic awareness. After taking deep breaths, follow this reflective sequence and ask yourself the following questions:

   1. What thoughts are present in your mind?
   2. What emotions are you feeling in your heart?
   3. What sensations are you noticing in your body?

   Each of these progressive questions is designed to deepen your understanding of yourself. They can help build personal insight, help you reset in the face of unrelenting tasks or goals, or help facilitate your journey to self-realization.

4) **Trust... but verify.** As you start to appreciate your somatic awareness, use the cues you glean from your body to spark conversations with a mentor, trusted colleague, supervisor, or family member to think about goals you want to set or actions you want to take. Use those conversations to explore, verify, and affirm how you feel.

5) **Journal.** As you become more attuned to your body, write down what you feel and where you feel it in a journal or personal notebook. After an extended period, review your entries to see if any patterns or trends might give insight into your values and needs or help you identify circumstances that would support your growth and evolution as a leader.

6) **Tune your somatic meter.** The best way to ensure you're properly attuned to your body is to make sure your body is in optimal condition. When your system is properly maintained, it makes it easier to decode information and discern how you're reacting to the world around you.

7) **Honor the truth.** Once you identify physical cues, move in the direction of what feels right. Then, trust your somatic wisdom to make powerful choices for your life and your career.

8) **Interrogate your relationship with the feminine and the masculine.** Regardless of what your gender identity is, investigate how you hold both masculine and feminine energy and how you treat others in your network. Make sure you create space for belonging for those who present and identify in different ways along the gender spectrum.

9) **Reframe sexual harassment training.** Sexual harassment prevention has been largely based on this idea: "Repression is the name of the game in the workplace." As a result, training is framed from the negativist perspective of what employees should *not* do. There is a good reason for this; employees need to know what impermissible behavior looks like. Yet, the prevalence of sexual harassment in the workplace suggests that the attempts to mitigate sexual harassment are not working to the extent we would like them to. I would like to see sexual harassment training expand to help people negotiate the under-discussed topic of intra-office romance and attraction. Educating professionals on the legal implications of harassing behavior is not enough. With people working together for long hours and sexuality being more recognizable than ever, I think it would help society in general if we could talk more about interpersonal dynamics and how each of us can manage romance, attraction, and desire more candidly. Sexuality is a part of the human experience, and if we acknowledge as much, we might be able to find more effective ways for all people involved.

CHAPTER 13

Perceptiveness & LGBTQ+ Leadership

If you were to ask people what they believe are the key attributes of leadership, they would probably list a number of characteristics before they mention the value of perceptiveness. But if we rebrand perceptiveness and look at it in different business contexts, we can see how this LGBTQ+ cultural value can benefit enterprising leaders of today.

GLOBAL AWARENESS

In our initial study on LGBTQ+ cultural values, we defined perceptiveness as the ability to be attuned to one's environment. From a macro level, perceptiveness means recognizing the social forces and social issues at play around us. Put another way, perceptiveness signifies having global awareness. As we live in an increasingly interdependent global society, it is imperative for leaders to have some sophisticated knowledge of what society is like and how it came to be.

Let's think back to the crucible that was 2020 in which the Black Lives Matter movement became front and center. The thing that was most surprising for so many of us in communities of color (besides the fact that violence against Black people at the hands of law enforcement seems to continue with impunity) is that so many people were *surprised*. Amidst the increased calls for police reform and racial equity, there was an inordinate amount of commentary in which people expressed outrage as though the violence against BIPOC people was new. Yet, even if we separated the excessive violence meted out against Black people by law enforcement from the state-sanctioned racial violence that has marked most of the Black experience in America, the issue is unfortunately not new. Police violence against racial minorities was documented as early as the 1920s and 1930s when state and federal agencies—including the National Commission on Law Observance and Enforcement established by President Herbert Hoover—began to examine police tactics and policing behavior.[163]

The same type of "implausible deniability" exists with respect to LGBTQ+ civil rights. In an era that was unsurprisingly lacking in LGBTQ+ rights legislation, a survey in 2019 showed that roughly 50% of Americans believed that federal legislation banned discrimination based on sexual orientation, when the law as it was written didn't carve out protections for gay people in the public sphere.[164] Even for landmark pieces of legislation like the Employment Non-Discrimination Act (ENDA), which was designed to provide legal protections for LGBTQ+ people in the workplace, there are enough religious exemptions for those protections to be tenuous at best.[165] This, friends, is the legal state of affairs for the lesbian, gay,

---

[163] Nodjimbadem, Katie. "The Long, Painful History of Police Brutality in the U.S." Smithsonian Magazine. July 27, 2017.

[164] Ipsos Poll Conducted for Reuters. "Stonewall Anniversary Poll 06.06.2019".

[165] Green, Emma. "America Moved On From Its Gay-Rights Movement— And Left a Legal Mess Behind." The Atlantic. August 17, 2019.

and bisexual community. If we look at legal protections based on gender identity, there are no federal laws explicitly protecting the transgender community from discrimination. As it stands, the fight for LGBTQ+ civil rights is far from over.

And while one might be forgiven for not reading legal briefs pertaining to the patchwork of LGBTQ+ laws across the country, the fact that a sizable segment of Americans was unaware that their LGBTQ+ friends, family, neighbors, and colleagues lack iron-clad legal protection is concerning. What the data points to and what social commentary tells us is that our understanding of each other and our unique cultural pathways is lacking. Leaders need to actively curate their global awareness, which means being aware: 1) that we all are different, and 2) that the worlds we inhabit are different, even if we live in the same neighborhood, work in the same enterprise, engage with the same people, or live in the same nation. By being aware of the social forces that different segments of our workforce have to negotiate, we can 1) create more understanding and inclusion in our organizations and 2) ensure that our organizations do not become inequitable microcosms of the world outside our doors.

EMPATHY

Global awareness makes it easier for leaders to connect with and show empathy towards their direct reports and colleagues. However, that begs the question: What is empathy? Empathy is the mindset and practice of honoring someone else's truth. If we break apart that definition, empathy has two crucial components. The first component is recognizing and perceiving someone else's truth. What this means is that regularly, we have to peek our heads above the clouds and take note of what's happening around us. We have to be aware of what's happening globally or socially and what's happening individually with the people in our sphere.

In other words, empathy means adopting a mindset where we open ourselves up to sensing, knowing, and hearing what other people are experiencing. Ironically, as LGBTQ+ people move throughout the global environment, they often have to familiarize themselves with other people's beliefs, perspectives, and experiences in order to gauge whether their environment is safe. In the process, LGBTQ+ people are primed to empathize as a means of survival; they empathize to build community, to carefully craft their personal boundaries, and to protect their personal safety.

That being said, empathy requires intentionality if we want to acknowledge the various realities that encircle us and the wondrous stories that reside in the people around us. In other words, empathy means adopting a mindset where we open ourselves up to sensing, knowing, and hearing what other people are experiencing. In order to be open to that possibility, we have to make the *decision* to be open to hearing people's stories. I liken this mindset to being an airline passenger and meeting the person sitting next to you: Do you shut down the possibility of conversation by putting on your earphones and focusing on work or a movie, or do you introduce yourself, ask fun questions, and try to make a new friend for the duration of the flight? If you make a choice to be open, then your actions and behavior will naturally align with this mindset.

When I coach leaders on empathy, I occasionally encounter a scrooge or skeptic who will say: "Are you asking me to be someone's therapist?" That question implies that by showing empathy, we are being asked to solve someone else's problems. Empathy is not about problem-solving, but rather facilitating human connection in a heart-based way.

The second component of empathy is the practice of honoring someone's truth. We can certainly have the mindset of being empathetic, but unless that energy is reflected in our actions, the other person may still not feel like they've been heard or understood. Practicing empathy is important to prioritize the other person's feelings instead of our own agenda. Empathy requires us to show curiosity, and we can't be empathetic and judgmental at the same time. If we stay connected to the heart and not the ego mind, our first goal is to listen and understand to the best of our ability.

As such, we would do well to remember one Joel-ism: "Empathy is about recognizing the core emotions in another person's experiences; it is not about the sameness of experience." It can often feel challenging to relate to someone because their life experience seems so fundamentally different from ours. I've had well-meaning strangers say they can't possibly understand what it's like to be LGBTQ+, but empathy is not the cerebral exercise of matching personal details (i.e. using the same cultural identifier, having the same cultural pathway, or living the same experience); empathy is about connecting hearts and listening to stories and understanding the deeper truth that binds us all. Although being Queer is a rich, complex, and wonderful experience, empathy with LGBTQ+ people is not as difficult as we make it out to be if we understand the core values of being LGBTQ+ or the core emotions that describe the LGBTQ+ journey. If you have ever felt different from the "norm" (although I feel quite normal in my Queerness), or if you have felt misunderstood for being who you are, then you have some inkling of what it's like to be LGBTQ+. On the same note, if you felt a powerful emotional attraction to someone that defied logic or societal expectation, or if you've ever thought words were inadequate to describe your persona, presence, or energy, there's a good chance you understand a semblance of what it's like to be LGBTQ+.

To be sure, perception is not the same as lived experience. But when we frame empathy in a way that gives breadth to the full range of emotional experiences, empathy connects people in ways they never thought possible. Instead of the bland familiarity that many of us have with our colleagues, we can use compassion to explore our shared humanity. Again, empathy is about recognizing the core emotions in another person's experiences; it is not about the sameness of experience.

Unfortunately, empathy gets sidetracked when the ego-mind supersedes the heart. To explain how to avoid what I call the "ego-mind trap," I will share a story involving my favorite mentor and the wisest person I know: my Mom.

Once upon a time, I was sharing some work stress with my Mom, and she immediately went into problem-solving mode. As she sensed me retreating from the conversation, the following exchange took place:

Mom:	Okay… I'm not hearing you say anything.
Me:	Well… I wasn't really looking for advice. I just needed to vent.
Mom:	I was just trying to help.
Me:	I know, but that's not what I need at this particular moment.

Let's just say that conversation was not a prime example of how empathy works.

But, fear not! Soon after that, I was on the phone again with Mom, and this time, I was talking about another work dilemma I faced with a different colleague. This time, Mom was quiet, and when I asked her for feedback, she responded: "Well… I didn't think I had permission to say anything." Again, this was not helpful.

But, the third time proved to be the charm. Mom and I were again discussing work, and this time, she said to me: "Okay… Before we begin, I need you to tell me what type of Mom you need for this conversation."

Puzzled, I said, "I'm not sure I follow. What type of Mom do I need? What do you mean?"

Mom:	"Several conversations ago, I tried to offer advice, and you didn't take to that too well. The second time, I tried to be quiet and listen, but you didn't like that version of me either. So… Here are the options: Do you want me to be a) Advice-Giving Mom, b) Ride-or-Die Mom, c) Kick Someone's Ass Mom, or

d) Active Listening and Understanding Mom? Those are your four options. Tell me which card to play, and we'll proceed accordingly."

I still laugh at that conversation today, not only because of how Mom responded but because of my surprise that she knew what "ride-or-die" meant. That aside, Mom demonstrated an important aspect of practicing empathy: recognizing what the situation dictates. In most instances, people are not necessarily looking for advice. Instead, they are looking for space to be seen and be vulnerable. As friends, colleagues, and leaders, we help create a safe space for people to be open. In turn, it creates an affirmative effect that validates the person's feelings and soothes their insecurities. In that space or cocoon, the person we're empathizing with will find the wherewithal to invoke their wisdom and apply it to any situation. Premature problem-solving or unsolicited advice short-circuits this process whereby a person realizes their power. Instead, good leaders use situational awareness to ask the other person what they need and respond accordingly. This allows the other person to summon their wisdom for their highest good. Perceptiveness doesn't mean being prescient; it means asking the other person for what they need and putting their needs first when they seek support.

INTUITION

In addition to global awareness and empathy, the third aspect of perceptiveness is intuition, or the ability to understand something quickly without resorting to cognitive reasoning. Intuition is instinctive; it is the tacit knowledge we have accumulated over a lifetime. It is the tried-and-true knowledge that we rely on to achieve daily tasks and meet strategic objectives. LGBTQ+ people must use intuition regularly when they identify allies, meet other community members, and discover safe spaces.

Some examples of tacit knowledge include the implied knowledge that helps you find your way home when your customary route is under construction or the understanding a seasoned consultant might rely on when they're first performing discovery with a new client. My Aunt Mickey uses her intuition to make the perfect savory cornbread that no one in the family can seem to duplicate. And while leaders should definitely engage in the deliberative and systematic thinking that allows us to be intentional and brilliant, we should not ignore the tacit knowledge or intuition that allows us to make decisions without the constraint of prolonged analytical reasoning.

As untethered as intuition may sound, imagine a world where everything we do requires deliberation. Imagine what our lives would be like if we had to think about brushing our teeth or eating lunch. Imagine the brain power we would have to expend to function. Our tasks would be never-ending and our lives would be utterly exhausting.

As leaders, we don't always have the luxury of time or infinite resources to make decisions. Sometimes we must make snap judgments based on our accumulated knowledge. It's important that we use our perceptiveness to strike the right tone or reach an accord when those situations arise. In those moments, our intuition is not based on whim or passing fancy; it is based on our lived experience and our prior knowledge, which inform what we believe to be correct.

Our intuition helps us to automate and ritualize certain aspects of our lives so that we devote our attention to crucial issues and reserve our energy for more complicated endeavors when necessary. When intuition is balanced with deliberate thinking, leaders can use their intuition to create and sustain a transformational leadership practice.

Additionally, our intuition can protect us from making poor decisions. Each of us has an emotional guidance system, or EGS™, that can lead us or steer us away from certain situations. Just like a GPS system that offers geographic guidance, our EGS™ provides leadership and insight to ensure positive outcomes. When we receive negative feelings, cues, or sensations, those are indicators that something is amiss or awry and probably not in our best interest. Conversely, when we receive positive feelings, surges, and sensations, that is a good indication that we are moving in the right direction. The more we use intuition (while not abandoning rationality) to inform our perspective, the more we, as leaders, can make sound decisions that support every employee in the organization. The topic of intuition is explored further in the chapter on somatic awareness.

Albert Einstein once wrote: "*The intuitive mind is a sacred gift and the rational mind is a faithful servant. We have created a society that honors the servant and has forgotten the gift.*" The mistake would be in thinking that intuition has no utility for leaders. As noted with the statistics shared previously, intuition is a critical component of leadership that remains under-discussed and undervalued. But as leaders look to new and unconventional ways to further their self-awareness and invigorate their leadership practice, they would do well to follow the lead of LGBTQ+ people, increase their perceptiveness, and honor their intuition more fully. Intuition is a misunderstood but sacred component of leadership.

Whether it is global awareness, empathy, or intuition, perceptiveness is part of the cultural genius™ that LGBTQ+ people rely on to be leaders in society. Perceptiveness informs their knowledge of the world and helps them be responsible global citizens; it deepens their capacity for empathy and strengthens their intuitive radar to make the best decisions about their lives and careers. As the world becomes more familiar with the LGBTQ+ community and culture, those same gifts can also benefit leaders who want to become more aware of the world around them. By increasing their level of perceptiveness, leaders can make positively impactful decisions because they better understand the society in which they live. Perceptiveness is the gift that Queer people have developed out of necessity, yet it is the example that leaders everywhere can learn from as they look to transform themselves and their organizations.

LESSONS IN LGBTQ+ LEADERSHIP:
PERCEPTIVENESS

In order to sharpen your level of perceptiveness, I offer the following recommendations:

1) **Study the world around you.** Take time each day to visit with people and consult with sources that expand your mind's aperture and help you visualize the world beyond your front door.

2) **Gather information from various resources.** Solicit information, data, and perspectives from a variety of places, and in particular, sources that amplify the perspective of non-dominant groups.

3) **Empathize, don't proselytize.** Use conversation to support someone else's vulnerability. Don't fall prey to advice-giving or personal coaching. Take time to listen deeply and understand the other person's needs in the moment.

4) **Take an empathy inventory.** Ask people in your circle of influence to rate your level of empathy and offer suggestions of how you can show greater empathy.

5) **Value your intuition.** Don't over-indulge in rationality at the expense of your intuition. Allow your spirit to speak to you in unfettered ways so you can hear your wisdom.

6) **Cultivate your intuition.** Take time to yourself every day to be present with your thoughts. Create space in your calendar for observation and reflection. Avoid cramming your calendar with back-to-back meetings where you don't have time to listen to your inner wisdom.

7) **Review what your intuition tells you.** As you honor your intuition, record the data that your intuition gives you. Take notes over time to see if there are any patterns or any places of divergence. Those trends will likely inform you of the actions you need to take and the guidance you need to honor.

CHAPTER 14

Interconnectedness & LGBTQ+ Leadership

Since their inception, social media apps and platforms have infiltrated our homes, lives, and daily interactions. As of April 2021, there were 4.48 million users of social media around the world.[166] That's a staggering number by any measure when you remember that social media was invented merely 25 years ago. Like many of you reading this page, I dabble in the social media ecosystem and have enjoyed getting the occasional exposé into people's lives.

But with my "friend" count approaching numbers I never thought it would, I started asking myself: Am I truly engaging people, or am I just a voyeur to the lives they choose to present? With technology and social media everywhere, are we as a species actually connecting to each other, or are we just connected? Are we simply voyeurs for each other? I liken this to a situation in which two or

---

[166] Deen, Brian. "Social Network Usage & Growth: How Many People Use Social Media in 2022?" Backlinko. October 10, 2021.

more people work for the same organization: Are we simply hallway associates (i.e. we speak to each other if we see each other in the hallway) or are we lunchtime buddies (i.e. we seek each other out to have lunch and catch-up about the weekend)? Are we just colleagues who know each other's titles and job responsibilities, or are we business partners invested in each other's success? The former applies passive association, whereas the latter implies familiarity and interpersonal engagement.

Part of the need for connection is due to the silent epidemic of loneliness. In the last 10 years, social scientists have noticed that loneliness has become a far-reaching crisis and a major public health concern. Loneliness is as detrimental to your health as smoking 15 cigarettes a day,[167] which could partly explain our fascination with "weapons of mass distraction" such as Facebook, Snapchat, Twitter, and Instagram. Consider the following statistics:

1. Seventy municipalities, schools, and businesses across Denmark have signed up for the National Movement Against Loneliness.
2. In May 2019, New Zealand's progressive Prime Minister Jacinda Ardern placed loneliness among the top five priorities in the national budget.
3. In January 2018, U.K. Prime Minister Teresa May appointed the world's first Minister for Loneliness.
4. A 2018 study of 20,000 Americans found that 46% felt alone sometimes or all the time and that Generation Y (1980–1996) and Generation Z (1996 onward) are lonelier and claim to be in worse mental health than their predecessors.

---

[167] Holt-Lunstad J, Smith TB, Baker M, Harris T, Stephenson D. Loneliness and social isolation as risk factors for mortality: a meta-analytic review. Perspect Psychol Sci. 2015 Mar;10(2):227–37. doi:10.1177/1745691614568352. PMID: 25910392.

5. In September of 2016, there were half a million young people in Japan who chose not to leave their house or interact with anyone for at least six months.
6. People who are lonely have a 26% higher chance of dying.[168,169]

As these statistics show, we are living in a world where the idea of interconnectedness feels fleeting—if not non-existent—for many people. And this was before the onset of Covid-19!

Perhaps our collective desire to thwart loneliness is why more and more employees are seeking greater connection in their places of employment? Or maybe the reasons are two-fold: Today's generation of emerging leaders not only want to support the sense of community and connection wherever they can, but also want to reject the staid and hierarchical form of leadership that has produced so much isolation in the workforce. As the *Harvard Business Review* quoted in 2017, social belonging (a form of interconnectedness) is a fundamental business need that is hardwired into our DNA.

Yet, 40% of people say they feel isolated at work.[170] Today's workforce wants engagement. In surveys of recent leadership competencies, employees want open, vulnerable, relatable, and personable leaders, and managers who display those traits increase team performance.[171] They want leaders who bring people together and are able to lead without being preoccupied with someone's title, rank, position, or identity. In addition, they want someone who understands that the organization's success depends on everyone's success at every level of the organization.

---

[168] Anonymous. (n.d.) The Loneliness Epidemic Is So Bad World Leaders Have Been Forced to Intervene. https://melmagazine.com/en-us/story/the-loneliness-epidemic-is-so-bad-world-leaders-have-been-forced-to-intervene

[169] CBC News. August 16, 2017. https://www.cbc.ca/news/health/loneliness-public-health-psychologist-1.4249637

[170] *Id.*

[171] Shaffer, E. & Neal, S. (2021). Why leaders must connect more during times of crisis. Catalyst.

Regardless of that logic, some would argue, why do we have to get to know our colleagues? As I've heard time and time again: "We're not at work to have friends...We're there because we have a job to do." But in reality, how can you do your job effectively if you don't have the relationships with your peers to support candor, trust, and openness? When we have nurtured our relationship with a colleague, we can discuss expectations, frustrations, and misgivings while knowing that the other person will be open to our feedback, constructive or otherwise. When we feel comfortable with our colleagues, we can be honest about mistakes or seek help without worrying about being judged or seen as incompetent. When we have an affinity for the people we work with, we will make the extra effort to support them because we know that in a team environment, each of us is defined by our collective success. Building relationships is not just about niceties or "lip service;" it is the pulse by which organizations grow and transform.

Yet, there is a deeper and more fundamental truth that we must recognize. Apart from our jobs and day-to-day responsibilities, we must recognize we are all connected and interdependent on each other in some way to survive in this world. Though we may think that our pathways are singular and distinct from one another, how we show up in the world profoundly impacts the lives of others. What greater example of that notion is there other than the COVID-19 pandemic that we have all endured? The decisions of our neighbors to wear masks, take precautions, be truthful about their health status, and get vaccinated have greatly impacted the livelihood of everyone and have determined our overall ability to stay safe and inoculated against a mutating virus. We need everyone to act responsibly if we are ever to be rid of COVID-19.

But the need for collective responsibility pre-dates COVID. Our ability to get through the day is predicated on the successful coordination of a number of events. Think about your day and what you routinely try to accomplish between the time you wake up and go to bed: the quality of your day is wholly dependent on multiple people honoring the professional obligations and social covenants we have dutifully established. If the subway doesn't operate efficiently, if people in the crowd don't abide by the laws, if the daycare center doesn't open on time, or if our spouse doesn't tend to his share of domestic duties, our day is dramatically different than what we thought it would be. In turn, our ability to achieve our goals is severely compromised. Whether we like it or not, we are part of an elaborate web in which our success is influenced, in part, by the ability of others to be accountable and honor their obligations.

Yet and still, we would be remiss to reduce our understanding of connectedness to our ability to perform tasks and fulfill job responsibilities. It is not just our "doing-ness" that connects and unifies us; it is, first and foremost, our "being-ness." As human beings, our ability to recognize our common connection, our oneness, and our universality will determine what kind of society we will have, what type of communities we will have, and what type of leaders we will be.

We have to unlearn what we have learned in order to be better leaders. Part of the "unlearning" we must undergo is thinking that our engagement in the business world is strictly transactional. Many years ago, I was invited to join a coaching outfit based in the Bay Area. They had a sterling reputation and worked for many "big name" companies in the Tech Industry. The coaching outfit preached "community," and in my initial emails with them, I thought: "Hey! This could be a great fit." At their next monthly meeting, I met their motley crew of consultants and coaches, and during introductions, I met "Jim," a fellow coach who also shared a passion for music and spirituality. As we finished our brief introductions, we exchanged numbers and made an appointment to talk again and further the conversation. Everything felt easy and mellow.

However, our next conversation had a completely different tone to it. Without exchanging pleasantries and barely saying hello, Jim asked me a number of questions in rapid-fire succession: "So…

What are your business goals for this year? Who are your top five business clients? What industries are you focused on?" It felt like Jim was trying to "size me up," and I quickly lost interest in the conversation as I realized that Jim was more interested in me building his book of business than befriending a business colleague. Our conversation lasted 15 minutes and felt cold, routine, and transactional. Jim didn't see me as a person; he saw me as a "means to an end."

Had Jim taken the time to get to know me, our conversation could have easily expanded into business prospects and, perhaps eventually, a business partnership. Yet, because his approach was so limited and so myopic, it killed any possibility of us engaging in further dialogue. When we focus on the transaction and not the person, we narrow the scope of opportunity and create one-dimensional interactions. If our interpersonal lens is too small, it restricts the points of engagement between two people and limits the realm of possibility solely to the business at-hand.

Conversely, creating space for broader human connection sets the stage for an ongoing relationship that can produce opportunity at the right time. For example, 12 years ago, I was hired as part of an external coaching team for a leadership milestone program. Six times a year, the coaching cadre would convene at a beautiful resort for a week to support senior associates in incorporating wellness rituals into their leadership practice. The coaching cadre worked alongside other vendors, all of whom were experts in motivational speaking, wellness, and holistic practices.

Throughout those visits, I became familiar with several vendors and started talking to them regularly. Yet, eager to avoid the customary and dry conversations about "work," I purposely avoided networking and talking "shop." Although a number of the coaches were there to solicit, I held back because I didn't want to come across as an opportunist.

Several years into the contract, I became friends with Annie, one of the directors at one of the partner firms. On the surface, she seemed quiet and formal, but during "off hours," she was warm, personable, and "real." During lunch one day, she asked if I had ever considered doing contract work with her firm, to which I replied: "I considered it but didn't want to be part of the mad rush of people trying to get new work from you. That's not me." Annie smiled and said, "I know, which is one of the reasons I like you… You're genuine and not just a self-promoter. I trust you to be a man of integrity, which is why I think you could do some great work for us."

As a result, Annie became a close friend and introduced me to several great business opportunities over the years. Because we focused on our shared humanity, we created a relationship that has survived the years and allowed us to become friends, confidants *and* trusted colleagues. I am definitely a better person and a better consultant/coach for having met her.

When we recognize our interconnectedness, we deepen our relationships and expand the reach of our impact.

INTERCONNECTEDNESS OF THE LGBTQ+ COMMUNITY

The LGBTQ+ community has firsthand knowledge of how interconnectedness can influence relationships. Although we are one community, we are many "people," and our journeys as bisexual, transgender, asexual, or Queer people are connected and intertwined. Although our identities related to gender identity, gender expression, and sexual orientation are unique, the histories and subcultures are connected in such a way that it would be difficult for any segment of the community to survive without the support and allyship of the other. For example, the LGBTQ+ community owes a huge debt of gratitude to the transgender community for its leadership and visibility during the early days of the LGBTQ+ civil rights movement. Without the transgender community, particularly transgender people of color, there would not have been the Stonewall rebellion. Without the Stonewall rebellion, the LGBTQ+ movement and the LGBTQ+ community would not exist in their current form.

And yet, there are other lesser-known examples of interconnectedness in the LGBTQ+ community that should be brought to light. In the 1980s, HIV/AIDS was known as "gay cancer." For several years, San Francisco had the highest density of HIV/AIDS-related cases.[172] When the LGBTQ+ community was ravaged by the HIV/AIDS epidemic, there were scores of nurses, doctors, and morticians who refused to treat HIV/AIDS patients. Without the necessary care to survive, gay male patients turned to lesbian women to provide the physical and emotional care they were denied in hospitals across the region. Dubbed in some areas as "Blood Sisters," lesbian women volunteered in massive numbers in both the United States and the United Kingdom to help HIV/AIDS patients stabilize their medical condition, process their trauma and grief, and in the most critical of situations, die with dignity.[173]

Further, these same lesbian volunteers donated blood when there was a shortage in supply and told gay men that they were loved and that they mattered. As Jad Adams, a noted British historian, wrote for his documentary, *AIDS: The Unheard Voices*, "[…]A lot of these men were not out to their families or were explicitly rejected by their families. They really needed the support that gay-friendly women could provide."[174] Although HIV/AIDS posed a significantly lesser risk to lesbian women than gay men, the "Blood Sisters" believed that the plight of gay men was interconnected to their struggle for liberation, affirmation, and equality.

---

[172] McFarland, Dr. Willi, MD, PhD (Ed.). City & County of San Francisco. "Atlas of HIV/AIDS in San Francisco 1981–2000." https://www.sfdph.org/dph/files/reports/RptsHIVAIDS/HIVAIDSAtlas1981-2000.pdf

[173] Lister, Kate. "The lesbian 'blood sisters' who cared for gay men when doctors were scared to."

[174] *Id.*

The stories of the Blood Sisters notwithstanding, the LGBTQ+ community can also offer a cautionary tale of when interconnectedness has been ignored to the peril of our collective political hopes and community calls for unity. Though it may seem like a distant memory for some, it wasn't that long ago that Congress debated the passage of the Employment Non-Discrimination Act (ENDA), which was written to prohibit discrimination in hiring and employment based on sexual orientation and gender identity. In 2007, ENDA was being debated in the House of Representatives. In an astonishing moment of Machiavellian politics, former representative Barney Frank (D, MA) supported a "gay-only version" of the bill, which excluded protections for transgender employees. At the time, Frank—a tremendous public servant who I respect—argued that the LGB version of the bill was the only politically feasible version of the bill that could become law at that time. Frank was the first openly gay member of the U.S. congress and a trailblazer for LGBTQ+ political activism, but his decision was a tactical error. Frank's comments created a firestorm and threatened to splinter the LGBTQ+ movement at a time when LGBTQ+ rights and initiatives remained unpopular with a majority of people in the U.S. For all of his political savvy and wisdom, one could fairly argue that Frank didn't fully see the interconnectedness between the LGB+ movement and the trans movement.

Remarkably, the introduction of the "trans-exclusionary" ENDA in the House prompted the creation of United ENDA, a coalition of 400+ organizations that emerged to fight trans exclusion. As Chris Johnson, a reporter with the *Washington Blade* would write, the 2007 ENDA fight turned out to be a watershed moment in LGBTQ+ activism. Since then, and only with a few notable exceptions, "there have been no instances of any gay activism or legislation that did not include trans people."[175] From what could've

---

[175] Johnson, Chris. "10 years later, firestorm over gay-only ENDA vote still informs movement." Washington Blade. November 6, 2017.

been a major debacle, the LGBTQ+ community decided to honor "interconnectedness" over political pragmatism and support nothing less than full inclusion for everyone in the community.

INTERCONNECTEDNESS IN LEADERSHIP

As leaders, it is important to recognize the power of interconnectedness when we build teams and foster a sense of community. We can't advocate for just one cause or one community without realizing that our journeys are intertwined. For example, when we seek to eradicate white supremacy, we can't ignore patriarchy, cisgenderism, or Christianism. Strangely, I have witnessed a number of pundits decrying white supremacy while still trafficking in bias towards other marginalized groups such as Jewish people. "Ism," in any form, perpetuates the illusion of separation, or the idea that we have no responsibility to care for others since our lives are separate and distinct. In the Christian Bible, one of the passages I love the most is taken from the New Testament (Matthew 25:40), which says, "...Inasmuch as ye have done it unto one of the least of these my brethren, ye have done it unto me." When reinterpreted for modern and non-Christian audiences, this passage offers one inescapable truth: How we treat those who are most vulnerable is how we treat the entire population. If we want to be leaders with great vision and integrity, we cannot dismiss those for whom we have disdain without undermining our integrity and lack of moral vision. We owe it to ourselves and those we lead to honor the humanity of all people, even in the most ignoble of circumstances.

History, circumstances, and stigma helped bring the various communities of the larger LGBTQ+ community together under one banner, one flag, and one cause: social liberation. However, the community's aggregation alone could not produce the sense of community that exists today without the conscious recognition of LGBTQ+ people that our journeys are connected. Over the years and through many hard-fought battles, we learned that we do best when we first see the humanity in each other. Although our community is not perfect, we recognize that our strength is reflected in how we care for the most vulnerable in our midst. Having endured countless attacks on our culture, Queer people have acted in ways to cultivate relationships and remind ourselves that interconnectedness requires deep engagement with each other.

As you think about your effectiveness as a leader, you may want to do something that would have seemed sacrilegious in the past: put away the leadership books that you got in business school, set your titles and egos aside, ignore the temptation to follow the scripted strategic plan, and ask the people around you: Who are you? How are you? What do I need to know about you to help you succeed? By asking those questions, we can transform the workplace from a place where we simply cross paths into a place where we grow, lead, and commune with each other.

LESSONS IN LGBTQ+ LEADERSHIP: INTERCONNECTEDNESS

In order to foster, maintain, and sustain interconnectedness in your organization, I invite you to consider the following:

1) **Look for connection points with people you meet.** Go beyond the typical business talk. As you engage people, listen for where they lived, grew up, or went to school. Listen for information about their family. Seek insight into their passions. Ask questions to learn more about the people you work with and the worlds they inhabit.

2) **Start small.** Begin with small topics to lead to deeper understanding. Interconnectedness doesn't mean you have to bare your soul or tell your deepest darkest secrets: it simply means cracking the door a little to lay the foundation for something greater. Start engagements by just saying hello or asking someone about their weekend. A slight shift in attitude can make a world of difference in how someone perceives you and how you work together.

3) **Model vulnerability.** Interconnectedness exists when people are being vulnerable. To foster vulnerability, don't be afraid to show who you are. If you occupy a position of power, the level of interconnectedness and vulnerability in your workplace will directly result from the openness *you* show in engaging your team and your peers.

4) **Use an intersectional lens.** Don't judge people based on first appearances or superficial or stereotypical measures. The person you believe to be different from you may share a lot in common with you if you remember that our identities are intersectional.

5) **Take a personal engagement inventory.** Take note of who you engage with and who you don't regularly. Do you notice any patterns? Are there any biases influencing your behavior?

Ask yourself: What can I do to be more inclusive in my interpersonal interactions?

6) **Use spatial intelligence to improve the sense of belonging.** Sometimes workspaces can be set up like fortresses, making it impossible to forge a human connection. Work with your colleagues to design the work areas in your organization to promote greater engagement. As a professor, I learned from my friend and colleague, Grant, to ask my students to rearrange the classroom on the first day of class to support their comfort and learning. As leaders, we should remember that our physical space can also impact how we connect with each other.

7) **Make dedicated time to focus on relationships.** While I wouldn't dare suggest that any leader ignore deadlines or forego taking action to complete projects, make sure you devote adequate time to gauge how your people are doing. Create space in your workday to have meaningful conversations.

8) **Practice allyship.** Allyship is not a noun; it's a verb. To support interconnectedness, focus on how you can take concrete action to support people in your organization. Being a true ally can eliminate divisions in the workplace and build more inclusion and equity, which are key ingredients for interconnectedness.

9) **Honor "being-ness," not "doing-ness."** Maintain a presence where people can see your humanity and recognize your concern for their humanity as well. Remind your peers that their value to the organization lies primarily in who they are, not what they do. Notice the positive impact and how your colleagues perform when they feel seen and valued.

CHAPTER 15

Non-Binary Thinking & LGBTQ+ Leadership

It's either up or down, left or right, or black or white. At times, those notions seem to be the way of the world. In so many contexts, we are offered two choices in terms of living and thinking. If you're on social media, you may get asked to "like" a post or "dislike" a related idea. If you're ordering food, you may be presented with the option of soup or salad. If you're getting to know a new romantic acquaintance, you may ask them if they prefer the mountains or the beach. If you are meeting a friend for "happy hour" at a bar, the drink menu may suggest either wine or beer. In so many ways, our social discourse and thinking operate in a binary fashion. There is often no in-between, which means that when choosing simple pleasures or engaging in simple conversation, the choices placed before us are simplistic at their best.

Yet, the LGBTQ+ cultural value of gender fluidity allows us to rethink how we approach binaries in leadership, whether it's related to gender norms or an analytical, problem-solving framework.

Examining gender fluidity is not necessarily an opening to challenge one's gender identity. It is the chance to reframe our *leadership identity* and explore how the value of gender fluidity inspires non-binary, "out-of-the-box" thinking so that we can transform our leadership practices.

MASCULINE AND FEMININE ENERGY

One of the ways in which society furthers polarity is in its treatment of masculine and feminine energy, yet this norm has not existed in every society. In many (but not all) of the indigenous First Nation communities of North America, the Two Spirit or gender non-conforming people, were the preeminent spiritual, artistic, and intellectual influencers for the community.[176,177] Once believed to be cisgender men who dressed in women's clothing, the Two Spirit people could be gender variant in several forms, whether in their social presentation or by virtue of their sexual or economic role within the family unit. In their full capacity, Two Spirit people were indigenous thought leaders who acted as shamans, presided over ceremonies, settled disputes, showcased craftsmanship, completed important domestic tasks, and exhibited servant leadership.[178]

From what we know, Two Spirit people were revered in First Nation or Native American communities because of their greater tolerance for human difference and ambiguity. Gender variation was commonly accepted among Native American societies, and

---

[176] There is evidence that Two Spirit people were designated as leaders among the Native American tribes of 1) the Great Plains and western Great Lakes regions of the U.S., 2) the lower Mississippi River Valley, 3) Florida and the Caribbean, 4) the Southwest and Great Basin, 5) California and Alaska, and 6) the western region of Canada. There does not appear to be evidence of Two Spirit people in the social hierarchy of tribes that were located in the northeastern parts of North America.

[177] Williams, W. L. (1992). *Spirit and the Flesh: Sexual Diversity in American Indian Culture*. Boston: Beacon Press.

[178] *Id.*

some Native American creation stories, like that of the Kamia, envisioned deities who were gender fluid or gender neutral.[179] In contrast to how conservative societies perceive gender today, historic Native American communities, by and large, believed that gender variant people possessed a divinely-ordained persona that should not be degraded or interfered with unless the community wished to be dispossessed of their special talents and wisdom. Further, where non-binary leaders were not explicitly incorporated into the community, a number of Native American societies recognized the importance and equality of both masculine and feminine energy. In Native American tribes such as the Mandan or Navajo, those who identified as men and/or women were undifferentiated, and the presence of gender fluidity elevated non-binary people to a special status within the community.[180] In many ways, Native American societies appeared to have a great appreciation for human diversity, and those who we would now call LGBTQ+ people (particularly those who are transgender) played a prominent role in leading those communities.

Yet, in modern, colonized, and religious societies, gender variance has been characterized negatively. As we see in traditional discourse, masculine energy and feminine energy (if they were even framed that way) were seen as two adjacent but fundamentally different ways of living and expression.[181] Embodied in the traditional (and cisgender) male and female bodies, masculine energy has often been described as assertive, strong, analytical, and directive, whereas feminine energy has often been described as collaborative, nurturing, intuitive, and heart-centered. Further, not only have those leadership models been valued differently within a patriarchal society, they have often been regarded as existing separately and distinctly depending on one's gender identity. For example, based

---

[179] *Id.*

[180] *Id.*

[181] Derksen, S. (2022, March 1). "Being and Doing: Integrating Masculine and Feminine Energies." Living Well Counseling Services. https://livingwellcounselling.ca/integrating-masculine-feminine-energies/

on the traditional gendered discourse, if I identify as a man, I am supposed to be self-reliant, non-emotive, unyielding, and forceful. I often laugh at the metaphor of the man who is lost on the road trip but is resigned to driving in circles simply because asking for help is seen as a sign of weakness. Although these notions seem reminiscent of a past era, the "toxic masculine" notion of leadership still radiates in some circles. As a staff attorney for an insurance company where I worked years ago, I was once presented with one of those "gotcha" questions during a company outing to see how I would respond to a particular legal issue. I began my response with "I think" and was later told that although my answer in its totality was correct, my opening salvo of "I think" showed "weakness" and a material lack of confidence. To say I was flabbergasted is an understatement.

In contrast, if a person identifies as a woman, they are expected to be conciliatory, deferential, supportive, and non-confrontational. I was raised by a strong woman in a family and community of strong women, so I've never expected women to be demure, passive, or insecure. That being said, what has been tragic is to watch how women (often women of color) have been treated in larger society for being impassioned, incisive, bold, or unflinching when brandishing the same leadership qualities for which men are celebrated. These gender norms and stereotypes pose problems not only for women worldwide but also foment a form of masculinity and masculine leadership that is heavy-handed, demotivating, and frankly passé. They place men in a restrictive box that is emasculating, socially archaic, and ill-suited for a generation of employees and global residents who value collectivism, consensus, and collegiality. Additionally, these norms alienate our friends, partners, and peers who are non-binary or gender non-conforming or those whose gender identity and gender expression are more fluid.

Yet, the irony is that gender fluidity not only applies to those who are expressly non-binary or gender non-conforming; it also applies to our general sense of self, the ways in which we relate to others, and the manner in which we lead. Given the rigidity with which gender is defined, it seems any one of us would be hard-pressed to honor, subscribe to, or maintain those norms based on our gender identity. When presented in a more progressive and balanced fashion, the values deemed masculine and feminine should hold sway for us all. From the masculine constructivist framework, we want our leaders to be analytical, audacious, proactive, and principled. We should want strong and immovable leaders, especially in times of adversity, or leaders who are resolute and steadfast in getting things done. From the feminine constructivist framework, we should want empathetic, resourceful, communicative, and community-minded leaders. We should also want leaders who are reflective, discerning, relational, engaging, and personable. Embracing both the masculine and the feminine allows people to be their best selves. The historical record is replete with instances of people who achieved significant milestones while breaking gender codes. Two great examples are Anthony Roth Costanzo, who had reached critical acclaim as an opera singer by singing notes that women generally sing, and Devrim Ozdemir, who became one of the first women to don a firefighter's uniform in Turkey in 2008.

The challenge is that those leadership qualities that are deemed to be feminine are not championed nearly enough, and in recent decades, there has been a lot more thought about the idea of feminine leadership and the value of the feminine principle. In 2016, former first lady Michelle Obama wrote a book about how she epitomized feminine leadership.

As it has been described, feminine leadership refers to the relational qualities of leadership. It describes the mindsets and practices related to sensitivity, compassion, empathy, communication, generosity, nurturing, collaboration, holistic thinking, vulnerability, and altruism. Typically, these skill sets have been dubbed "soft skills" because they speak to how people work; they are different from "hard skills" or the technical expertise needed to complete certain tasks. However, as stated previously, soft skills are not only important to today's leaders, employees, change agents, and global contributors. They are essential for everyone. If we are sensitive to the needs of the people we serve, we can design better products and services to improve their lives. When we are compassionate or empathetic with the people we work with, we can work together more effectively. If we are generous or altruistic in sharing our time and talent, we can help others to grow. If we employ holistic or systemic thinking, we will develop sustainable solutions. Finally, if we show vulnerability, we can increase psychological safety and help ourselves obtain the support we need.

As we think about how to build better leaders, I would encourage our leaders to remember that masculine and feminine leadership principles are socially constructed. Strong leaders adopt a blended or gender-fluid approach that recognizes the value of both masculine and feminine leadership and disrupts the notion that certain traits are reserved for only certain people depending on where they exist on the gender spectrum. Masculine and feminine leadership are not about gender as much as they are about one's energy and consciousness. In fact, the value of gender fluidity gives us the freedom to move beyond masculine and feminine categories and be more holistic in our leadership approach.

THE CHALLENGE OF BINARY THINKING

As we discuss masculine and feminine leadership and the duality they represent, the challenge, of course, is that the world we inhabit cannot be described in simplistic or dualistic terms. Homo sapiens is a complex species, and each of us is more than just a simple choice between two seemingly opposing imperatives. The world, in its varied dimensions, cannot be placed neatly into two poles or two camps or treated as the by-product of outdated binary thinking.

Much of this polemic has its origins in the centuries-old belief that an eternal struggle exists between two opposites—one good and one bad, one superior and one inferior, or one endearing and one alienating. The concept of dualism, for example, suggests that regarding any phenomenon, there are two heterogeneous, irreducible components that are necessary to understanding the whole.[182] In the time of Plato and Aristotle, dualism was invoked to explain how we as humans should explain our existence and discuss the mind in relationship to the body. There have also been elements of dualism encapsulated in different religious traditions. For example, in Hinduism, the Dvaita Vedanta philosophy believes that God exists as two distinct realities. Alternatively, Taoism holds the belief that the two principles of Yin (dark, negative, and feminine) and Yang (bright, positive, and masculine) influence the destiny of every living thing.[183] In the modern era, the French mathematician and philosopher René Descartes asserted that the mind and body were separate and distinct, with the mind being the seat of self-consciousness, self-awareness, and intelligence.[184] At its core, dualism is a cosmology that holds that harmony in the world and life is achieved by the interplay between two competing or opposing parts. As we think about the values of the LGBTQ+ community, gender fluidity affords leaders the ability to go beyond socialized norms and embrace the full spectrum of powerful leadership.

Yet, when extended beyond spirituality, philosophy, or mathematics, duality has also created an analytical framework that reduces complex systems and ideas to rudimentary dimensions that belie the world in which we live. As risky as it is to venture into this topic

---

[182] Stitch, Stephen S. & Warfield, T. A. (Eds.) (2002). *The Blackwell Guide to Philosophy of Mind*. Hoboken, NJ: Wiley.

[183] Fang, Tony. "Yin Yang: A New Perspective on Culture." *Management and Organization Review*. 8.1 (2015): 25–50.

[184] Robinson, H. (2016) Dualism. In E. N. Zalta (Ed.). *The Stanford Encyclopedia of Philosophy*. Stanford, CA: The Metaphysics Lab.

in today's social landscape, think about the binary posed by the U.S. political system. For a country that portrays itself as the most democratic in the world, it seems odd to have 333 million people represented primarily by a two-party system. Because of a binary system that forces voters to make false choices, many political commentators believe the U.S. political structure contributes to polarization. As the thinking goes, the two-party system has created a dynamic whereby the Democratic and Republican parties have tried to be all things to all people, thereby increasing the amount of alienation that voters within each party feel. In a 2012 survey that measured political attitudes, Americans were further estranged from the political party that most closely espoused their beliefs than citizens in any other comparable democracy.[185] Voter alienation is believed to fuel voter apathy, which has been at significant levels in recent election cycles. In 2020, 79.4 million Americans who were eligible to vote failed to cast a ballot.[186] In 2018, 120 million voters did not participate in the midterm elections, and in the 2016 presidential election, around 100 million eligible voters did not vote in the presidential election. Any electoral observer or lover of democracy should ask themselves: How is this evidence of a healthy democracy? In short, our democracy looks very "undemocratic" as it consistently ranks among the lowest in voter turnout among democratic nations in the world.[187] Although the U.S. electoral system is hampered mightily by voter suppression and structural inequalities that impact working-class, BIPOC, and young generational voters, American civic engagement

---

[185] Rodden, J. (2018, November). Keeping Your Enemies Close: Electoral Rules and Partisan Polarization. Stanford University. https://ces.fas.harvard.edu/uploads/files/events/rodden_anxieties_november2018.pdf

[186] Hauwa, A. (2021, March 16). "How the Biden Administration Can Tackle America's Turnout Problem." Center for American Progress. https://www.americanprogress.org/article/biden-administration-can-tackle-americas-voter-turnout-problem/

[187] *Id.*

is negatively affected by a binary political framework that fails to represent the lofty, broad, and diverse sensibilities of the American electorate. In very real ways, binary thinking is creating undesirable outcomes that affect us personally, interpersonally, and systemically.

Beyond the cultural wave of black or white paradigmatic behavior, binary thinking also represents the coping mechanism many have adopted to survive in a hyper-stimulated society. As I have shared with my students, we live in a world of mass distractions where advertisers, newscasters, vendors, promoters, and influencers are constantly vying for our attention. Further, many of us have jobs where our employers are demanding twice as much as they did 10 years ago. Consider the following statistics about the American labor force just in the last decade:

- The number of super commuters, or those who travel more than an hour and a half, has increased by 31%.[188]
- The average American work week is 47 hours. Americans put in 260 more hours than the average British worker and almost 500 hours more than most French citizens, according to the International Labour Organization.[189]
- Nearly 1/3 of American workers skip lunch breaks altogether, while 50% of workers take a half hour or less to eat.[190]

---

[188] Popov, I. & Salviati, C. (2019, March 24). "Traffic, Trains, or Teleconference? The Changing American Landscape." Apartment List. https://www.apartmentlist.com/research/traffic-trains-or-teleconference-the-changing-american-commute

[189] Abadi, M. (2018, March 18). "11 American work habits other countries avoid at all costs." https://www.businessinsider.com/unhealthy-american-work-habits-2017-11

[190] Bresiger, G. (2014, February 2). "Millions of Americans skipping lunch to work: study." https://nypost.com/2014/02/02/millions-of-americans-skipping-lunch-to-work-study/

In short, Americans seem preoccupied. If we have to contend with a world where our lives are constantly in motion, literally or figuratively, then binary thinking provides us the mental shorthand to decipher, decode, and respond quickly to information in our environment. In other words, in order to avoid information overload or the feeling of being overburdened or overwhelmed with the world's complexity, binary thinking provides a seeming mental respite for a frenzied society.

The challenge, however, is that with binary thinking, we get acclimated or accustomed to the status quo. With binary thinking, we may find ourselves retreading old norms and behaviors that have outlived their usefulness or have proved ineffective. As leaders, we may hold on to ideas and norms that are symbolic but have no value other than they hearken back to a romanticized era known as the "good ol' days." In those instances, the focus is more on tradition than innovation, and many leaders hold onto those traditions while posing a great risk to themselves and those they claim to serve.

For example, I remember working with members of a senior leadership team at an engineering firm who said they wanted to create a more equitable organization while emphatically saying they did not want to disrupt the company culture. It was a fascinating sentiment that revealed their limiting beliefs and the limited capacity for non-binary thinking. As with any opportunity or dilemma, we could always find the proverbial middle pathway or magic doorway if we took the time to question our mental models and the conceptual frameworks to which we attach ourselves. It took us some time to help the leaders realize that the "either/or" dialectic they created stymied their growth and limited their chance of becoming the inclusive organization they envisioned. Yet, once the leadership eschewed the binary thinking that had become their norm, they realized that in seeking greater diversity and inclusion for their organization, they were ironically plagued by a lack of non-binary thinking. As a result, they adopted a pluralistic analytical approach.

The leaders looked at their strategic initiative more expansively, which helped them re-engineer their culture, improve the level of belonging, and capitalize on the markets where they had been losing ground. To this day, they remain one of our favorite clients.

If we as leaders can recognize the LGBTQ+ cultural value of gender fluidity and understand its larger implication—the importance of going beyond binary thinking—then we can craft innovative solutions to address the world we live in today. When we let go of binary thinking, we can interrogate the "sacred cows" and seemingly unassailable truths to visualize new possibilities. Another way of thinking about this concept is through the lens of full spectrum thinking. Full spectrum thinking is a critical analysis that renounces rigid or categorical thinking and thus rejects false clarity. It avoids the type of presumptive, stereotypical, or superficial deliberation that is so characteristic of binary thinking. As futurist Bob Johansen wrote in his book *Full-Spectrum Thinking*:

> The future will be a global scramble that will be hard to categorize. You will need a full-spectrum mindset to have any hint of what is going on. The scramble will be fraught with toxic misinformation (not necessarily intentional), disinformation (intentional), and distrust. In this future, it will be very dangerous to fit new threats or new opportunities into old categories of thought... Full-spectrum thinking will be required in order to survive.[191]

Full-spectrum thinking is the type of thinking and social interpretation that gender-fluid, non-binary, and gender non-conforming people engage in every day by virtue of their existence. Because transgender and non-binary people reject categorical thinking that reduces gender to either male or female, they have the cultural

---

[191] Johansen, B. (2020). *Full-Spectrum Thinking: How to Escape Boxes in a Post-Categorical Future*. Oakland, CA: Berrett-Koehler, 7.

appreciation, personal affinity, and mental aptitude to facilitate fluid, full-spectrum thinking. Due to their cultural journey, transgender and gender- fluid people regularly invoke full spectrum thinking to inform their daily perspective and navigate a contentious social environment. As such, the LGBTQ+ value of gender fluidity connotes the new age leadership practice that can help leaders see patterns, think systemically, and operate imaginatively. As Johansen reminds us, rigid categorical thinking leads to certainty but doesn't lead to clarity. In the modern world, the value of gender fluidity has implications on how we think, assess, and interpret phenomena around us. Gender fluidity invites us to adopt a full-spectrum mindset in ways we envision ourselves and in ways in which we lead others.

Unfortunately, the business world is littered with obituaries of organizations that neglected "out of the box" thinking and failed to innovate. In 2010, the video-renting giant Blockbuster Video filed for bankruptcy after failing to consider developing a streaming service. When Netflix approached Blockbuster in 2000 with an offer to sell the company to Blockbuster, leaders at Blockbuster rejected the offer because they didn't want to get involved with a "niche business."[192] And as they say, the rest is history. In 2001, Polaroid, the instant camera company, filed for bankruptcy because it failed to anticipate the growth of the digital camera. As business reports suggest, Polaroid was so focused on its past success that it failed to innovate or recognize emerging trends in the technology space. Fortunately, Polaroid has rebranded itself to produce new instant cameras, pocket printers, and phone photo scanners to introduce

---

[192] Satell, G. (2014, September 5). "A Look Back At Why Blockbuster Really Failed and Why It Didn't Have To." Forbes. https://www.forbes.com/sites/greg-satell/2014/09/05/a-look-back-at-why-blockbuster-really-failed-and-why-it-didnt-have-to/?sh=3ad82eb11d64

its line of products to a new generation of customers.[193] Thirdly, Borders Books became an international sensation as a book and music retailer by offering customers a large collection of books worldwide. However, when Borders failed to provide e-reader books and services, the retailer accumulated too much debt, closed all of its stores, and sold its customer lists to Barnes & Noble for a paltry $13.9 million. When organizations fail to entertain the broad possibilities with respect to their products and services, and leaders fail to recognize different ways of achieving their vision or mission, they run the risk of becoming irrelevant. Binary thinking is a surefire way for leaders to lose their audience and block their sense of innovation.

Yet, there are leaders and companies that have demonstrated the value of non-binary thinking and created a great social impact. In 2011, Impossible Foods emerged as a plant-based-food distributor by asking, what I assume, was a fundamental question: As more and more people feel torn between a meat-based diet and a vegetarian diet, what if those same consumers could experience both in the same meal? What if consumers could still enjoy some of their culinary favorites—which may include meat—while consuming a plant-based meal? Because the founders challenged the very nature of the dichotomous dilemma before them, they were able to develop a product that reduces greenhouse gases, conserves water, and preserves natural habitats. Other plant-based food distributors like Beyond Meat have achieved similar results and are valued in the billions of dollars. As we can see, non-binary thinking furthers innovation and can generate great social impact.

Often, in leadership circles, emerging leaders may follow the same path and make the same choices they have seen others make on the road to success. To be sure, emulating what works is not a

---

[193] Djudji, D. (2021, August 26). "The Story of Polaroid: From Empire to Bankruptcy and Back Again." Photography. https://www.diyphotography.net/the-story-of-polaroid-from-empire-to-bankruptcy-and-back-again/

bad thing. It's just that singular or binary choices are not the *only* options. In those moments when we are presented with two choices, it behooves us to take a step back and question that very paradigmatic model. Robert Frost once extolled the virtue of taking "the road less traveled," but that may be problematic if we, as leaders, don't conceptualize that there are "dozens of roads" and envision the multitude of options before us. What we "see" is often a function of our limited thinking. As the LGBTQ+ community would remind us, social conventions, traditions, and normative ways of thinking do not always represent the world in all its splendor. When it comes to being more fluid in our thinking, I invite leaders to remember the creed of Ralph Waldo Emerson, who wrote: "Do not go where the path may lead… Go instead where there is no path and leave a trail."[194] Whereas the former Frost-ian poetic anecdote suggests choosing the less popular of two dichotomous alternatives, the latter quote by Emerson invites us to think outside the box. In essence, the LGBTQ+ value of gender fluidity asks us to broaden our perspective and not limit our leadership capacity by the "tried-and-true" or "dead-end" choices that society would place before us. The non-binary perspective and gender fluid experiences of the LGBTQ+ community remind us that we are at our best when we embrace nuance and complexity and acknowledge all of who we are: masculine, feminine, and everything in between. And they remind us that the best way of leading is to question, challenge, and disrupt black-and-white thinking at every opportunity we get.

---

[194] Atkinson, Brooks (Ed.) (2000). *The Essential Writings of Ralph Waldo Emerson*. New York, NY: The Modern Library.

LESSONS IN LGBTQ+ LEADERSHIP:
GENDER FLUIDITY

1) **Illuminate the concept of feminine leadership.** Introduce your team to feminine leadership principles and highlight how feminine leadership attributes can benefit the organization. Reiterate that the new age leadership modes like feminine leadership or gender-fluid leadership are not about gender; they symbolize a consciousness that is important for the 21st century.

2) **Take inventory of the "sacred cows"** or tradition-bound norms and practices within your organization.

   - Rate the effectiveness or value of those traditions. Then, ask yourself: Who is being served by these traditions?

   - Based on your assessment results, invite others to brainstorm with you to determine how those traditions may be revised, modified, or eliminated to increase a sense of belonging, purpose, and productivity in your organization.

3) **Create an innovation platform** for your organization and assess your innovation readiness gap. You may use the following questions as your rubric:

   a) Is "out of the box" thinking part of the normative culture?

   b) How do you support your people in generating innovative, "out of the box" ideas? How is this type of thinking incentivized?

   c) How are you vetting talent for innovative thinking?

   d) Does the structure of your organization support innovation?

   e) Is innovation a metric in your performance and talent management system? If so, how do you measure innovation and creativity?

f) What incubators have you provided for innovation? Are these incubators equitably accessible? Do those incubators leverage the expertise of all people throughout the organization?

g) What is your system for assessing and developing innovative projects?

h) What innovative projects are in development? How do those projects get funneled to the proper people/departments?

i) What is your current innovation portfolio?

4) **Examine your mental models.** Investigate how they may influence your thinking and perception of others. Choose one or two strategies you will adopt to expand your thinking.

5) **Curate curiosity.** Get in the habit of asking thought-provoking questions and facilitating meta conversations. Good examples of generative questions are:

- Why did we decide on that course of action?
- What assumptions am I making as I think about this issue?
- Is what I am thinking really true?
- Why, as an organization/group/enterprise, did we adopt that approach?
- Is this process/norm/behavior still working?
- For whom is this norm/behavior/practice beneficial?
- Who is excluded by operating/thinking in this way?
- What if we tried _____?
- What if we "tried on" a different mental model?

6) **Bring other people to the table.** Binary thinking becomes the norm when you engage in "group think" among a homogenous group. When you don't engage others who may have a different perspective, it can be easy to fall into the same paradigmatic rut where two limited perspectives dominate your analysis. Leveraging the insight and expertise of a heterogeneous group can mitigate binary thinking and also disrupt personal or group bias.

7) **Engage in deep listening.** When I was getting certified as a mediator, we were assigned an essay entitled "The Twelve Signs of Non-Listening," based on *Messages: The Communication Skills Book* by McKay, Davis, and Fanning.[195] Essentially, the article documented how humans avoid deep listening in conversation. Depending on the time and circumstance, we may be thinking about what we're having for lunch or the vacation we have planned for the weekend. Depending on the person, we may be predisposed to disagree with or challenge their assertions. Depending on the time of the day and our mood, we may try to categorize or squeeze what we're hearing into dichotomous thematic boxes to save time and/or mental stamina. However, being reductionist can rob us of the detail, nuance, or context to understand valuable perspectives. When engaging our clients, peers, or direct reports, it is critical to give the conversation the space and time necessary to understand the dynamics in their full breadth without resorting to black/white thinking.

8) **Avoid the Dunning-Kruger effect.** Known for popularizing science, astrophysicist Neil deGrasse Tyson, often recites one of my favorite quotes: "The great challenge in life is knowing enough to think you are right but not knowing enough to know you are wrong." Tyson's quote summarizes the Dunning-Kruger effect, which is a cognitive bias in which people with limited knowledge can overestimate their knowledge or competence about a particular topic.[196] In the Google era, where people can quickly fact-check and superficially become experts on anything under the sun, the Dunning-Kruger effect can lead people to adopt beliefs or characterize social or organizational dynamics

[195] McKay, M., & Davis, M., Fanning, P. (1995). *Messages: The Communication Skills Book*. Oakland, CA: New Harbinger.

[196] Cherry, Kendra. (2021, August 6). "The Dunning-Kruger Effect." VeryWellMind. https://www.verywellmind.com/an-overview-of-the-dunning-kruger-effect-4160740

in overly general terms ripe with binary thinking. As a leader, create the space for yourself and others to explore topics more fully before arriving at conclusions that may be simplistic, erroneous, or off-kilter.

9) **Evangelize non-binary thinking.** In championing non-binary thinking, illustrate the ways in which non-binary thinking can support your current work and projects. Exhibit non-binary thinking in your behavior as a way of modelling that type of thinking for others.

CHAPTER 16

Creativity & LGBTQ+ Leadership

One of the most understated and under-appreciated dimensions of leadership is creativity. Creative energy exists everywhere, but is still hard to discern. When most people think of creativity, they think of music, the arts, film, theater, dance, graphic design, poetry, or storytelling. In that sense, creativity is seen as the hallmark of the privileged few. In that vein, creativity represents the boundless ability to connect and express oneself emotionally for those who see themselves as artists. Yet, when conceptualized more broadly, creativity is simply the art of doing something differently than it has been done before. Without a doubt, the LGBTQ+ community has made an invaluable and indelible contribution to the arts and art allows us to invoke all of our senses and experience life in a three-dimensional way.

However, such a wondrous definition of art makes it hard for leaders to recognize their own creativity. If you have difficulty drawing a straight line (as I do) or feel clumsy with words or would prefer to sing only when no one else is around, it may feel challenging to understand how to incorporate creativity into our leadership practice.

At the root of creativity is the ability to create: to build something anew or to create something in a mold or fashion that has never been done before. As a leader, you have the opportunity to generate a new idea or way of doing things or to take an existing concept, product, or practice and make it better. That is what artists do all the time: they envision a new song or piece of art or a form of movement that has never been visualized. Or, they take an existing art form and make it relevant for new audiences and generations. For example, one of the reasons why sampling in hip-hop music is so inventive is because it takes a musical element and uses it in a different way than was intended. It's like going to an antique store or a junkyard and finding an old relic that can then be used as part of a new art display or part of a new machine. Creativity can both be the introduction of a new phenomenon or the reinterpretation of something already familiar to us. In either case, creativity expands our imagination and embellishes our experience of life.

LGBTQ+ people, like other underrepresented groups, have to be creative every day in order to live, enjoy, and navigate modern society. As influencer Rigel Gemini once wrote, we as LGBTQ+ people exhibit creativity in the creation of ourselves.[197] People identifying as LGBTQ+ give themselves the freedom and creative license to present, describe, and regard themselves in whatever medium they choose. As LGBTQ+ people, we get to use creativity in order to express our unique cultural heritage through the arts, clothing, personal presentation, and language. We've used creativity to describe our persona since the heteronormative and cisgender cultures we inhabit have linguistic conventions that are inadequate in describing who we are

---

[197] Gemini, R. (2016, July 29). "Why Are Queer People Creative?" https://www.rigelgemini.com/home/2016/7/29/why-are-queer-people-creative

as a population. Transgender and gender non-conforming people have taught us how to be expansive in our use of language in order to more appropriately represent the full spectrum of gender identity and gender expression. Further, our creativity has allowed us to create norms, tools, and conventions to escape detection, harassment, and discrimination in those places where we have not felt safe. For example, in Chapter 12, I discussed gay men signaling to each other using handkerchiefs to communicate their affectional preferences discreetly.

Following the example set by the Queer community, today's leaders can use creativity to reimagine the workforce, reimagine the work we do, and reimagine how we engage with each other. And based on the LGBTQ+ community's appreciation for creativity, this cultural staple can be instructive in terms of aesthetics, personal transformation, generating courage, and engaging in effective problem-solving.

AESTHETICS

Creativity can enhance productivity when it's used to improve one's environment. However, it may not always be obvious how the aesthetics of our environment can influence us on a day-to-day basis. For me, the lesson started with an experience close to home.

When my mother moved to Charlotte for her retirement, she moved into a beautiful new home in one of the fastest growing parts of the city. The house was a new construction, and she customized a few elements to make the property her own. Unfortunately, she wanted to bring all of her old furniture from Milwaukee to Charlotte to fill her new space. Ever the practical person and suddenly beset with a retiree's budget, Mom was not eager to spend more money if she could avoid it. While I understood her reasoning, I pleaded with her to bring some new energy into the space. Understandably, the idea of bringing old furniture to a new space was too much for my modernist sensibilities. As a result, I made it my mission to decorate the interior and advise on everything from the wall color and rugs to the artwork and furnishings. It was a painstaking task: Mom had a hard time matching my enthusiasm and visualizing my proposed design concepts without proofs or mock-ups.

Yet, despite Mom's nonchalance, I worked diligently and eagerly, constantly asking her for input and approval as I made my way from one room to the next. At one point, Mom just told me to "do my thing," and eventually, the house felt like a home. Although we joked that the house could be featured in *Southern Woman* magazine or something of the sort, her neighbors and guests were exceedingly complimentary. One day Mom said to me admiringly, "I think you missed your calling. I think you could've been an interior designer," to which I responded, "Nah, this is just the benefit of having a gay son." And in the weeks and months that ensued, I witnessed Mom settle into her space and seem much more at ease than I had seen her in years. Often, she would call me from her favorite place in the sunroom while she was reading, crocheting, or just enjoying the sunlight. I could tell that her new environment helped her to ease into retirement and better acclimate to her new city and surroundings.

Aesthetics are important when setting a tone for greater learning, productivity, and engagement. If you were to walk into a room that was disheveled, dirty, or disorganized, I doubt you would stay for long or feel inclined to do your best work. But even if the environment is clean, the question remains: is it likely to stimulate safety, calm, or productivity? Will it make others feel connected? Is the environment vibrant, colorful, and eye-catching? Or is it bland, antiseptic, or too corporate? These are essential questions to remember when we gather or organize our space. When we come together for any occasion, it is important to have intentionality and to design our areas in a way that furthers a connection. In her book, *The Art of Gathering: How We Meet and Why It Matters*, Priya Parker wrote that every event should have a clear, identified purpose.[198] The workplace *definitely* has a clear purpose. If the meeting space should have a definite purpose, then the immediate environment should be designed to maximize that purpose and further vitality. The notion of aesthetics is where creativity can be of great use to leaders who want to enhance productivity, commitment, and connection.

Unfortunately, creativity can be one of the first casualties when leaders try to inspire their workforce. Years ago, I remember when we had a firm retreat planned for our legal department. Other departments had excursions that took them to fancy resorts, beachfront property, mountainous getaways, or splashy cities like Vegas or Miami. As part of the labor and employment division, we earned a trip to, you guessed it, a 3-star hotel in suburban Minneapolis. There were no parks, beaches, or mountains, and we spent most of that 3-day retreat inside a large corporate boardroom with dim lighting, cold air, and drab colors. My boredom didn't kill me, but the banality of the occasion nearly did.

While leaders should prioritize psycho-social measures, they should also look for ways to create stimulating and aesthetically pleasing environments. Research shows that high-quality indoor environments with scenic views, stimulating decor, and human-centered design can help employees become more productive.[199] In addition, when people work in more beautiful environments and are closer to nature, their sense of well-being improves dramatically.

That is not to say that every workplace needs to look like the Taj Mahal. But the work environment should be comfortable and alluring. Even small steps like adding flowers to the workspace or adding natural light can increase brain activity and lower cortisol, the body's

---

[198] Parker, Priya. (2008). *The Art of Gathering: How We Meet and Why it Matters.* New York: Riverhead Books.

[199] Balch, O. (2016, Feb. 10). Does a pretty office make a productive workspace? The Guardian. https://www.theguardian.com/sustainable-business/2016/feb/10/office-beautiful-pretty-views-employees-productive

stress hormone.[200] In fact, engineers and urban planners are building new office buildings that incorporate scenic views, green space, spacious interiors, and natural elements. For example, the Chiswick Business Park in West London was built to rave reviews with its beach pit, ponds and lakes, adult amusement park, and petting zoo to help workers relieve their stress from the day. It almost seems to be the corporate rival of Michael Jackson's Neverland Ranch. Airports like San Francisco International Airport have remodeled their terminals to include regional fauna, yoga rooms, and a smart design that makes people feel connected with the environment. As a leader, you don't have to get your interior design "degree" like me; you simply have to recognize that the safety and comfort of your employees are affected by physical ambiance. In studying the LGBTQ+ cultural value of creativity, leaders can prioritize aesthetics in a way that enhances productivity and well-being.

PERSONAL TRANSFORMATION

Naturally, when we think about the LGBTQ+ cultural value of creativity in leadership development, the most obvious connection is how to use creativity to lead *others*. However, creativity is also a gateway to personal transformation. As an executive coach, I once worked with a C-level executive who was visibly frustrated with his employer, a fact which surfaced early in our engagement. With all of his business experience and my supposed coaching wizardry, he could not find his way out of a particular predicament. He was a wonderful client and an aspiring musician/songwriter to boot, but I could see the strain his career was taking on him and his progress

---

[200] Datz, T. (2015, Oct. 26). Green office environments linked with higher cognitive function scores. Harvard T. H. Chan School of Public Health. https://www.hsph.harvard.edu/news/press-releases/green-office-environments-linked-with-higher-cognitive-function-scores/

in our coaching sessions was starting to stall. As he sat with me in a coaching session on one particular summer day, let's just say that his workplace environment was still striking a sour chord.

Then suddenly, I had a bright idea! And with the skeptical face he used to greet most of my bright ideas, our conversation went something like this:

The Executive:	Okay, Joel, what are you thinking?
Me:	Why don't you write a song?
The Executive:	Excuse me? Did you say "write a song?"
Me:	Yes, write a song about your current situation. Writing about it might help you develop a different perspective.
The Executive:	You know, this takes the cake, but I like where you're going with this.

Sheepishly, the executive began writing a song, and guess what? It worked! The next time we met, he found a different way of analyzing the problem and discovered a new way of solving the larger, more significant issue. Although he never performed his ditty for me, I marveled at how the creative process—both in his leadership approach and my coaching practice—helped him enhance his leadership capability and showcase his personal transformation.

Of course, that coaching engagement was not the first time I had seen a person grow from honoring their creativity. As a youngster, I began my journey with creativity when I discovered my fascination with words. I found conventional language limiting and intuitively bent words and phrases to convey meaning. With an introduction to Dr. Seuss and a love affair with poets like Sonia Sanchez and Langston Hughes, I discovered that I had a calling in poetry and the linguistic arts.

Over the years, I learned how to honor my craft and protect my artistic energy. Writing poetry is not a linear process, nor is it a completely functional process where you immediately get out what you put in. When I try to force poetry or make it sound a certain way, it suffers every time. It sounds contrived and formulaic. Yet, when I remain humble and patient, my poetry seems more organic and natural. I learned that the creative process has its own timetable and that I have to honor poetry whenever it arrives. To the chagrin of my family and friends, that often has meant writing poetry at inopportune times, such as 4 a.m. or 11 p.m. or when I'm at a family function or sitting at a table in a busy restaurant. I've written poetry on napkins and receipts, matchboxes, or even my palms when I needed to record a rhyme or lyric. I've left voicemail messages for myself when I caught a melody or a tune and was worried about forgetting it. I realized in my teenage years that art comes through you and not from you. All art comes from a higher source, and when art presents itself, our job is to simply move out of the way mentally and allow it to express itself in whatever form it wants to be conveyed. I realized that poetry does not come from me. Instead, I am simply the vessel through which it is delivered to the world. In the process of my artistic maturation, I learned better patience and humility. I became very familiar with my talents and acutely aware of my abilities. Discovering my art is as close to a spiritual awakening as anything I've ever experienced.

When the poetry is being transmitted or "downloaded," as I like to say, the feeling is very intuitive. When my poetry is flowing, it's like watching a cascade of words and interlocking expressions stream endlessly through my mind. At times, the phrases feel other-worldly. For example, on my spoken word CD "Simplexity," I wrote the following stanza for the title track:

> "Love can take you into a ravine
> With air the color of tornado green.
> Not everyone has the same pedigree
> At least on paper

To some, love is just a caper
Love is like poetry:
People treat it as a competition, even though it's meant
to be shared
And over time, I got indifferent and got scared."

Upon hearing that, a friend asked me: "How the hell did you think of the phrase tornado green?" I really couldn't give an answer. When I'm in tune with myself, words and phrases just show up in my mind based on the lived experiences, emotional vibrations, and fragmented feelings I've had. They show up at my spirit's door without any forewarning, and it is my decision whether to breathe them in or let them die. The words are prepackaged, and the associations I draw can be easy and luxurious or raw and edgy. In any situation, the words are drawn from a reservoir that I am simultaneously conscious but not conscious of, consumed with but not consumed by. As fast as some inspiration comes, it can also leave quite quickly if I'm not present with my breath or feelings or the energy surrounding me. As a creative, you indulge until your truth is set free.

A phenomenon started to take place when I began producing spoken word CDs; I started seeing colors in my mind. For example, for my first spoken word CD, which was metaphysical, abstract, and reflective, the color I kept seeing was blue. With my second CD, with themes related to healing and transformation, I kept seeing the color purple, representing wisdom and spirituality. During my third CD, which spoke of love, sex, and sensuality, the color that flooded my mind was red, with its associated meanings of passion, rage, and torment. The process of perceiving colors and receiving sensory stimulation while engaging one cognitive pathway is known as synesthesia. The first time I heard someone mention this phenomenon was hip-hop & R&B music producer/artist Pharrell. In my 20s, I started to see my poetry as a gift rather than a hobby or side talent.

In the years ahead, I often turned to my poetry whenever I felt stuck. For example, in the short time I practiced law, I would often write poetry when I was bored at work. Writing poetry helped me unlock my brain and think more analytically, especially when tasked with writing legal memos and briefs for the stodgy partners in my law firm. Writing poetry helped me to process my emotions when I fell in love, when a close relative transitioned or passed, or when I experienced something in nature that felt supernatural. As an LGBTQ+ person, creativity didn't feel odd or eccentric or inaccessible. To the contrary, it felt as natural as any of my other endeavors, and I often wondered why society seemed to portray creative pursuits such as singing, film, dance, acting, and poetry as "gay." I felt bad for my peers who couldn't explore their creative side for fear of being deemed Queer, but I also felt lucky to belong to a community where my interests didn't have to be condensed solely into sport, bravado, or gamesmanship. Art and creativity gave voice to my soul and spirit. I learned that creativity not only transforms the world; it also transforms the artist or the creator.

One area where art is particularly transformational is in public speaking. As a professor, I have taught storytelling for leaders for nearly seven years. As my public speaking mentors Amy and Michael Port reminded me, speaking is not just about making a statement; it's a performance. In my class, I spend the first three weeks helping the students to find their voices and claim their stories. From there, we work on helping them to embellish their story in a way that makes people want to listen. In those sessions, I see students transform from the heady, introverted, and self-conscious creatures who enter my room into the empowered, mesmerizing, and thoughtful influencers I know them to be. Not everyone has the same artistic talent, but everyone has the capacity to be creative if they honor themselves, recognize their unique abilities (whatever those might be), and work to improve their creative expression. If I can develop my poetry and storytelling to the point where people routinely ask me to share it, then I know that any leader can elevate their art (whatever form it comes in) to create positive change in the world. As Tolstoy wrote, changing the world is about changing oneself.[201] Fortunately, leaders can use the LGBTQ+ cultural value of creativity to spur their own evolution.

BUILDING COURAGE

In addition to improving aesthetics and facilitating personal transformation, leaders can use creativity to build courage. Since the dawn of humankind, art has been used as a rallying cry to galvanize the masses, provide social commentary, and move people to righteous action. Creativity has been the artful medium for speaking truth to power or challenging those in positions of authority to act with greater integrity and moral consciousness. As a kid, I remember my Uncle Phil playing songs like "What's Going On?" by Marvin Gaye or "War" by Edwin Starr as a way of stoking the fire and reminding ourselves never to be satisfied with the crumbs of social equality. Of course, it didn't hurt that the messages were folded into soulful melodies and head-bobbing protest anthems that made it easy to "groove" and "collude" for social justice. When done mindfully, art has always had the ability and freedom to describe the world with searing clarity and unapologetic charm. In my estimation, art is often the first clarion call in the battle for justice and equality.

To that end, LGBTQ+ people have historically used their creativity in order to speak truth to power. During the Harlem Renaissance, the historical period in the U.S. when Harlem was the cultural hub for some of the nation's most riveting and provocative music, poetry, film, and literature, LGBTQ+ artists used their art to protest Prohibition, celebrate Queer sensibilities, and highlight

---

[201] Moore, C. (Ed.) (2006). Leo Tolstoy: Spiriting Writings. Maryknoll, New York, NY: Orbis Books.

racial justice. In fact, the philosophical curator, architect, and "dean" of the Harlem Renaissance Alain Locke, was a self-identified Queer Black man.

Yet, Locke was not the only visible or recognized LGBTQ+ artist during the Harlem Renaissance. In America's most famous Black neighborhood, LGBTQ+ artists were in the vanguard of the Harlem Renaissance, and it's not an exaggeration to say that the Harlem Renaissance would not have taken place were it not for the LGBTQ+ people. LGBTQ+ artists like Richard Bruce Nugent were unafraid of embracing their sexual identity, which was a revolutionary act at a time when many Black leaders denounced Black Queer people for corrupting the puritanical image they wanted to portray to the white establishment. As an illustrator, painter, writer, and dancer, Nugent declared forcefully: "It has never occurred to me that [my sexuality] was anything to be ashamed of..."[202]

Other LGBTQ+ artists would follow suit. For example, Claude McKay was a bisexual poet who wrote openly about same-sex desire, and writer Nella Larsen was a novelist whose book, *Passing*, had clear lesbian overtones.[203] Whether it was Nugent, McKay, or Larsen, LGBTQ+ artists used their creativity to fortify their courage, defy the existing social order, and protest stigmatization.

Other LGBTQ+ artists like James Baldwin wrote fiery speeches about the social trauma they faced living in America and dealing with the twin rods of racism and heterosexism. A self-proclaimed maverick who sometimes felt "remote" from the LGBTQ+ community, Baldwin also wrote candidly about sexuality. In discussing sexual politics in his powerful novel Giovanni's Room, Baldwin wrote:

---

[202] Shareef, M. "Black and Queer in the Harlem Renaissance." Queer Majority. https://www.queermajority.com/essays-all/black-and-queer-in-the-harlem-renaissance

[203] Larsen, Nella. (2003). *Passing*. New York, NY: Penguin Books.

The question of human affection, of integrity, in my case, the question of trying to become a writer, are all linked with the question of sexuality. Sexuality is only a part of it. I don't know even if it's the most important part. [But] it's indispensable.[204]

Baldwin would go on to say about American society:

It's very frightening. But the so-called straight person is no safer than I am really. Loving anybody is a tremendous danger, a tremendous responsibility... The terrors homosexuals go through in this society would not be so great if the society itself did not go through so many terrors which it doesn't want to admit. The discovery of one's sexual preference doesn't have to be a trauma. It's a trauma because it's such a traumatized society.[205]

In his irreverent and defiant way, Baldwin interrogated society's treatment of the LGBTQ+ community and consistently questioned the gap between America's lofty principles and its history of sordid racial and heteronormative practices.

While some of Baldwin's contemporaries, like the poet Langston Hughes and the playwright and writer Zora Neale Hurston, were more private about their sexuality (though they are widely believed to be Queer), others such as Lorraine Hansberry, Alain Locke, and Countee Cullen were far less ambiguous about their sexual orientation. Each of them made contributions that shifted the artistic landscape, whether it was Hurston's book "Their Eyes Were Watching God,"[206] Lorraine Hansberry's play "A Raisin in the

---

[204] Baldwin, J. and Troupe, Q. (2014). James Baldwin: The Last Interview and Other Conversations. Brooklyn, New York: Melville House Publishing, pp. 62–63.

[205] *Id.*

[206] Hurston, Z. N. (1998). *Their Eyes Were Watching God.* New York, NY: HarperCollins.

Sun,"[207] Countee Cullen's poem "Heritage,"[208] or Langston Hughes' poem "I, Too."[209]

Other LGBTQ+ artists like Gladys Bentley, a non-binary blues singer who dominated the New York City club scene in the 1920s and 1930s, continued to push back against the strain of cisgender normativity that was being touted by Black political leaders such as Adam Clayton Powell.[210] Described by Langston Hughes as "an amazing exhibition of musical energy," Bentley was simply the most audacious of Queer artists who sought to be themselves.[211]

And yet, Bentley's creative expression was part of a larger cultural milieu that featured parties, gatherings, and events that exclusively catered to the LGBTQ+ community. In the early 1920s, the Hamilton Lodge Ball became known as *the* event for the LGBTQ+ community and is considered one of the earliest precursors of the modern ballroom scene, though Black Queer Ballroom Culture began in 1869.[212] Known officially as the "Masquerade and Civic Ball" but derisively as the "Faggots Ball," the Hamilton Lodge Ball attracted "effeminate men, sissies, 'wolves,' 'fairies,' 'faggots,' the third sex, 'ladies of the night,' and male prostitutes… for a grand jamboree of dancing, lovemaking, display, rivalry, drinking, and advertisement."[213] In 1937,

---

[207] Hansberry, L. (1994). *A Raisin in the Sun*. New York, NY: Random House.

[208] Cullen, C. (2021). *Color*. Berkeley, CA: West Margin Press.

[209] Hughes, L. (1994). *I, Too, Am America. The Collected Poems of Langston Hughes*. New York, NY: Vintage Books.

[210] Waxman, O. B. 2021, Oct. 11. "The Overlooked LGBTQ+ History of the Harlem Renaissance." Time Magazine. https://time.com/6104381/lgbtq-history-harlem-renaissance/

[211] Shareef, M. "Black and Queer in the Harlem Renaissance." Queer Majority. https://www.queermajority.com/essays-all/black-and-queer-in-the-harlem-renaissance

[212] "What Black History Month Doesn't Teach You About the Harlem Renaissance." 2012, Feb. 24. Black Youth Project. Retrieved from http://blackyouthproject.com/what-black-history-month-doesnt-teach-you-about-the-harlem-renaissance/

[213] *Id.*

nearly 8,000 guests attended the annual event,[214] and scenes such as the one described at the Hamilton Lodge Ball played out all over the country in places like Chicago, New Orleans, and Los Angeles. Though social by nature, these events challenged the status quo and provided a safe haven for artists and LGBTQ+ creatives who used their art to critique society thoughtfully and strategically. Instead of placing themselves before a firing squad or putting themselves in harm's way, these visionaries knew that their art could simultaneously be eloquent and subversive. They were political strategists as much as they were artists, and they used their art courageously to speak to people in ways that political placards and bullhorns could not. And yet, they used their art in ways that only masters of their craft can.

Engaging in creativity can help embolden us to meet problems head-on and take on greater challenges. Even for the stewards of the Harlem Renaissance, critiquing and challenging the status quo through song, word, dance, or film wasn't easy. The role of art is not just in delivering the message but in calling forth the courage to speak in a vulnerable way. As a leader, taking on creative challenges may also help you find the courage to have difficult conversations, take on unforeseen challenges, or speak truth to power in a way that is honest, strategic, and disarming. That is the lesson we take from the pioneers of the Harlem Renaissance: They were courageous truth-tellers, and the critical and questioning nature of LGBTQ+ creatives has carried itself forward to the modern day.

PROBLEM-SOLVING

In essence, what the truth-tellers of the Harlem Renaissance exemplified was leadership, and the LGBTQ+ community has shown an ability to lead through its creative exploits while using creative means to achieve its objectives. Leadership is oft-times the ability to create solutions where there appear to be no clear options. Therefore,

---

[214] *Id.*

being creative is not just about artistic pursuits but also about creating new ways of thinking or generating novel ideas to address existing challenges. It is problem-solving at its best. When the AIDS Coalition To Unleash Power (more popularly known as ACT UP) was first organized in 1987, the U.S. government was extremely passive and dismissive in its response to the AIDS epidemic. And truthfully, that characterization may still be too generous given the feckless actions taken at the time. As a result, ACT UP was formed to wage a multifaceted, multilateral campaign. But make no mistake about it: *how* they waged that campaign was one of sheer creative genius. Today, ACT UP remains an international, grassroots political group working to support progressive policies and end the global AIDS pandemic.

Despite the white savior model that the media tried to push, ACT UP had no single leader. Instead, figures such as playwright Larry Kramer (who I have the utmost respect for) served as guest speakers on a rotating basis. It was a decentralized network of activists who worked independently on various issues. As one historian wrote, ACT UP was so diffuse that everyone thought that what they were doing and their friends were doing was an ACT UP-sanctioned activity.[215] ACT UP existed everywhere, and its breadth made it particularly effective.

In becoming a broad-based movement, ACT UP harnessed the cultural sensibilities of the entire community. ACT UP relied on a diverse group of leaders to challenge the existing HIV/AIDS-biased laws and policies on the books. For example, Karin Timour was a straight ally who made it possible for thousands of HIV patients to get private health insurance. Everyone who attended an ACT UP meeting knew someone who had been sick or had died, and the

---

[215] Miss Rosen. (2021, Sep. 6). "How ACT UP Transformed the Landscape of Art and Activism in the Age of AIDS." Blind Magazine.

group derived its power from the multicultural factions that organized for its benefit.

In truth, ACT UP was not for the faint of heart. Meetings with ACT UP resembled public squares where activists debated each other in British parliamentary style about tactics, ideas, and targets. The conversations, at times, were shouting matches, but they produced the direct-action strategy for which ACT UP became known. ACT UP's campaign was multi-layered: it directly challenged the hospitals, churches, pharmaceutical companies, political officials, and media who condescended to the community or stood idly by as more people died from HIV/AIDS. In some bold demonstrations, ACT UP shut down the Grand Central Terminal in NYC, protested at Wall Street and New York City Tri-state area homeless shelters, and picketed St. Patrick's Cathedral in Manhattan. ACT UP also blocked the Champs-Elysees in Paris, staged a "die-in" at President George Herbert Walker Bush's vacation home, and even showed up en masse to a New York Mets baseball game.[216]

Further, ACT UP also made brazen and creative use of art, graphic design, photography, and iconography to spread its message. Whether through the slogan "SILENCE = DEATH," the pink triangle graphic that commemorates LGBTQ+ persecution during the Nazi era, or photo exhibits of HIV/AIDS patients fighting for their lives, ACT UP activists used creative elements to raise awareness and garner support.

While a number of institutions branded ACT UP's tactics as vulgar and excessive, the network was relentless and helped to produce systemic change. Some of ACT UP's tactics would be borrowed later by climate change activists in the 2000s, activists protesting the International Monetary Fund and World Bank in 2000, and Black

---

[216] France, D. (2020, Ap. 13). "The Activists: How ACT UP—the coalition that fought against AIDS stigma and won medications that slowed the plague—forever changed patients' rights, protests, and American political organizing as it's practiced today." The New York Times. https://www.nytimes.com/interactive/2020/04/13/t-magazine/act-up-aids.html

Lives Matter protesters in 2020. In terms of its legacy, ACT UP achieved the following:

- It instituted clean-needle exchange programs
- Made experimental drugs available to those facing certain death
- Protected efforts to disseminate generic drugs to the Global South
- Stopped pharmaceutical companies from price-gouging
- Helped restore the AIDS Drug Assistance Program

As of the publication of this book, ACT UP chapters around the world are still active in varying capacities.

Using the centuries-old practice of civil disobedience, ACT UP creatively remade the art of political organizing in America. By foregoing consensus, employing direct action, empowering people from all different walks of life, crafting unflinching art, and allowing members to set its agenda, ACT UP was led creatively and used creativity to end the HIV/AIDS crisis in the United States. It took the community's concerns directly to the pulpits, storefronts, board rooms, media offices, and public spaces around the world. ACT UP helped to remake political organizing as we know it and is another example of how LGBTQ+ people—whether in relation to aesthetics, personal transformation, courageous action, or problem-solving—have used creative thinking and artistic expression to make the world a more beautiful and humane place.

Naturally, not all LGBTQ+ people have a penchant for certain creative pursuits. Still, I believe that all people—especially Queer people—have an enduring capacity for creative energy and expression. Creativity, at its core, is about defying convention and imagining new possibilities. Given that LGBTQ+ people have historically been outside the norm in terms of behavior, it is not surprising that LGBTQ+ people may be more inclined to use their creative abilities more intentionally. The opportunity is for leaders to generate their creativity to transform the way we live and work in the 21st century.

LESSONS IN LGBTQ+ LEADERSHIP: CREATIVITY

1) **Find your muse.** Find a source of inspiration to help you explore, discover, hone, and master your creative talents.

2) **Stick with your creative routine.** Commit to it for at least six months. Notice the areas in which you change, grow, and evolve over time.

3) **Uplevel your norms and practices to include creativity.** Work with colleagues to find areas to enliven your meetings, person-to-person engagement, and physical workspace.

4) **Beautify your workspace.** As a leader, find ways to make your working environment more attractive. Not only will your colleagues be more productive, but it will also help you be a more enthusiastic and effective leader.

5) **Find a new creative hobby.** Step outside your comfort zone and find an art form that will help you normalize taking risks and chances.

6) **Build up your creative courage.** Use creative energy to think about ways to be more strategic in dealing with complex issues and difficult people. Use creative expression to build your courage, confidence, and ability to speak the "truth" in difficult situations.

7) **Perform a creative audit.** Assess what areas of your leadership practice or what areas of your organization's leadership culture are stale, antiquated, or ineffective. Re-examine your ways of direct engagement and introduce creative elements to take your leadership practice to the next level.

8) **Invite your people to bring their creativity out of the closet.** Encourage risk-taking and model courageous behavior to support your people in resuscitating their creativity and applying it to the workplace.

9) **Introduce a creative element to your brand.** Find ways of using creativity to showcase who you are.

10) **Push creative problem-solving.** When attempting to solve issues, don't fall into old patterns, traditions, and ways of thinking. Take a step back and ask yourself how you could approach the problem and the problem-solving process differently.

BARRIERS TO RECOGNIZING LGBTQ+ CULTURAL GENIUS™

In the same way that counter-culturalists, intellectuals, creatives, and change agents help inspire vibrant communities, the LGBTQ+ community is helping to transform the world in a positive and irrepressible way. By virtue of our culture and lived experience, not only have LGBTQ+ people brought considerable talents and gifts to the world, but we have also helped to inspire a way of living that encourages others to be liberated and proud of who they are. Our culture is wise and ebullient, rich and steadfast, principled and adaptive. It radiates with social justice and advocacy. It inspires resilience and creativity. It streaks with flair and zeal. It rests upon freedom and courage and self-realization. In sum, LGBTQ+ culture not only possesses norms and values that have been reinforced for centuries, but it also possesses an inextinguishable light that has flourished in the darkest of times and the most brutal of circumstances, without even the slightest bit of affirmation from those with privilege. The culture and community exist not only because of the struggles we've endured, but most certainly in spite of them.

Even more, the LGBTQ+ community has provided countless examples throughout our community's journey of transformational leadership. We have lifted as we have climbed. We have danced as we have walked. We have persevered though we have stumbled. Our example is a beautiful case study of living humanly, of how to feed and nurture the soul by trusting your instincts and following the path of your cultural pedigree. And yet we have provided a blueprint for the world of how to live generatively and intentionally. Our faith in ourselves has made us who we are and has helped remake the world. That is what I call our cultural genius™: our ability to transform the ecosystem around us by relying on our unique sensibilities and artistic aptitude.

Those LGBTQ+ leadership sensibilities or competencies could transform any system or organization. If those cultural norms and values are approached with curiosity, intrigue, and humility, each provides guidance for leaders seeking growth, maturation, and personal expansion. It is by growing internally that we grow immeasurably. For those who prefer an aesthetic that asks us to be the best version of ourselves, there is no better example (although there are definitely comparable ones) of self-mastery, self-actualization, and liberated leadership than that of the LGBTQ+ community.

Despite those factors, there are still forces in society that make it difficult to recognize the virtue of LGBTQ+ people. Whether it is homogenization, stereotyping, religious bias, or cultural dismissiveness, LGBTQ+ people—as has been the case throughout our history—continue to face social and political opposition. Though the tactics and the actors have changed, the motivation has remained the same: to stamp out a culture whose very existence threatens a world order that is over-invested in conformity, repression, and subjugation. There are three significant ways in which the contributions of LGBTQ+ people get obscured, and we, as leaders and global citizens, must mitigate those factors. If we address the discriminatory practices and dismantle some of the philosophical rationales for anti-LGBTQ+ bias, we will not only further LGBTQ+ liberation but help formulate a progressive and freedom-loving society. Section 4 of this book is written to help leaders, global residents, LGBTQ+ people, and our allies identify the critical dynamics that obscure our beauty so our cultural genius™ can be fully leveraged by anyone anywhere on the planet.

CHAPTER 17

Here, There, & Nowhere: Recognizing the Diversity Within the LGBTQ+ Community

I have a little experiment I'd like to try with you. Close your eyes. Then, create a picture of what an LGBTQ+ person looks like in your mind.

Going well? Good. Now I want you to think of a famous Queer person... anyone... it doesn't matter who.

Still with me? Excellent. Now, I want you to envision how the world sees the quintessential LGBTQ+ person. Breathe. You're doing great.

Now, I want you to ask yourself: What did the person look like in all those images? What kind of clothing did they wear? What tone or attitude did they strike with their posture? What could you tell from their eyes? And what was their ethnic background? What was their gender? Did they come from a certain socio-economic background? Were they a person with a disability? What were their pronouns? Were they cisgender or non-binary? Where did they live?

Chances are you had a particular image in mind when I asked you those questions. And if you had an image of a middle-class, white, able-bodied, cisgender gay man from Western Europe or North America, I can hardly blame you. For all of the wonderful diversity in the LGBTQ+ community, the consistent avatar for all things Queer is the person I just described. It doesn't mean that there is something wrong with you if you are a middle-class, white, abled-bodied, cisgender man from Western Europe or North America. The challenge is that if you do not fit this profile, you are rendered invisible by a persistent narrative in which *that* cultural identity in its totality has not only become the norm but the standard for all things LGBTQ+. This dynamic not only makes it difficult for the community to fully express its beauty, but it also makes it difficult for people outside of our community to recognize the breadth of the Queer community and the extent to which LGBTQ+ culture intersects and reinforces other cultures around the globe.

Further, it makes it hard for those of us who are non-white, non-male, or non-cisgender members of the LGBTQ+ community to navigate it unabashedly. Admittedly, I am very comfortable in my LGBTQ+ skin, but I've personally had numerous experiences where other LGBTQ+ people have somehow assumed I wasn't gay. Whether it was Milwaukee, Boston, Saint Paul, or Miami, I remember going to LGBTQ+ establishments and having the bouncer warn me politely that the bar I was attending was LGBTQ+. In fact, when I was in Saint Paul, the bartender informed me that I might be more comfortable elsewhere since most of their clientele was Queer. Strangely, no other patron got the advisory. I assured the bouncer that I was perfectly okay associating with LGBTQ+ folk, as long as they didn't stereotype me as they just had.

Our community is intersectional and as diverse as any on the planet. Yet, from somewhere in the ethos, we are maintaining the false illusion that the LGBTQ+ community—globally and otherwise—is white-centered and cis-normative. As a result, this image is being telegraphed to the outside world and coloring (no pun intended) the faulty perception of who we are.

This truth could not have been more apparent than when I became a member of the San Francisco LGBTQ+ Speakers bureau. One week, four Queer BIPOC people and I were assigned to a well-known public high school on the western side of the city. During our presentation, we introduced ourselves and shared information about our lives, hobbies, careers, community interests, and identities. Afterward, we entertained questions from the students for about 35 minutes on a wide range of topics. As usual, we found the students to be thoughtful, intelligent, and blunt in their questioning. Many of them had met or known LGBTQ+ people. Some of them were LGBTQ+ themselves, and as we called on each student one by one, you could tell by their facial expressions that questions were racing through their adolescent minds.

However, one student (let's call him Charles) had his head down most of the time. Finally, after the questions stopped coming and there were a few seconds of silence, Charles's arm shot up as though he was responding to a military drill. Eager to hear his question, one of the other speakers called on him, and with a quizzical look, he asked: "If all of you are LGBTQ+ or whatever, why is it that all we see are white people when it comes to LGBTQ+ stuff?"

His question broke the ice. All of the speakers doubled over in laughter. The question spoke to a reality we all knew too well, and as we collected ourselves, we all said in unison: "Oh, Charles, we don't have enough time to talk about that."

But oh, do we need to. Charles's question was one I had entertained throughout my youth. When I started to question whether I had "Jedi" sensibilities (i.e., I was gay/Queer), part of what made it difficult for me to see myself as an LGBTQ+ person (besides techno music) was the fact that I didn't see any LGBTQ+ person in popular media who also looked like me. At the time, I used to joke that LGBTQ+ people must've been a lost tribe from Scandinavia based on the homogenous portraits and depictions I saw around me.

It reminded me of a book I read in college, which highlighted the lack of intersectionality in our discussions around culture and identity. When I enrolled in a Black womanist course at the University of Minnesota, I had the privilege of reading the following womanist anthology: "All the Women Are White. All the Blacks Are Men, But Some of Us Are Brave."[217] It was an illuminating collection of essays highlighting Black women's challenges in having their stories recognized in movements dominated by white women (feminism) and Black men (racial equity).

Similarly, racial and gender minorities can find it difficult to have their voice recognized in a community that supports differences but whose cultural sketch doesn't always reflect that diversity. Like any cultural group, the LGBTQ+ community can, at times, function like the larger society in which it sits. In a world beset by inequity and social privilege, marginalized communities can resemble or recreate the systems we purport to change.

HOMOPHOBIC IMPERIALISM

At the same time, LGBTQ+ rights opponents have also sought to paint the LGBTQ+ community as Eurocentric in order to insulate themselves from any accusations of bias or prejudice. For example, some leaders—particularly in the Global South—have argued that "gayness" is a European or Western imperialistic value imposed nefariously on certain societies. As the thinking goes, "homosexuality" undermines traditional cultures or the foundation of a natural

---

[217] Hull, G. T., & Scott, P. B., & Smith, B. (1993). *All the Women Are White, All the Blacks Are Men, But Some of Us Are Brave.* New York, NY: Feminist Pres at CUNY.

and just society. When President Barack Obama visited his ancestral homeland of Kenya in 2015, he drew the ire of conservative African leaders who said the gay-affimining head of state was "offending African values."[218] This thinking helps perpetuate the myth that LGBTQ+ values are inherently foreign and that LGBTQ+ people are predominantly Eurocentric.

Ironically, many leaders fail to realize that the homophobia that exists in places like India and sub-Saharan Africa was produced by American and European colonialism. As researcher Sylvia Tamale would write:

> Is it not the mother of all ironies for a Bible-wielding African politician named 'David' dressed in a three-piece suit, caressing an iPhone and speaking a colonial language, to condemn anything for its un-Africanness? Another irony lies in the fact that, in African countries, ideological and political groupings, civic associations, cultural, linguistic, and religious organisations that are staunchly opposed in their world views quickly rally together in their opposition to non-conforming sexualities. Hence, 'progressive' social groups (for instance, children's rights activists) have become strange bedfellows with the most oppressive regimes in Africa in condemning and attacking such sexualities.[219]

It is worth noting that prior to colonialism, same-sex activity was accepted in many societies, including African cultures, where men enjoyed consensual sexual relations in the military or fraternal

---

[218] Honan, Edith & Mason, J. "Obama in Kenya says gays need equality, draws African criticism." Reuters. July 25, 2015. https://www.reuters.com/article/us-obama-africa-gay/obama-in-kenya-says-gays-need-equality-draws-african-criticism-idUSKCN0PZ0MZ20150725

[219] Tamale, Sylvia. "Exploring the contours of African sexualities: Religion, law and power." African Human Rights Law Journal. Volume 14: No. 1 (2014). http://www.ahrlj.up.ac.za/tamale-s

organizations. In numerous tribal societies, men participated in homosexual activity while otherwise conforming to the traditional ways of life.[220] Additionally, a number of African people like the Yoruba—have historically and consistently used language and vernacular that has explicitly referred to same-sex relations and gender variance.[221]

Further, gender-variant and same-sex relations existed in other parts of the pre-colonial world, including Samoa, Tonga, Tahiti, and Hawaii, to name a few. For example, in pre-colonial Hawaii, the *aikane* was a friend and companion of the chief, who sometimes engaged in sexual relations with the chief. In Samoa, the "Fa'afafine" was the name given to biological men who identified as women. Identified as possessing a special gift or talent at an early age, the Fa'afafine dressed and presented as women in rituals and ceremonial affairs and also performed the tasks of men if needed. In the pre-colonial world of the Americas, many indigenous and First Nation cultures held gender-variant members ("two-spirit" peoples) in high esteem as artistic or spiritual leaders who contributed mightily to the vitality and growth of the community.[222]

So, in truth, same-sex relations and gender variance are not new to Polynesia, Africa, Asia, or the Indigenous world of the Americas. In fact, it is because of the sexual and gender fluidity in pre-colonial societies that many colonialists believed that subjugation of the Global South and West was necessary. As a result,

---

[220] "Why anti-gay sentiment remains strong in much of Africa." The Conversation. June 10, 2015. https://theconversation.com/why-anti-gay-sentiment-remains-strong-in-much-of-africa-42677

[221] Alimi, Bisi. "If you say being gay is not African, you don't know your history." The Guardian. September 9, 2015. https://www.theguardian.com/commentisfree/2015/sep/09/being-gay-african-history-homosexuality-christianity

[222] Burton, Neal. "Gender Variation and Same Sex Relations in Precolonial Times." Psychology Today. April 25, 2020. https://www.psychologytoday.com/us/blog/hide-and-seek/201707/gender-variation-and-same-sex-relations-in-precolonial-times

European colonizers exacted brutality on local populations in the form of extra-judicial killings, barbarism, or oppressive penal codes. For example, in 1513, the Spanish colonizer Vasco Nunez de Balboa is believed to have fed 40 "two-spirit" indigenous people in the Panamanian region to his dog pack (though these claims have been disputed by some). In 1861, during its colonization of India, the UK established Section 377 to outlaw any sexual relations that were deemed "against the order of nature," based on England's first sodomy law that was enacted in 1533.[223] Section 377 was the basis for much of India's anti-LGBTQ+ jurisprudence until it was overturned in 2018, nearly 160 years after it was enacted. Similar laws still exist in places like Singapore and Myanmar.

In many ways, European colonialism was not just about the economic and cultural exploitation of native societies; it was also about the repression of sexual and gender norms that were seen as deviant to highly religious, patriarchal, and white supremacist cultures in Europe and abroad. Perhaps there is no greater illustration of the European colonial legacy of anti-LGBTQ+ bias than the fact that of the 70+ countries that currently ban homosexual relations, more than half of those are former British colonies or protectorates.[224]

Unfortunately, colonization and the exportation of homophobia/transphobia have extended into the 21st century. In the early 2000s, realizing they were losing ground in the U.S. on issues such as abortion and LGBTQ+ rights, Christian conservative groups sought to re-establish their legitimacy by directing their attention to the Global South. Countries like Uganda, Ghana, Nigeria, and Zimbabwe were seen as new and fertile territories to propagate anti-LGBTQ+ bias and raise money for their floundering initiatives back home.

---

[223] Rao, Rahul (2020). *Out of Time: The Queer Politics of Postcoloniality.* Oxford University Press. pp. 7–9.

[224] Han, Enze & Joseph O'Mahoney. British Colonialism and the Criminalization of Homosexuality: Queens, Crime and Empire. Routledge (May 2018).

Whether historic or New Age, the colonializing efforts of influencers in the states and Western Europe have created the impression that sexual and gender fluidity is either absent in the Global South or that it never existed, thereby making it easier for the LGBTQ+ community to be racialized as white-dominant.

FRAMING LGBTQ+ PEOPLE AS AN EXTERNAL THREAT

Of course, the puritanical efforts abroad, in places like Southwest Asia, Eastern Europe, and Sub-Saharan Africa, have run parallel to efforts in North America and Western Europe to repress LGBTQ+ sensibilities. In addition to the religious dogma that preached against so-called LGBTQ+ immorality, the U.S. government also played an important role in depicting LGBTQ+ culture as subversive. In the mid-20th Century, World War II and the New Deal created numerous career opportunities for LGBTQ+ employees in state and federal governments. Over time, militants and pugnacious statesmen such as Wisconsin senator Joseph McCarthy labeled gay men and lesbians as national security risks and communist sympathizers.[225] With the increasing visibility of LGBTQ+ culture in the 1950s and 1960s, the government conflated LGBTQ+ culture as a national security threat, or as some would call it, the "Lavender Scare." As a result, at the behest of government officials such as U.S. Senator Joseph McCarthy, F.B.I. Director J. Edgar Hoover, and American prosecutor Roy Cohn, President Dwight D. Eisenhower instituted Executive Order 10450, purging nearly 5,000 LGBTQ+ civil servants from government service.[226] Similar initiatives were taken up

---

[225] Johnson, David K. The Lavender Scare: The Cold War Persecution of Gays and Lesbians in the Federal Government. Chicago: University of Chicago Press, 2009.

[226] *Id.*

at the state and local level, and with government incursion into civil liberties at an all-time high, LGBTQ+ people were understandably reticent to be visible.

For modern-day LGBTQ+ people of color (POC), the Lavender Scare came against the backdrop of Jim Crow. It represented a "double-bind" dilemma with serious negative implications and no obvious solution. People of color didn't have the latitude to express their sexual freedom, much less the ability to declare their sexual identity. Reliant on their families to overcome racism, many Queer POC (QPOC) stayed in the closet, further reinforcing the narrow view of the LGBTQ+ community as being predominantly white.

As a result, some may ask: Do Queer people of color have any responsibility for the enduring "white-centeredness" of the LGBTQ+ community if POC failed to come out? Naturally, Queer people of color have an opportunity to use their personal agency—when comfortable and ready—to embrace who they are and to proactively disclose their identity to whomever they choose. The failure to do so concedes a stereotypical narrative that the LGBTQ+ community is only white or Eurocentric.

However, questioning the role of Queer people of color in portraying a racially-diverse community assumes that BIPOC communities do not come out when, in fact, BIPOC communities come out at higher rates than their white counterparts.[227] Further, we cannot ignore the synergistic effect that racism and heterosexism play in painting LGBTQ+ culture as white exclusive. If we know LGBTQ+ history, then we should know that BIPOC people helped lead the charge at transcendent moments. The Cooper Do-Nuts uprising in Los Angeles in 1959, the Compton Cafeteria revolt in San Francisco in 1966, and the Stonewall rebellion in New York in 1969 would

---

[227] Gates, Gary J. (2017). "In U.S., more adults identifying as LGBT." Gallup. https://news.gallup.com/poll/201731/lgbt-identification-rises.aspx. Accessed on March 9, 2022.

not have been possible were it not for the leadership and courage of Queer people of color.[228]

Further, people of color also achieved important LGBTQ+ milestones. For example, before Harvey Milk made his mark as one of the most venerated leaders of the LGBTQ+ movement (and deservedly so), José Sarria was the first openly gay person to run for office in 1961. Although Sarria didn't win his election for San Francisco city supervisor, he defied convention: He was Latino and worked as a drag queen at a local bar.

There were other LGBTQ+ trailblazers as well who were also people of color. The same-sex marriage movement didn't begin in Massachusetts in the 2000s; it began with the humble yet assertive activism of Donna Burkett and Manonia Evans, a Black lesbian couple who sought a marriage license in 1971 in my hometown of Milwaukee. Burkett and Evans took the case to court when their marriage license application was denied.[229]

Examples of other obscure Queer BIPOC pioneers include people like Maxine Doyle Perkins, a Latino transgender woman who risked imprisonment to advocate for LGBTQ+ rights in North Carolina. Given the nickname of "Notoria" and described by the *Charlotte Observer* as a "hopeless homosexual," Perkins was prosecuted in 1961 for having sex with a man in Charlotte's Uptown district and sentenced to 30 years in prison for sodomy.[230] Perkins's case received national attention because she defied gender norms and refused to be misgendered (she alternated between dresses and suits during her court appearances and refused to answer to any name

---

[228] Marsha P. Johnson, Sylvia Rivera, and Stormie DeLarvarie are widely believed to have started the Stonewall rebellion.

[229] James, Scott. "Queer People of Color Led the L.G.B.T.Q. Charge, but Were Denied the Rewards." New York Times. June 22, 2019.

[230] Burford, Joshua. Interview with WFAE on January 8, 2018. *South Bound Preview: Historian Joshua Burford Recalls Trans Woman's Courage In 1960s Charlotte.* https://www.wfae.org/tags/maxine-perkins

but "Maxine"). The case also garnered attention because the punishment levied against Perkins was so severe. Perkins only served two years of her sentence, and due to her case, jail sentences for homosexuality were reduced to between four months and 10 years. Although the reduced prison time was of little consolation, Perkins's shero-ism laid the foundation for the freedoms LGBTQ+ people enjoy today.

Whether it's Martha P. Johnson, Jose Sarria, Donna Burkett, Manonia Evans, or Maxine Doyle Perkins, LGBTQ+ history is littered with dozens of invisible stories of leadership and courage from around the world. Every segment of the community was intimately involved in our collective liberation. When historical accounts such as 2015's *Stonewall* movie whitewash the movement, they do a disservice to LGBTQ+ people of color and the LGBTQ+ community overall.

TRANS-INVISIBILITY

While racial minorities have been obscured in honoring the beauty and vitality of the LGBTQ+ community, we must also acknowledge the relative invisibility of women, transgender people, and other sexual minorities in LGBTQ+ cultural profiles. As noted previously, transgender people and sex workers played prominent roles during various social flashpoints, whether at Cooper's Do-nuts, Compton Cafeteria, or Stonewall. If this is true, why has it been so difficult for mainstream society to recognize the transgender experience?

In short, one of the reasons is that people still confuse gender identity with sexual orientation. Although both identities challenge traditional gender norms, the cultural pathway of transgender people—while parallel to that of sexual minorities—is distinct from the cultural pathway of gay, lesbian, or bisexual people. Gender identity refers to one's personal concept of gender, which may or may conform to traditional gender norms. Sexual orientation is defined as one's romantic, affectional, and familial connection to a person of the same sex. The two concepts may be difficult to understand for a society that is still relatively illiterate when it comes to gender and sexual fluidity.

Further, research about the LGBTQ+ community may exclude demographic questions that focus on transgender people. Surveys designed for LGBTQ+ audiences may lump the LGBTQ+ community together while ignoring the health, employment, and income disparities between various subgroups, including transgender people.

Finally, the LGB+ community has not always done a great job creating space for the transgender community to be heard. To be clear, cisgenderism has been a problem among sexual minorities as well, even dating back to the earliest moments in modern LGBTQ+ history. For example, I'd be remiss if I didn't note that while the Compton Cafeteria revolt was in response to police harassment, the Compton Cafeteria itself was popular among transgender people because they were not welcomed in gay and lesbian establishments in San Francisco.[231]

These factors have contributed to trans invisibility or a phenomenon where the histories, stories, and achievements of transgender people have been rendered obscure within the LGBTQ+ community and society in general. In order to fully appreciate the talents of LGBTQ+ people as a whole, transgender people cannot be an afterthought; they need to be fully illuminated and intentionally displayed.

BI-ERASURE

Similarly, bisexual people have also faced obscurity and dealt with double marginalization; the experience whereby a minority is further minoritized within their community. Ironically, although over

---

[231] Stryker, Susan. *Transgender History*. First Printing edition. Berkeley, CA: Seal Press, 2008.

half of LGB+ people identify as bisexual, they are often treated as a footnote to LGBTQ+ history and culture.[232] In other instances, bisexuality is delegitimized or regarded as a temporary cultural "bus stop" en route to the "final destination" of identifying as gay or lesbian. The practice of minimizing the bisexual experience is known as bi-erasure. It contributes to an image of the LGBTQ+ community in which lesbian women and gay men are at the forefront, to the exclusion of bisexual people.[233] As a result, bisexual people face severe health disparities compared to lesbian women and gay men, including higher rates of depression and anxiety.[234]

SIGNS THAT INCREASED VISIBILITY IS OCCURRING

Despite the vestiges of trans invisibility and bi-erasure, we are seeing attitudinal shifts in our greater society where people realize the LGBTQ+ community is multi-faceted. For example, in the 2021 Gay and Lesbian Alliance Against Defamation (GLAAD) Acceptance Survey, which annually measures general attitudes towards LGBTQ+ inclusion, 37% of non-LGBTQ+ respondents stated they understood that the LGBTQ+ community is comprised of different sub-groups with different needs. That figure increased by eight percentage points from the 2020 GLAAD Acceptance report.[235]

Also, we are seeing progress in balanced LGBTQ+ representation in entertainment and visual media. According to GLAAD's annual report, *Where We Are On TV*, 2021 saw increased LGBTQ+ representation. According to GLAAD's report:

---

[232] Williams Institute. UCLA School of Law. "How many people are Lesbian, Gay, Bisexual, and Transgender." April 2011. https://williamsinstitute.law.ucla.edu/publications/how-many-people-lgbt/

[233] Erasure of Bisexuality. GLAAD. https://www.glaad.org/bisexual/bierasure

[234] *Id.*

[235] Accelerating Acceptance 2021. Gay and Lesbian Alliance Against Defamation. www.glaad.org/sites/default/files/AA2021_Final.pdf

1. In the 2020–21 season, bisexual+ characters made up 28 percent of all LGBTQ+ characters on all three television platforms (broadcast, cable, and streaming), representing a two-percentage increase from the previous year.

2. Across all three platforms, there were 29 regular and recurring transgender characters. These characters included 15 trans women, 12 trans men, and two non-binary, trans characters.

3. For the fourth year, GLAAD identified asexual characters on TV, including a single asexual character on Netflix's since-canceled *BoJack Horseman*. Moreover, a lesbian asexual character was said to be included in 2022 primetime scripted cable programming.

4. Of the 773 series LGBTQ+ regulars counted on broadcast television, 46 percent (354) of those characters were people of color, a one-percentage-point decrease from the previous year's record high of 47 percent. The racial diversity of LGBTQ+ characters on all platforms increased.

5. The percentage of series regular characters with a disability slightly increased, up to 3.5 percent from the previous year's 3.1 percent.[236]

For more information, please consult GLAAD's 2021 *Where We Are On TV* report.

Fortunately, depictions of LGBTQ+ in entertainment and media are starting to reflect the full diversity of the community.

---

[236] Where We Are On TV—2020. Gay and Lesbian Alliance Against Defamation. https://www.glaad.org/whereweareontv20

WHY RECOGNIZING LGBTQ+ DIVERSITY IS IMPORTANT FOR LGBTQ+ HUMAN RIGHTS

If we want to appreciate the cultural genius™ of LGBTQ+ people fully, we have to become more aware of LGBTQ+ diversity in order to discern how those gifts can be manifested in a myriad of ways. LGBTQ+ diversity is not a feel-good measure; it has direct consequences for LGBTQ+ civil rights and political advocacy. If we want to build more effective coalitions in support of LGBTQ+ rights, building an authentic and all-embracing image of LGBTQ+ people is tantamount to greater integration into all aspects of society. The following story demonstrates the need for more inclusive storytelling related to all people within the LGBTQ+ community.

When I lived in Kansas City in the early 2000s, I was a member of the board of the local Human Rights Campaign chapter, which is a national organization dedicated to LGBTQ+ rights. One month, in anticipation of a trip to Kansas City, the HRC national president, Joe Solmonese, asked to meet with local Black leaders to discuss how to build a stronger coalition. It was a courageous act and a powerful move on the part of Solmonese and HRC, one that assuaged at least some of my fears in supporting the organization. Given that I was the only Black person on the local board, my fellow board members asked if I would be comfortable organizing meetings between the HRC president and Black representatives in Kansas City. Like a number of mainstream LGBTQ+ organizations, HRC had failed to cultivate relationships with the Black community in Kansas City. In their wisdom, they assumed that Black leaders meant talking to Black religious leaders.

Within two weeks, I managed to organize a meeting with Black leaders, which included members of the Urban League, the local chapter of the NAACP, local elected officials, local business leaders, and members of the clergy. However, I counseled HRC representatives that in meeting with any community group, there needed to be an identifiable shared interest. Even with good intentions, sending out a request to meet with Black leaders could be seen as haughty unless it was framed as an opportunity to support the Black community as well. Initially, the invitation sounded imperial, and no leader from any community would welcome being "summonsed" to a meeting whose purpose was vague and ill-defined. The question that had to be answered for the Black leaders was: "Who is HRC, and why should we meet with them?" With some finessing, I crafted a message where the purpose of the meeting was to build dialogue between various community groups around Black empowerment and LGBTQ+ inclusion.

When the meeting began, each of the assembled leaders opened the conversation with the customary introductions, indicating who they were and what organization they represented. Yet, in short order, the dialogue turned to the more robust topic of allyship.

Astutely, many of those gathered noted the false polemic of talking about the Black community and LGBTQ+ community as separate when there were people who belonged to both. From there, the Black leaders offered some telling insights which had been articulated by other BIPOC people and me before: Firstly, the Black leaders wanted to know why the image of the LGBTQ+ community was so homogeneous. In their eyes, they wanted HRC and other LGBTQ+ organizations to diversify their spokespeople, leadership, and marketing.

Secondly, the Black leaders wanted to know what was being done to support Black LGBTQ+ people from the LGBTQ+ side. While they recognized they had an obligation to continue to dismantle homophobia in the Black community, they also wanted to hear HRC's commitment to dismantling racism in the LGBTQ+ community.

Finally, they noted that as long as the LGBTQ+ community continued to portray itself as an upper-class movement of white men, it would be difficult to get coalitional support from other marginalized groups. As the leaders noted, it's difficult to stress the urgency of supporting LGBTQ+ rights when the profile of the people who are said to be disadvantaged consists of people who are supremely privileged in society according to race and gender. Nevertheless, the meeting was extremely thoughtful and candid, and to his credit, Solmonese said he left the meeting more informed than before.

The feedback from Black leaders in Kansas City speaks to why it is so important for our society to appreciate the full diversity of the community. To begin with, LGBTQ+ people are a part of every conceivable demographic. There is no community in which Queer people are not members. Because of that fact, leaders need to recognize that LGBTQ+ people do not just fit one profile. We are Asian, and we are bisexual. We are full-bodied, and we are disabled. Some of us are working class, and some of us are undocumented. We are feminine and masculine and neither. Some of us are elderly; some of us were just born. We are transgender, and we are lesbian. We span the globe, and we span the human spectrum of diversity.

When that diversity is minimized or misrepresented, or erased and over-shadowed, it not only undercuts our ability to showcase our diversity and cultural genius™, it also undermines our ability to demonstrate the social and political threats to our existence. While I would never argue that LGBTQ+ liberation is unimportant for people who have privilege (racial, gender, gender identity, or otherwise), portraits of the community that overrepresent "the rich, male, cisgender, or white" give an impression that our community is not vulnerable. They give the impression that the LGBTQ+ community is a special interest group as opposed to a misunderstood and oppressed community.

Some have argued quite plausibly that the movement for LGBTQ+ rights has been accepted much more quickly by mainstream society since the most visible vanguards of the movement have been cisgender white men. In other words, racial and gender privilege accelerated LGBTQ+ acceptance in ways that underrepresented communities pushing for racial and gender equity could not. In a study of implicit bias based on various diversity dimensions, researchers discovered that implicit bias shifted more rapidly on sexuality than towards any other diversity topic between 2007–2016.[237] Based on the imperfect society we know, the studies make sense: If Americans, most of whom are white, are uncomfortable with examining their racism and sexism, they are more likely to support people who look like their family members and/or neighbors as opposed to BIPOC people whose racialized experiences they have barely begun to understand.

Yet, as the U.S. becomes more racially diverse and less gender-stratified, relying on white or male privilege to sustain acceptance is not a sound strategy. Not only does the LGBTQ+ community have an opportunity to build stronger relationships with communities of color, it also has a responsibility to support racial and gender equity to improve the lives of Queer communities of color and those who are disabled or financially insecure. These objectives can only be achieved by recognizing and highlighting the full diversity within the community.

As irrepressible as LGBTQ+ people can be, there is no amount of vigor, flair, and resilience that can fully diminish the amount of anti-LGBTQ+ bias in the world. Yet, when the intra-communal diversity of LGBTQ+ people is displayed in a revealing and compelling way, the world sees itself in us. We are not the other. We are not alien lifeforms. We are poetic extensions of the people they see every day. Additionally, when the world sees our full diversity, it can fully appreciate our talents and use them to the best of our ability.

However, when the world does not fully appreciate our diversity, it can conjure up unique ways to disparage our talent. LGBTQ+ people are more likely than non-LGBTQ+ people to be

---

[237] Schmidt, Samantha. "Americans' views flipped on gay rights. How did minds change so quickly?" Washington Post. June 7, 2019. https://www.washingtonpost.com/local/social-issues/americans-views-flipped-on-gay-rights-how-did-minds-change-so-quickly/2019/06/07/ae256016-8720-11e9-98c1-e945ae5db8fb_story.html

unemployed and at risk for poverty. Transgender people are chronically underemployed,[238] and bisexual people are at a greater risk for poverty than other sexual minorities.[239] Further, for those LGBTQ+ people who are employed, they may be *uncomfortably* employed as LGBTQ+ workers encounter hostile work environments riddled with bias, discrimination, and microaggressions. According to a study by the Human Rights Campaign Foundation in 2021, 45% of LGBTQ+ people are closeted at work, and at least 1 out of 8 LGBTQ+ people report feeling exhausted from hiding their gender identity or sexual orientation.[240] Moreover, only three Fortune 500 companies are headed by openly LGBTQ+ people, and less than .3% (yes, you read that correctly) of Board directors were openly gay in 2020.[241,242] How can organizations fully leverage the genius of LGBTQ+ people when LGBTQ+ people are still fearing discrimination in the workplace?

The first step is recognizing that the experiences of LGBTQ+ people in the workplace can differ based on the subgroup to which an employee belongs. LGBTQ+ people of color are three times more likely to face discrimination based on gender identity and sexual orientation than their white counterparts.[243] The degree to which

---

[238] When compared to cisgender people, transgender people are 11% less likely to be employed. "Transgender Americans are more likely to be unemployed and poor." The Conversation. https://theconversation.com/transgender-americans-are-more-likely-to-be-unemployed-and-poor-127585

[239] O'hara, Mary Emily. "Study: Bisexual community faces more poverty than lesbians and gay men." them. https://www.them.us/story/bisexual-community-poverty

[240] Fidas, D., Cooper, L. (2019). *A workplace divided: Understanding the climate for LGBTQ+ workers nationwide*. Human Rights Campaign Foundation.

[241] Aspan, M. (2020, June 16). *Fortune 500 CEOs praise landmark LGBTQ+ antidiscrimination ruling*.

[242] *Fair representation might lead to better outcomes in times of crisis*. (2020, April 7). Out Leadership.

[243] *Discrimination in America: Experiences and views of LGBTQ+ Americans*. (2017). National Public Radio, the Robert Wood Johnson Foundation, and the Harvard T. H. Chan School of Public Health.

LGBTQ+ employees hear jokes against gender and sexual minorities differs depending on the group to which they belong.[244] Moreover, transgender workers face unique bias where co-workers may protest bathroom accessibility, incorrectly designate gender pronouns, or ask inappropriate questions. If leaders don't recognize the diversity within the community, they will be ill-prepared to create distinctive approaches to further inclusion and belonging for all members of the LGBTQ+ community. More directly, they will fail to truly appreciate how Queer people can help them remake their leadership practice.

---

[244] In terms of 53% of LGBTQ+ people have heard lesbian and gay jokes, 37% have heard bisexual jokes, and 41% have heard transgender jokes. Fidas, D., Cooper, L. (2019). *A workplace divided: Understanding the climate for LGBTQ+ workers nationwide.* Human Rights Campaign Foundation

LESSONS IN LGBTQ+ LEADERSHIP: HONORING DIFFERENCE

1) **Identify biases.** What biases, if any, do you have towards each subgroup within the LGBTQ+ community? Where do those biases come from?

2) **Deactivate biases.** What will you do to deactivate those biases? Create an action plan for acknowledging, examining, and dismantling those biases.

3) **Recognize the various communities of the LGBTQ+ community.** Which subgroups are you most familiar with? Which groups are you least familiar with? What steps can you take to become a better ally to each of the groups that make up the larger LGBTQ+ community?

4) **Educate yourself.** Learn about the cultural experiences of each LGBTQ+ cultural group, including Queer people of color, women, lesbians, bisexuals, asexuals, transgender people, and intersex people.

5) **Meet with each subgroup of the LGBTQ+ community to understand their unique experiences within the organization.** Partner with employees and leaders from that community to create strategies for eradicating bias, accelerating career growth, and developing leadership opportunities.

6) **Create an LGBTQ+ employee resource group for your organization.** Ensure that your affinity group is dedicated to nurturing the psychological safety of *all* LGBTQ+ employees.

7) **Donate to under-served and under-funded LGBTQ+ organizations.** Seek out and support organizations that represent the full spectrum of LGBTQ+ diversity.

8) **Volunteer with LGBTQ+ organizations.** Look for groups to join in your local area.

9) **Seek, hire, and retain LGBTQ+ people.** Create a community of LGBTQ+ vendors and business partners to support your business.

CHAPTER 18

B.C.D.: Neutralizing the Weaponization of Religion

Undoubtedly, it's happened to you…

You've been engaged in a socially charged conversation with someone who has strong religious convictions. No…scratch that: *extremely* strong religious convictions. As you discuss a "controversial" social issue (like, oh, I don't know, anything related to LGBTQ+ rights), and as you cite statistics or offer personal anecdotes or appeal to your fellow conversationalist's sense of fairness, the discussion abruptly ends when the other person says, "You are wrong because the Bible says ___."

Omg! You had no warning. Who knew your "friend" had the Bible in her back pocket? Is this not unfair or what?!

It's startling. As you reflect, you realize that although contentious, the exchange has had ripples of illumination and has served as a rare but delicious forum for dialogue. But once that pivotal phrase is uttered, the conversation suddenly dovetails and tragically… stops. You want to respond, but with the full weight of the Bible being pushed against your assertions, your arguments start to feel slight, insignificant, or paltry. You cringe at the idea of "arguing with God" and quietly slip into the shadows, convinced that you should never discuss this issue—or any issue—that flouts religious doctrine. Your friend revels in this small "victory" and, without being overly smug, looks at you resolutely as if to say, "Silly mortal... How could these truths not be self-evident?"

If you've experienced this before (and I'm sure you have), there is a name for this social phenomenon: Biblical Conversation Death, or "BCD." Biblical Conversation Death occurs when religiosity is leveraged in a diverse conversation as a means of silencing or pre-empting opposing arguments.

BCD is not simply sharing religious beliefs or cultural perspectives, nor does it occur exclusively with the Christian Bible or with people who identify as Christians. BCD is a euphemism for any conversation where religious zealotry is designed to minimize dialogue, specifically concerning LGBTQ+ issues. The same phenomenon could occur with the Torah, the Koran, the Bhagavad Gita, or the Tipitaka. BCD doesn't speak as much to the social views people may hold as it does to the process they engage in when discussing polemics in society. BCD implicates not only those who "weaponize" religion or religious texts but also those who willingly capitulate to religious arguments as if religious arguments cannot be deftly, respectfully, and successfully challenged.

Here are some examples of how BCD occurs in everyday conversation:

Scenario One

Lupe: I haven't completed my ballot and Voting Day is Tuesday.

Tina: I know. I'll be so glad to not get inundated with any more mailings, especially around Prop B.

Lupe: I know! Prop B seems to be the hot-button issue.
          I don't know why people are so upset about it. What's
          the big issue if children are taught about gay families
          in school?

Tina: It's a huge issue! I don't want my kids to be taught to
          accept immoral lifestyles. It's wrong.

Lupe: How is it wrong? Prop B is just about expanding
          children's knowledge about other people and
          other families.

Tina: The Bible says it's wrong. That's all the proof I need.

Lupe: Okay, well, I can't argue with that.

Scenario Two

Warren: Hey Bud, are you going to Tim's "Going Away" party?

Jared: Eh, I think I'll pass.

Warren: The guy has worked for the company for 25 years. You
          won't even come by to say "thank you?"

Jared: Not if his partner, boyfriend—or whatever you would
          call him—will be there. Being a Christian, I can't
          support that.

Warren: Oh… Okay. That makes sense.

In each scenario, the exchange ends abruptly once a declarant invokes the "Bible" or religion. "Death" in diversity conversations occurs when dialogue becomes neutered for fear of engaging in a discussion with religious overtones or when religiosity is invoked to dismiss social issues, particularly LGBTQ+ rights, and those arguments go unchallenged.

BCD is not the support or gracious recognition of someone else's religious beliefs. Instead, it is the belief—either by the proponent or the recipient, explicitly or implicitly—that religious dogma (by virtue of them being religious) is unassailable and superior to the ideology, needs, or social aspirations of others, especially those who are LGBTQ+. Here are a few examples to illustrate the difference between the two:

Example A (two neighbors):

Jalen: I won't let my son be a member of the Boy Scouts if they accept homosexual Scoutmasters.

Corinne: Why? They're just people like you and me.

Jalen: I'm sorry, but that's how I feel as a Christian.

Corinne: Well…I'm a Christian, and I don't agree with that at all, but you're entitled to think whatever you want.

Assessment: Not BCD.

Example B (three friends):

Laura: Do you guys still want to go with us to the amusement park this weekend? The boys are so excited.

Meredith: We're game.

Tara: I would, but I heard the park hosts LGBTQ+ events every year.

Laura: LGBTQ+ events? What am I missing?

Meredith: Yeah, I'm not following.

Tara: Well, I don't want to support a business that promotes that lifestyle.

Meredith: You mean the Gay Day event? From what I understand, the amusement park just sets aside one day to welcome LGBTQ+ patrons. It happens all across the country with other amusement parks.

Laura: How is it promoting a lifestyle because they have a "Gay Day?"

Tara: The Bible says very clearly that people who condone immoral lifestyles are just as guilty as those who

	engage in the lifestyle themselves. The Bible is clear. I know I'm right on this.
Meredith:	(thought bubble) *"I don't think the Bible says that, but I don't know what to say."*
Laura:	(thought bubble) *"She seems so adamant about it, so she must be right. These types of conversations make me uncomfortable. But, if I disagree with her, it'll just be awkward."*
Laura:	Okay. I see your point.
Tara:	Whew! I was worried for a moment that you guys thought differently. We have to be vigilant about this kind of stuff, especially with kids.
Meredith:	(thought bubble) *"I couldn't disagree more."*
Laura:	Yep.
Verdict:	Definite BCD.

In Example A, Carol responded from a place of strength, not fear. Although she disagreed with Ted, she didn't retreat. She recognized Ted's beliefs but also affirmed her perspective. The conversation didn't suffer from Biblical Conversation Death. Instead, it was a cultural exchange that had run its course.

The second example, however, illustrates what can happen when religiosity is raised as a rhetorical panacea to LGBTQ+ issues. People will either retreat because they lack the temerity to challenge the assertions or because they see religiosity as an occasion to suspend their critical thought process. In Example B, Laura and Meredith were trying to placate Tara instead of offering an honest critique of Tara's statements. When a person feigns agreement to pacify a religious conservative, or when a religious conservative treats their position on LGBTQ+ rights as indisputable, there is definitely a case of BCD.

BCD is manifested between religious adherents and agnostics, or religious conservatives and LGBTQ+ people, as well as people of the same religious faith. Not surprisingly, people of the same faith can have differing views on what their religion teaches, as some people are strict constructionists (they read religious texts literally) while others are loose constructionists (they read religious texts figuratively). The one constant variable is that LGBTQ+ issues seem to be disproportionately ripe for BCD.

BCD IN THE SOCIAL CONTEXT

BCD occurs not only in the individual context or in one-on-one conversations but also in the larger social context when lightning rod issues (particularly LGBTQ+ issues) are advocated. From a macro perspective, BCD heightens social sensitivities, restrains LGBTQ+ rights, and fuels political debate.

Think not? In 2013, the United States Senate passed the Employment Non-Discrimination Act, which makes it illegal for most private-sector employers and government sector employers on the local, state, and federal levels to discriminate against employees on the basis of sexual orientation and gender identity.[245] However, the legislation was not politically feasible until exemptions were written into the law for religious organizations. As it stands, if religious organizations believe that homosexuality is sinful, they can refuse to hire a prospective LGBTQ+ employee because they are LGBTQ+. Religious exemptions are "needed" because, as members of the Traditional Values Coalition have argued:

> The Employment Non-Discrimination Act discriminates against Christian daycare, Christian parents, Christian business owners, and the rights of religious freedom.[246]

---

[245] As of February 2014, the legislation is still pending in the U.S. House of Representatives.

[246] *Traditional Values Coalition* on Friday, December 6th, 2013, in a fundraising email, Tampa Bay Times PolitiFact.com.

Many legislators and conservatives agreed with this argument. Senator Rand Paul of Kentucky argued that from the perspective of non-profits, "hiring gay people would burden the employer's exercise of religion."[247] In advance of the Senate vote on ENDA, the Becket Fund for Religious Liberty expressed concern "that the law does not provide religious liberty protections where they are warranted."[248]

That is the alternative way BCD manifests itself. If a person doesn't rely on "morality-based" arguments or scripture to refute calls for LGBTQ+ inclusion, they will argue that supporting LGBTQ+ rights impedes "religious freedom." And, of course, since this country was founded based on religious liberty, no reasonable person would dare argue with someone protecting religious liberty, right? This rationale is just another derivation of BCD used to denigrate LGBTQ+ rights. As Rev. Harry Knox maintains:

> Religious liberty is a notion precious to our democracy, closely tied to the First Amendment's guarantee of free exercise of religion. Its integrity is worth fighting for. [However] I have long been troubled that some people of faith invoke religion as a crutch to justify ignorance or dislike of LGBTQ+ people.[249]

John Witte, director of the Center for the Study of Law and Religion at Emory University, agrees:

---

[247] Meckler, Laura. "Religious Exemptions at Center of ENDA Debate." The Wall Street Journal. Washington Wire. November 1, 2013. <http://blogs.wsj.com/washwire/2013/11/01/religious-exemptions-at-center-of-enda-debate/>

[248] Gryboski, Michael. "Religious Exemption in Employment Non-Discrimination Act 'Terribly Broad,' Denounced NYT Editorial." Christian Post. November 6, 2013.

[249] Knox, Harry. "Unholy Religious Exemptions." The Baltimore Sun. December 9, 2013.

> [Interestingly] a religious organization is perfectly fine with hav-
> ing the Civil Rights Act in place and saying that religious dis-
> crimination in general is not something that we want to allow
> in our community, but a religious organization has to have the
> ability to engage in religious discrimination in its core religious
> employment decisions.

In anticipation of LGBTQ+ political victories, some conservatives have gone even further and have tried to apply the religious
exemption argument in a broader social context. In the Winter of
2014, numerous bills were introduced in statehouses across the U.S.
that would allow employees and business owners to shirk their professional duties and avoid providing goods or services to LGBTQ+
people if those acts violate their "sincerely-held religious beliefs."[250]
For example, if a lesbian couple entered an auto dealership to buy
a new car, a car salesman could decline to work with them if he
objected to "homosexuality." A bill introduced in the Kansas
Legislature—House Bill 2453—was based on similar precepts.
When asked to explain the basis for the legislation, one Kansas state
legislator argued implausibly:

> It's not that we want to discriminate against someone because
> they're gay. We just don't think you should be coerced [to provide
> service to LGBTQ+ customers]… against your sincerely held reli-
> gious belief.[251]

More and more U.S. states are drafting "religious liberty" legislation that would make it permissible for business owners and

---

[250] Margolin, Emma. "Religious liberty bill opens door for LGBT discrimination." MSNBC. February 6, 2014. <http://www.msnbc.com/msnbc/bill-opens-
door-lgbt-discrimination>

[251] Margolin, Emma. "Religious liberty bill opens door for LGBT discrimination." MSNBC. February 6, 2014. <http://www.msnbc.com/msnbc/bill-opens-
door-lgbt-discrimination>

professionals to discriminate against LGBTQ+ employees *and* consumers if they have a moral objection to "homosexuality," including Ohio, Idaho, Mississippi, Arizona, and Oklahoma.[252]

Brilliantly, opponents of LGBTQ+ rights are using the "religious exemption" argument preemptively and have reframed the issue. LGBTQ+ people are no longer victimized; they are "victimizing" those who simply want to uphold their religious beliefs, even though no LGBTQ+ rights initiative has ever come close to establishing an official religion or rewriting traditional religious doctrines. As my friend Kenya remarked satirically, "Discrimination isn't really discrimination if you're doing it for God. Obviously."

Clearly, the point of the legislation is not to appeal to reasoned intellect but to silence the rights and speech of LGBTQ+ people and their allies as they advocate for full inclusion. That is an example of BCD on a much larger scale.

Given the patent contradiction of the "religious freedom" argument, it raises questions about the secondary dynamic of BCD: the general reluctance of people to question or challenge religious-based arguments against LGBTQ+ initiatives. Why are people so hesitant to push back against extremist religious views or contorted interpretations of religious text? Why do people defer to religious ideologies when someone mentions the Bible or religiosity?

"I think it's an issue of courage," says Billy, a noted diversity leader at the University of California-Berkeley. "People are afraid for their immortal soul, and if they disagree with anyone's religious beliefs, it feels as though they are questioning God. I'm an atheist, but before becoming atheist, it was difficult to throw off the yoke of religiosity to counter religious arguments and not feel conflicted or guilty. I think it's hard for many people to argue against religiosity if they grew up in a religious household."

---

[252] "Opponents seek responses amid court setbacks." Associated Press. San Francisco Chronicle. February 16, 2014, p. A14.

Certainly, it's hard to rationally argue when religiosity has such a strong emotional undercurrent. Religious views can be presented as unassailable. But isn't it odd to assert that everyone should abide by one particular religious doctrine? Religious fanaticism and zealotry is extremely dangerous and runs counter to one of the core principles (religious freedom) this country was founded upon.

As a spiritual person, I think you can appeal to one's logic without sacrificing one's spiritual beliefs. And as a progressive person, you can affirm the dignity of someone's religious beliefs without co-signing their political arguments.

Nonetheless, BCD persists. Thankfully, I achieved my breakthrough in the Fall of 2005. At the time, I was asked to speak to a Human Sexuality class at the University of Missouri-Kansas City. Most of the students seemed shy about discussing LGBTQ+ issues. Now, if you enroll in a human sexuality course, I believe you should expect to talk about LGBTQ+ issues at *some* point. So, I could understand the surprise if the topic for the lecture that week was "renewable energy," but with the course titled "Human Sexuality," I think you've been given fair notice that a gay/queer guest speaker might appear.

Despite that notion, people seemed very uncomfortable. I was part of a four-member panel of LGBTQ+ people who were asked to talk about their lives and to help dispel myths about sexual orientation and gender identity. As everyone introduced themselves, the panelists fielded questions from the class about what it means to be LGBTQ+.

The other panelists seemed rather apologetic for being LGBTQ+ and if I'm speaking honestly, "being apologetic for who you are" is not a sentiment I share.

Clumsy introductions aside, the class started to ask questions, some of which were fairly pedestrian while others were truly bizarre. Here are some examples:

"When did you know you were gay?"
"In your relationship, who's the man, and who's the woman?"
"Do you hate women?"
"What do LGBTQ+ people do for fun?"

In diversity circles, we're taught to meet people where they are. However, I also believe you have to lead people where you want them to go. And so, as we took turns answering the most fantastical lot of questions related to the LGBTQ+ community I had ever heard, I noticed that one lady in the rear of the room was sitting with her arms crossed. It was obvious that she was stewing, and when she finally raised her hand, I knew she had something compelling to say:

I don't condone homosexuality. So, I wonder if any of you were raised as Christians and how you reconcile being Christian and being gay?

Two of us had indicated that we were raised as Christians. As I pondered the question, I listened intently as one of the other panelists offered his response:

Well, I believe that God made me this way, and I think you can be gay and Christian without there being an issue.

If I were an Olympic judge, I'd probably give the response a six. Although the response was thoughtful, it didn't challenge the underlying premise of the question: Why is Christianity (or any religion for that matter) the litmus test for determining whether gayness, transgender-ness, or Queerness is okay? But I listened and sat quietly.

Meanwhile, the lady with the folded arms seemed unconvinced and appeared to be moving in for "the kill." As she continued her line of questioning (in a way that would make any litigator proud), she responded very forcefully:

Well, the Bible says homosexuality is wrong, and you seem to be glossing over it.

Bereft of bible quotes (egads!), my co-panelist stumbled through his response. We had clearly reached a stand-off in the class. Both parties seemed to be dueling, and my Christian co-panelist had gone down pretty quickly in a heap of LGBTQ+ smoke.

Once that tortured exchange was over, the folded-arm lady (who was now leaning forward over the desk) directed the following question at me:

Lady: Mr. Joel...you said that you were raised as a Christian.
            How would you square your lifestyle with the
            teachings in the Bible? I'm really curious...

And that was the moment when I realized that I was *not* supposed to have a response. Like any LGBTQ+ diversity dialogue with religious overtones, that was the precise moment when I was supposed to capitulate and fall victim to... you guessed it... "Biblical Conversation Death." The room fell silent, and all eyes fell on me as the lady laid down her supposed conversational "Ace" card.

But having become trained to recognize BCD, I began my line of questioning:

Me: Thank you for your question. I'm curious: Why are
            you asking me about the Bible?
Lady: Why? Um, well, because the Bible is the word of God.
Me: Well, I respect your faith, but you talking to me about
            the Bible is like going to China and discussing the
            U.S. Constitution.
Lady: Come again? (giggles in the class).
Me: I appreciate that you're a Christian and that your faith
            is important to you. But, it's *your* faith. It is not mine.

We don't live in a theocracy, and I think it's ill-advised
to apply your religious views to everyone or in every
context. That's why I mentioned China... I wouldn't
go to another country and apply our cultural norms
to them. Nor do I feel you should apply your views
to me. Your interpretation of the Bible tells you one
thing. My interpretation, if I were to call myself
Christian, tells me something different. Either way,
I think it's important to recognize that the Bible, at
least in my eyes, is not the final authority, or even a
topic of relevant discussion.

After the meek responses I had gotten earlier, there was suddenly
a flurry of raised hands as more people wanted to talk. It seemed my
statement gave the other students in the classroom license or permission to challenge traditional norms about religion and sexuality. But
although the "temperature" in the class had risen appreciably, our session quickly ran out of time. So, in my final statement, I offered this:

Gayness is not something I need to apologize for. It's just as normal to me as breathing. And although we have different worldviews, what's most important is to continue the dialogue.

As I walked out of the class, the professor said to me discreetly,
"That was the best class we've had all semester!" All I could think
was: "Wow... Thank God I don't have to come back next week.
I might have to wear a bulletproof vest."

As I walked to the parking garage, I heard someone shout: Hey!
As I turned around, I quickly found myself in Round 2 of the conversation I had in the classroom.

Unidentified Person: Hey, Mr. Brown... I want to talk to
                         you! (It was the folded-arm lady, and as

	she approached me, I didn't know if she was going to tackle me or pummel me. I kept thinking, 'I wish the professor was here now.' Nonetheless, the conversation continued).
Lady:	You seem to have some pretty strong views.
Me:	As do you. But at least you expanded your worldview, right?
Lady:	Well… I'm really mad.
Me:	Well… I'm sorry you're mad. But I hope you learned something. I certainly did. Have a good night.
Lady:	Good night to you too.

And with that, I drove home, relieved that folded arm lady didn't become a "fighting fists" lady and happy that the world could create enough space for a "folded arm" lady and a Gay "guest speaker" to co-exist peacefully. It is possible, and can even be easy, to further dialogue or neutralize manipulative rhetoric that is based on rigid religious doctrine. Religiosity in and of itself is not negative or unwelcome, but Queer sensibilities should not be the conversational doormat on which religious people wipe their feet to silence the beliefs of LGBTQ+ people. If we want to educate society about LGBTQ+ leadership competencies, then we have to employ a more deft way of diffusing religious-based rationalizations that argue to the contrary.

BCD has entered conversations I've had with friends, acquaintances, and even strangers on aircraft during transcontinental flights. The quandary that I've had has been: Do I stop talking to these people (which is difficult when they're family or squeezed next to you on a Boeing-737), or do I speak my truth? In the end, I've always chosen to wade into those uncomfortable waters, and more times than not, I feel like I'm a better global citizen for it.

However, dialogue can quickly become a debate when egos are involved. Discussing a polarizing issue can lead to gamesmanship instead of give-and-take. In the LGBTQ+ socio-political context, using the retort, "Well, the Bible says..." is one of the ceaseless ways in which people try to achieve "conversational conquest." And once that happens, the implication is: "Game. Set. Match."

But there's no need for anyone to lose, nor is there any reason for the conversation to end. You, too, can be a conversational stalwart if you recognize when your cross-cultural exchange is derailed by zealotry. Recognizing the warning signs of Biblical Conversation Death will help you acclimate to the conversational dynamic and redirect your energy to fostering a genuine dialogue instead of falling victim to religious sloganeering. The unspoken fallacy of BCD is that within the context of the cultural exchange, religious arguments are presented (and accepted) as though they are infallible and irrefutable when they are just additional points for discussion.

It's always amazing to me that the most intelligent and articulate people can easily become mum when diversity and inclusion topics surface. However, we don't learn from each other when we hide behind fear, recycled rhetoric, or the seemingly impenetrable walls of our calcified positions. Engaging in cross-cultural dialogue doesn't require a Ph.D., just curiosity, courage, and a sense of adventure.

I am deeply spiritual, and my spiritual practices are very important to me. Spirituality is wonderful, but it should appeal to the better angels of our nature and not a primal need to wage war with words. If you're in a conversation and someone starts to wind up with their religious rationale, don't fret. Don't run. Don't retreat. Be undeterred. You owe it to yourself and your God and the Goddesses above to speak your truth and be heard when others speak theirs. In order to see the value of LGBTQ+ people and their leadership pedigree, we need more diversity, difference, and dialogue (a process I coined with a colleague) and less BCD.

LESSONS IN LGBTQ+ LEADERSHIP:
DIVERSITY DIALOGUE

1) **Religiosity should not be feared.** When a person invokes their religious beliefs, the conversation doesn't have to end as though having the dialogue will invite the wrath of God. Instead, use the opportunity to be curious. Ask the person to explain their religious beliefs without condemning their religion. You are modeling inclusivity by showing some intrigue and interest, which will lower defenses and create a pathway for true intercultural dialogue. And to have a true dialogue, both parties have to:

2) **Take the opportunity to share personal experiences.** Someone sharing their religious background shouldn't silence you or give you a bad case of BCD. Rather, it is an invitation for you to share your beliefs and perspective in a non-judgmental way. Without disparaging or ridiculing the other person's views, share your cultural views in a forthright and honest way. Reiterate that:

3) **Spirituality and Queerness are not mutually exclusive.** Sometimes religious opponents of LGBTQ+ rights discuss religion as though all religions condemn LGBTQ+ people or that all people within a particular faith interpret the religious text similarly. We know this to be false. Scholars such as Rev. Peter J. Gomes and Bishop Carlton Pearson (among many others) have long preached the notion that faith-based teachings are LGBTQ+-affirming. Further, there are dozens of LGBTQ+-inclusive spiritual spaces worldwide; in the U.S., more than half of LGBTQ+ adults identify as religious.[253] The notion that LGBTQ+ people are somehow a-spiritual or a-religious is a stereotype that undergirds BCD and must be stripped

---

[253] Conron, Kerith J., Goldberg, Shoshana K., and O'Neill, Kathryn (2020). "Religiosity Among LGBT Adults in the US." UCLA School of Law Williams Institute. https://williamsinstitute.law.ucla.edu/wp-content/uploads/LGBT-Religiosity-Oct-2020.pdf. Accessed March 9, 2022.

away if we want to avoid disingenuous religious rhetoric about LGBTQ+ rights.

4) **Remember the goal.** At all times. The goal of the conversation is not to convince someone of your views but to change the dynamic. If someone has strong convictions, the chances that you are going to change their mind are slim to none. The more important goal is to change the dynamic: to facilitate a conversation and exchange where that person can express their views AND you can express your views graciously but unabashedly. BCD often inhibits mutual dialogue because people fear engaging in conversation with impassioned zealots for fear of offending them or because the conversation has morphed into an academic conversation (as opposed to a diversity conversation) outside their scope of knowledge.

5) **Don't engage in a debate** about a particular religion unless you are really prepared to engage in what could be a hotly-contested and emotionally-charged conversation. Conventional wisdom says that if a person shares their religious beliefs, they are okay with you inspecting and challenging them. However, as with most things, the approach has to be delicate. Instead of making bold pronouncements (e.g., "That's not what the Bible says!"), ask questions. Use statements such as "I feel" or "My understanding is…" An example of this would be:

Person A: I think homosexuality is wrong.

Person B: But *my understanding* is that Jesus said nothing about homosexuality. I *feel* that selective reading of the Bible is dangerous.

Realize that this tact can have diminishing returns, which may lead you to:

6) **Reframe the conversation.** Often, the context for intercultural religious conversations is not exclusively religious. More often

than not, discussions like these take place in a social setting where the context is non-religious, and the accepted norms transcend religious doctrine. Therefore, reframe the conversation, so the focus is turned away from religion and put on the social situation. Let me offer an example:

Years ago, I served as a consultant to an energy company based in the Midwest, where an employee objected to an LGBTQ+ history month celebration because it "conflicted" with her religious beliefs. The employee quizzed management: "Why is this company celebrating an immoral lifestyle?" My response to her was simple:

> I appreciate how you feel, but this isn't a church...this is the workplace. Your employer has made a decision to embrace diversity, including sexual orientation. As an employee here, you're not being asked to support an 'immoral lifestyle.' You're being asked to support an inclusive environment.

In that example, I didn't engage in a conversation with the employee about her religious beliefs because they were not the pre-eminent issue. Instead, I reframed the conversation to focus on employee engagement, workplace diversity, and the organization's values. By doing so, I avoided BCD and a potentially messy conversation that would have drawn the attention away from our agenda. In other words, I caution you to:

7) **Avoid moving the goalposts.** Discussions about LGBTQ+ rights can morph into conversations that focus more on debating the finer points of religious doctrine than discussing the socio-political events at hand, which puts the LGBTQ+ rights supporter on the offensive and becomes a losing rhetorical proposition. The point of the conversation is not to prove your bona fides as a religious scholar but to share different viewpoints and participate in a balanced dialogue. Too many times, participants

in social debates get seduced into debating the finer points of religious texts without any skill, warning, or desire to shift the conversation in that direction. LGBTQ+-related conversations that invoke religion should not become discussions about religion per se, but religiosity, or the way religion is wielded in society, particularly to thwart an appreciation of LGBTQ+ leadership culture. In the midst of any diversity dialogue, you may want to:

8) **Pause and take breaths.** Pausing and taking breaths can help you maintain your equilibrium and reset your center. If you feel upset during a conversation or find yourself falling prey to BCD, take a moment to pause and gather your thoughts. Breathe deeply as you regain your composure. And, where all else fails...

9) **Disengage... disengage... disengage.** If you don't see daylight and the conversation has become a monologue of unbridled piety, or if you find yourself back-peddling, acting tongue-tied, or feeling plagued by conversational paralysis, disengage. When conversations reach an impasse, it is best to withdraw from the exchange and allow for a "cooling off" period before continuing the dialogue at an appropriate time (should that time arise).

CHAPTER 19

ISM: Dismantling the Systemic Oppression of LGBTQ+ People... One Word At a Time

I hope this is not a controversial statement: LGBTQ+ people across the world have faced discrimination, oppression, bias, and recrimination for hundreds of years. For what it's worth, I do not feel this statement is debatable.

However, in trying to highlight the cultural genius™ of the LGBTQ+ community, and in responding to challenges against the latest vestiges of LGBTQ+ hostility, I've noticed public commentators using semantics to downplay the biased actions and statements of others. Let's delve in, shall we?

For anybody who is familiar with American comedy, a flashpoint emerged in 2021 when comedian Dave Chappelle made what many thought were transphobic comments against the Transgender community in his comedy special "The Closer." And while I agree that the tone, tenor, and nature of Mr. Chappelle's comments were indeed insensitive, transphobic, and hurtful towards the transgender community, the purpose of this chapter is not to give voice to one comedian's comments but to highlight the disingenuous ways in which LGBTQ+-hostile behavior has been analyzed.

When disparaging comments are made about LGBTQ+ people, and someone (maybe even an LGBTQ+ person) asserts that those comments are homophobic, biphobic, lesbophobic, or the like, one of the first lines of defense is to argue: "Hey, I'm not homophobic. I'm not *scared* of gay or LGBTQ+ people. I just have different beliefs." And once the underlying idea of *fear* is addressed, it's as if the underlying actions or beliefs that warranted critique have become negligible. In other words, it's as if the biases themselves have been purged of any negativity based on a technicality. So, not surprisingly, at the height of the Chappelle controversy, many comedians, including HBO's Bill Maher, dismissed the notion that Chapelle was transphobic because he didn't technically show fear of transgender people. In an interview on CNN with former CNN commentator Chris Cuomo, Maher explained his reasoning further when discussing criticism levied at Chapelle by LGBTQ+ activists:

Bill Maher: Well, first of all, you say "Going after," and you used terms like "homophobia." I was speaking recently about phobia. That's a word that's traveled quite a bit from its original meaning… A lot of mission creep on that word. Phobia, it's become really just a way people—a word they use to say, "I don't like something."

Cuomo: That's right. It's not a fear.

Maher: Phobia means an irrational fear. Spiders, arachnophobia, you have an irrational fear. Okay, germaphobia. I see all the hand sanitizers here. To me, that would be germaphobia.

Cuomo: But those are only for shaking hands with me.

Maher: I see… Which I never was worried about and still am not (joking). But he's not afraid of homosexuals. Or it's not transphobic. It's that this trans stuff is very new.

I don't think he, or myself, or any other, again, right-thinking person, thinks there aren't such things in the world as people who are trans, who are born in a body that doesn't align with what their brain is telling them. That's okay. But now we're talking about children!

It's interesting. Someone I know, a woman in her 40s, said to me somewhat recently at a dinner party that, when she was a kid, she was what they used to call a "Tomboy."

She said, "I never was interested in wearing a dress. I only wore pants until I was like 14 or 15." She said, "If I was around today, they would have made me into a boy, here in California."

That's what we're talking about. This is new. So, don't put it into this category of "This is settled science." We've been—we—anything that deviates from the one true opinion on this means, you're some horrible bigot and transphobic. That's not what's going on here.

And I don't think Dave Chappelle is transphobic. I mean, a lot of that special is talking about his opening act, who is trans, okay? It's just like… Can we take a breath? Maybe we are going too far with the children part of this. Kids should not be really making decisions about their gender. I mean, Mario Lopez was almost canceled for suggesting that maybe three-year-olds shouldn't decide their gender.

This is not crazy stuff that makes you a bigot.[254]

When convenient, those dismissive of LGBTQ+ culture like to be literal in their counter-arguments to suggest they don't actually "fear" LGBTQ+ people. According to Maher, Chapelle's anti-trans rhetoric was not transphobic because he actually knows and has "befriended" transgender people. The semantics game that Maher employs is maddening to say the least, especially as he confuses gender expression for gender identity and conflates the idea that young people are being forced to "choose" their gender.

If we want to diagnose the issue correctly, then we have to use the right resources, knowledge, and language. I wouldn't expect a doctor to use a video game controller to diagnose someone with the flu. Similarly, we can't expect an imprecise term to properly describe the nature and impact of biased terms and behavior, especially when the person's behavior comes from having privilege.

According to the Merriam-Webster dictionary, homophobia refers to "an irrational fear of, aversion to, or discrimination against homosexuality or homosexuals."[255] Additionally, Merriam-Webster also defines transphobia as "the irrational fear of, aversion to, or discrimination against transgender people."[256] When reading those definitions, people will immediately seize upon the word "fear" and dismiss any notion that their behavior is fear-based.

The reaction is predictable but short-sighted. In the West, LGBTQ+ people have more visibility than they ever have. According to new studies, more people are identifying as LGBTQ+ than ever

---

[254] Hains, Tim. "Bill Maher on Dave Chappelle/Trans Issues: The Word 'Phobia' Has Seen A Lot of Mission Creep." RealClear Politics. November 18, 2021. https://www.realclearpolitics.com/video/2021/11/18/bill_maher_on_dave_chappelle_and_trans_issues_the_word_phobia_has_seen_a_lot_of_mission_creep.html

[255] Merriam-Webster's dictionary of English usage. (2021). Springfield, Mass.: Merriam-Webster, Inc.

[256] Ibid.

before,[257] and gayborhoods such as Hell's Kitchen in New York, Uptown in Oakland, and Zona Rosa in Mexico City appear to be as popular as ever. With the ubiquity of the LGBTQ+ community creating more touchpoints, one could argue that mainstream society is at least more *familiar* with the community and, thus, less concerned about interacting with the community in social and professional situations. If we take the argument one step further, if mainstream society is comfortable interacting with marginalized groups, it's dubious to say that fear or *phobia* of that group exists.

The problem with this rationale is that it flies in the face of our historical record. There are a number of marginalized groups whose presence has been commonplace in the social landscape who have nonetheless engendered hate, bias, discrimination, and violence. For example, Asian and Black people have been in North America for centuries, yet they have faced racial animus consistently for the better part of U.S. and Canadian history. As a matter of fact, according to FBI crime statistics, the hate crimes against each group in the United States rose 70% and 40%, respectively, in 2019 and 2020.[258] These statistics highlight that familiarity with an ethnic group does not necessarily lend itself to holding that ethnic group in high esteem. In America, there is a saying, "Familiarity breeds contempt." If a group is thought to be threatening the existing social order, then groups with privilege may be more apt to showcase biased behavior to thwart the disfavored group's level of influence. Despite the presence of LGBTQ+ culture in popular culture, there are still signs that LGBTQ+ people face imminent danger. Some examples of these dangers include Uganda's anti-homosexuality bills, subversive discourse by Brazil's

---

[257] Schmidt, Samantha. "1 in 6 Gen Z adults are LGBT. And this number could continue to grow." Washington Post. February 24, 2021. https://www.washingtonpost.com/dc-md-va/2021/02/24/gen-z-lgbt/

[258] Mangan, Dan. "Hate crimes against Asian and Black people rise sharply in the U.S., FBI says." CNBC. August 30, 2021.

former president Jair Bolsonaro, or the new wave of religious exemption bills being passed in the U.S. to allow discrimination against LGBTQ+ people.

Increased contact with a marginalized group does not mean that the group will be respected more. Moreover, increased contact does not mean that fear or irrational thought doesn't exist or that the fear is not rooted in a deeper emotion right below the surface. Fear has a symbiotic relationship with anger because both can stem from a loss of control. Anger is produced when we lose control or face circumstances threatening our autonomy. The failure to protect our autonomy can trigger a fight or flight response which shows up as anger. At the root of this response, however, is a fear that absent some intervening force, we may lose further control and risk being victimized. The fear reinforces the anger, and the anger becomes an expression of the fear.

People who engage in homophobia or transphobia may not directly fear the LGBTQ+ person they encounter. In fact, due to stereotypes, a hostile non-LGBTQ+ person may view LGBTQ+ people as weak or docile when they meet them one-on-one. Yet, what they really fear is not the chance encounter, but a society in which LGBTQ+ people wield more socio-political power. They lament a society in which their jokes or aggressive behaviors are no longer tolerated. Those who are hostile feel sad because the world no longer feeds their bias. They feel isolated in a world that sees LGBTQ+ people in their full humanity. Those who are unpleasant to LGBTQ+ people fear a world that requires them to evolve and grow.

From a socio-political standpoint, the fear is based on a specific cosmology that views LGBTQ+ cultural genius™ as an insurgency. If your worldview is based on a zero-sum gain, which says that one group must lose in order for another group to gain, any social indicator that LGBTQ+ people are normal and natural—even something as simple as an LGBTQ+ person drawing breath or minding their own business in an otherwise free society—can be seen as an existential threat to one's well-being. The fear comes not so much from the individual, but the perceived threat of the whole. That is why homophobia and transphobia are such powerful terms; they underscore how anti-LGBTQ+ bias is not just disdain, but a deep-seated hatred against anything that challenges existing religious, patriarchal, and white supremacist norms.

According to the Johns Hopkins manual on mental health disorders, a phobia is an uncontrollable, irrational, and lasting fear of a certain object, situation, or activity.[259] And while bias certainly seems senseless on a personal level, especially to those of us on the receiving end of it, to see it simply as a form of irrational thought or discourse underestimates the nature of the oppression itself. That is why the term phobia, as linked to anti-LGBTQ+ attitudes and behaviors, is applicable but largely insufficient in describing the societal forces that animate so much of the anti-LGBTQ+ (and specifically trans-hostile) rhetoric and policymaking we see today.

Of course, prejudice by any name or semantic configuration is an unreasonable practice. Even if we ignore the sheer brutality of it, prejudice is a waste of individual time, money, and energy. Collectively, it is a waste of human potential, ingenuity, and life. Imagine what our world would look like if we applied the power given to warfare, division, oppression, and internecine conflict to address some of our more pressing problems like climate change, housing, poverty, and education. I remember thinking about this during a trip to Tulsa, Oklahoma, which I visited to commemorate the 100th anniversary of the largest race massacre in U.S. history. In 1921, Tulsa was a booming and prosperous city. As of 2021, it is a city at a crossroads, still trying to reconcile a hopeful future with a tragic past. Even as it brims with new coffee shops and pubs, an

---

[259] John Hopkins Medicine. https://www.hopkinsmedicine.org/health/conditions-and-diseases/phobias

energetic LGBTQ+ artistic center, and glistening new buildings that dot its downtown district, Tulsa lies in the shadow of what it should be: a city that should be on par with major metropolitan areas in the country. As with all U.S. urban centers, it is a city still laboring from the virus known as racism.

Our world suffers in much the same way. If we raised our consciousness and mitigated our prejudices, we would be much more advanced as a species. The world would look dramatically different. Most importantly, our understanding of prejudice and bias would be more nuanced and sophisticated.

Understandably, our concept of the world and the dynamics within it has to start somewhere. The word "homophobia" was first introduced by the late George Weinberg, a New York-based psychotherapist who coined the phrase in 1965 when he was invited to speak before the East Coast Homophile Organization.[260] Weinberg, who ironically identified as heterosexual, was so dismayed at the pushback he received when he wanted to invite a lesbian colleague to a dinner party that he developed a new term to describe the experience. As Weinberg would later recount in an interview with Gregory Herek, a professor of psychology at the University of California at Davis, "It was a fear of homosexuals, which seemed to be associated with a fear of contagion, a fear of reducing the things one fought for—home and family [to something inconsequential]. It was a religious fear...[that] led to great brutality, as fear always does." The term homophobia appeared for the first time in print in 1965 when gay activists who met with Weinberg used the term to reference the fear that straight men have when they believe their associates might be gay.

Similarly, words documenting the hatred and fear of lesbian and bisexual people have a parallel history and construction. Natalie

---

[260] Grimes, William. "George Weinberg Dies at 87; Coined 'Homophobia' After Seeing Fear of Gays." New York Times. March 22, 2017.

Gittleson was the first person to use the term lesbophobia when she described the "pernicious lesbophobia spreading from coast to coast" in the 1970s.[261] Later, author Jane Czyzselska would label lesbophobia as "homophobia with a side-order of sexism."[262] Comparably, although used by bisexual activists for decades, the term biphobia was popularized by researcher Kathleen Bennett in 1992 as the "denigration of bisexuality as a valid life choice."[263]

The genesis of the term transphobia is much less clear. Still, Julia Serano, one of the more influential thought leaders on transgender rights, argues that transphobia is a corollary of sexism and the direct result of people who have insecurities about gender and gender norms.[264] Transphobia started appearing in LGBTQ+ rights discourse in the 1990s, and the terms biphobia, lesbophobia, and transphobia are predicated on the notion that LGBTQ+ prejudice is rooted in fear and expressed as hate. The use of the root word phobia is not meant to exclusively describe a psychological disorder as much as it is meant to describe the unyielding animus towards LGBTQ+ people.

Based on their origins, homophobia and transphobia have understandably been used to discuss the mentality of people who traffic in anti-LGBTQ+ bias. Yet, there needs to be a phrase and lexicon that describes the systematic impact that anti-LGBTQ+ bias has on the community and world at large. Much like the conversations around race that led to a more multi-layered and structural

---

[261] Gittelson, Natalie. *The Erotic Life of the American Wife*, Delacorte Press (1972), pg. 222.

[262] Czyzselska, Jane. "Lesbophobia is homophobia with a side order of sexism." The Guardian. July 9, 2013. https://www.theguardian.com/commentisfree/2013/jul/09/lesbophobia-homophobia-side-order-sexism

[263] Greenesmith, Heron. "We Know Biphoba Is Harmful. But Do We Know What's Behind It?" Rewire News Group. April 25, 2018.

[264] Serano, Julia. *Whipping Girl: A Transsexual Woman on Sexism and the Scapegoating of Femininity*. Seal Press, 2007.

understanding of racism, the analysis of anti-LGBTQ+ bias must also reflect the integrated and deeply-embedded nature of LGBTQ+ bias in the systems that uphold our society.

Fortunately, we have language that honors the experience of LGBTQ+ people and fully contextualizes the animus the LGBTQ+ community receives. More resonant than the phobic language that has dominated the mainstream treatment of LGBTQ+ civil rights struggles, the phrases heterosexism and cisgenderism more accurately describe the system that creates, cradles, and churns the LGBTQ+ animus that is manifest at the interpersonal, institutional, and systemic levels in our society.

In 1971, gay rights activist Craig Rodwell developed the phrase heterosexism, which refers to a caste system of attitudes, policies, norms, and behaviors in favor of people who identify as heterosexual. This system works to the direct detriment, disadvantage, and degradation of those who identify as LGBTQ+, and when not disrupted, it creates psychological, psychosocial, and psychosomatic harm. Psychologically speaking, heterosexism induces what is known as minority stress, or long-term social anxiety, created by a lifetime of harassment, maltreatment, discrimination, and victimization.[265] Psychosocially, heterosexism creates a dynamic whereby social interaction with non-LGBTQ+ people can feel unsafe and dangerous. In a 2017 study by National Public Radio, more than half of LGBTQ+ Americans reported being harassed or subjected to violence based on their sexual orientation or gender identity.[266] Four years later, GLAAD reported that social media sites were essentially unsafe for LGBTQ+ people, with 64% of LGBTQ+ users reporting harassment

---

[265] Dentato, M. P., Ph.D., The minority stress perspective. Psychology and AIDS Exchange Newsletter. American Psychological Association. April 2012.

[266] Neel, J. "Poll: Majority of LGBTQ+ Americans Report Harassment, Violence Based on Identity." National Public Radio. November 21, 2017. https://www.npr.org/2017/11/21/565327959/poll-majority-of-LGBTQ+-americans-report-harassment-violence-based-on-identity

and hate speech, far more than any other identity group online.[267] Psychosomatically, heterosexism helps create health disparities for LGBTQ+ people and foments violence against LGBTQ+ individuals. In a 2021 study by the Williams Institute at UCLA, it was discovered that LGBTQ+ people were four times more likely to be victims of violent crime than non-LGBTQ+ people.[268] Semantically, historically, socially, and philosophically, heterosexism goes far beyond the superficial rationalization of anti-LGBTQ+ bias as people simply disagreeing or having "different beliefs."

In reality, heterosexism is not just an ideology but a constellation of practices that inherently rely on bias and discrimination to maintain order and repress anyone who fails to conform to heterosexual norms related to love, life, and sexuality. In this analysis, heterosexism is not just a fear-based temperament, but a host of actions taken individually *and* collectively in society to scorn LGBTQ+ people in every facet of life. Like racism, heterosexism is self-perpetuating and unrelenting, the vestiges of which will appear as normal to everyday citizens who have become immune or desensitized to LGBTQ+ hostile sentiment, behavior, and speech. For example, when I get asked if I have a girlfriend or hear fresh-faced young people say, "Oh, that's so gay!," those could be deemed low-level examples of heterosexism. Likewise, when we see lesbian couples being denied permission to adopt or bisexual people being told that they are confused about who they are, we are witnessing the harmful elements of a heterosexist system that seeks to perpetuate itself by denying LGB+ people the rights and privileges their heterosexual counterparts enjoy.

---

[267] Diaz, J. "Social Media Hate Speech, Harassment 'Significant Problem' For LGBTQ+ Users: Report." National Public Radio. May 10, 2021. https://www.npr.org/2021/05/10/995328226/social-media-hate-speech-harassment-significant-problem-for-LGBTQ+-users-report

[268] Williams Institute. UCLA School of Law. October 2, 2020. https://williamsinstitute.law.ucla.edu/press/ncvs-lgbt-violence-press-release/

Heterosexism is part of a system, and without any intervening action, systems fail to correct themselves.

Relatedly, cisgenderism has a similar theoretical foundation, except that the beneficiaries of cisgenderism are those whose concepts of gender and gender identity comport with traditional or societal expectations. The term cisgender is believed to have been first adopted by German sexologist Volkmar Sigusch, who wrote the essay "the Neosexual Revolution." Cisgender refers to those whose gender is the same as what was presumed at birth. The prefix "cis" is Latin for "on the same side as" and together with the English word gender, refers to those whose gender conforms to the traditional gender binary belief system. Trans people suffer from cisgenderism when they are misgendered or referred to using the wrong pronouns or when people suggest that being transgender is "not really a thing." When comedians or laypeople make fun of transgender people, it debases their humanity and treats them as caricatures. The ridicule and mockery of trans, non-binary, and non-gender-conforming people creates a climate whereby it becomes easier to harm them. As I've noted elsewhere in this book, violence against transgender people is at an all-time high, with trans women of color bearing the brunt of the violence against the community. Trans people of color also suffer from overkill, or a phenomenon where anti-trans violence is characterized by excessive beating and shooting.[269]

If we use the correct terminology to understand the systemic, institutional, and interpersonal risks that LGBTQ+ individuals face, then we can do more to protect these communities so that the world may benefit from their genius. Using simplistic arguments that over-emphasize "phobia" and "fear" or the lack thereof makes

---

[269] Stotzer, R. L. (September 2017). "*Data Sources Hinder Our Understanding of Transgender Murders*". American Journal of Public Health. **107** (9): 1362–1363. doi:10.2105/AJPH.2017.303973. ISSN 0090-0036. PMC 5551619. PMID 28787204.

it difficult to have a candid and honest conversation about the perils that affect the LGBTQ+ community.

Further, heterosexism and cisgenderism foment internalized bias among LGBTQ+ people that may lead individual members of the community to devalue who they are as well. Internalized bias results in Queer people disavowing their connection to the community, excessively criticizing Queer culture and LGBTQ+ leaders, stereotyping other LGBTQ+ people and Queer culture, showing contempt for perceived LGBTQ+ spaces, or reducing the culture to a single element. It's one thing for mainstream society to negate LGBTQ+ leadership principles; it is something sad and disheartening to hear other Queer people dismissing their own cultural gifts by virtue of their failure to examine their own internal bias against the community. All in all, the effects of heterosexism and cisgenderism affect the Queer community externally and internally such that non-LGBTQ+ people—*and* LGBTQ+ people—may misrepresent or ignore the gifts and talents with which we have been culturally endowed.

When comedians (or laypeople) such as Dave Chapelle ridicule LGBTQ+ people—specifically transgender people—they are indulging in cisgenderism and heterosexism based on the salient notion that their prescribed notion of gender identity, gender presentation, and sexual orientation is superior. No half-baked apology or embellished friendship with a member of the LGBTQ+ community will change that. No social status or marginalized identity—racial or otherwise—excuses one's behavior in a progressive society when your actions amplify historical systems of oppression. Chapelle's satirical nature doesn't give him creative license to traffic in bigotry, especially when he positions himself in his routines as a social commenator and less as an entertainer. And make no mistake about it: cisgenderism is just one side of the same systematic prism that reinforces patriarchy, classism, white supremacy, religious fanaticism, heterosexism, ableism, and nationalism. I have historically been a fan of Chapelle, but Chapelle's Blackness doesn't absolve him of criticism and trans identity doesn't make his comments any less problematic. The discourse just shows the double standard with which we regard harmful rhetoric towards gender non-conforming people. When pundits like Bill Maher make exaggerated arguments that the country has become "too soft" or that they are the victims of "cancel culture," they are creating a false equivalency between social accountability and the very cisgenderism they consciously support. They are further marginalizing the experience of LGBTQ+ people by co-opting language and applying it lazily. If we want to show greater appreciation for LGBTQ+ culture and its transformational leadership capacity, then we also have to show greater humility and care in recognizing the hardships that LGBTQ+ people endure. Our understanding of systemic oppression has to advance. The set of phobias related to society's opinion of LGBTQ+ people highlight the biases that non-LGBTQ+ people suffer from, but it falls short of fully documenting the world that constantly challenges and contests the right of LGBTQ+ people to *be*. Those challenges do not define LGBTQ+ people, but we do not exist apart from those challenges. If we want to learn to more fully appreciate who LGBTQ+ people are, then we cannot dismiss the forces they have had to overcome.

So what do we do when we encounter unapologetic bias of the peculiar kind? We have to understand the arguments against us and retake control of the narrative. Queer people are far more than the one-dimensional caricatures that some would make us to be. Cisgenderist jokes in a just society are just jokes made in bad taste. Transphobic jokes in a cis-heteronormative society are daggers that get trans people murdered. We have a right to be outraged but we also have a history of being strategic, and I would caution anyone who supports trans rights to really examine the social container we are in. Feigning victimhood has become fashionable and trying to silence anyone's art or opinion—as distasteful as it might be—only plays right into their sense of self-righteousness and martyrdom.

The deeper problem is a matter of emphasis: we need to shine more light on the actual lives of members of the Queer community than high-profile figures who will use the spotlight to generate sales and more publicity. I fully support the right of people to critique, protest, or boycott any establishments and/or person who traffics in cisgenderist rhetoric, but we also have to be careful not to amplify their platform. We should be more strategic and find ways to elevate our stories and narratives away from the reactionary bent of the news media, which has never been a reliable friend to our community and whose top priority has always been to sell entertainment at the expense of offering thoughtful and equitable social commentary. To our allies and the reasoned people of the world: I'd like to see more Queer-normative dialogue, more transgender comedians, and more spaces where trans people can share their stories away from the transphobic glare of the comedic stage. Again, we should implore and dictate that society focus more on the gifts that LGBTQ+ people provide and less on the passé tradition of recycling queer jokes when someone needs to score a few cheap points. That behavior is hurtful and dangerous, but not more dangerous than the persistent practice of keeping LGBTQ+ gifts a secret. Let's name heterosexism and cisgenderism when they occur, but let's not forget that our community was born out of beauty: LGBTQ+ wisdom has existed for over a millennia and can be transformational for a lifetime.

LESSONS IN LGBTQ+ LEADERSHIP:
ALLYSHIP AND CULTURAL HUMILITY

1) **Be a detective:** Dedicate an hour every week for the next three months to understand the experiences and perspectives of LGBTQ+ people. Speak to people in your network or circle of influence. What do you notice? Identify common themes.

2) **Study the definition of heterosexism and cisgenderism** and make sure you understand the different levels involved (e.g., individual, interpersonal, institutional, and structural) with each historically-based system of oppression. Identify three examples of both heterosexism and cisgenderism at each level of analysis.

3) **Think about your perceptions related to gender, gender identity, gender expression, and sexual orientation.** Where do they come from? What messages from your family of origin or your place of origin have influenced your understanding of gender, gender identity, gender expression, and sexual orientation? In addition, ask yourself:

   • What makes this self-interrogation process easy for you?
   • What makes it difficult?
   • What are the concepts/ideas that you are struggling to understand?

4) **What will you do to manage your bias?** Identify three strategies that you can take in the next 30 days to de-bias your speech, thoughts, and behavior. Find an accountability buddy to discuss your journey, share your insights, and troubleshoot areas of discomfort. Find time to discuss your beliefs with a trusted colleague/peer/friend in the next 30 days.

CONCLUSION

CHAPTER 20

The Wisdom of Queer Folk: The Dance of the Last Homosexual

As a Black gay child from the Midwest, I was always curious to know what it meant to be me. I suppose every child spends some part of their lifetime asking themself: "Who am I and where do I belong?"

As I got older, the questions persisted. As I performed my research and conceived this book, I spent a lot of time thinking about how this book could be of service to the community. First and foremost, I believed this book could have a human rights purpose: to illuminate the cultural values of the LGBTQ+ community in order to foster greater cultural understanding of LGBTQ+ people and to help insulate Queer people from further incursions against their liberties, rights, and freedoms. I hoped people would see our humanity and also see themselves. I believed the book could be a springboard for helping to reduce the stigmatization that

LGBTQ+ people face by describing LGBTQ+ culture in a more positive, complex, and nuanced way than how the culture is treated in mainstream society. I hoped by virtue of this book that I would be the last "homosexual"—the stereotypical and unsophisticated parody of LGBTQ+ culture—that anyone would ever encounter

Secondly, I hoped the research study could help usher in a new era of LGBTQ+ pride. As I intimated, naming cultural values—especially when one of the identified values is pride or authenticity—could have a liberating and positive effect on the everyday lives of LGBTQ+ people.

Thirdly, I believed that a more explicit and culturally intelligent discussion of LGBTQ+ cultural values might begin to help mainstream society further appreciate the depth and complexity of the Queer experience. If non-gay people are exposed to Queer culture from a values-based perspective and start seeing LGBTQ+ people as members of a multi-faceted community, then there is hope that Queer people will face less discrimination and be revered for the beautiful people we are. In many instances, I believe what people fear in LGBTQ+ people is what they have failed to discover and negotiate within themselves.

Yet, as the book and its accompanying research evolved, I realized my short-sightedness. The task of reframing LGBTQ+ culture not only benefits LGBTQ+ people; it also benefits humanity and a version of humanity that has been bereft of many of the things we stand for. In essence, the LGBTQ+ community has designed a social model, or a way to live, that creates space for more of our humanity. We have created a leadership model for how we, as modern-day professionals, community representatives, business professionals, and organizational executives, can collectively move our world forward. As one of the most persecuted and misunderstood groups on the planet, our cultural milieu has shaped us in ways that have fostered our liberation. It only makes sense to share these liberatory notions, which form the fabric of our culture, with the world in order to facilitate our liberation as a species. Our leadership competencies, our cultural genius™, and our unique way of being are needed by the world in order for our society to become a beloved community.

In my eyes, this is a timely endeavor. As we witness more deprivation, who couldn't benefit from more equity or diversity or inclusion? Who doesn't want to exhibit more pride, freedom, zeal, and creativity? Who doesn't yearn for increased self-realization, agency, nurture, or care? Who would dismiss the value of perceptiveness, resilience, or the power of being authentic? Who doesn't believe the world is hurting because of its lack of a sense of community, its disavowal of the feminine, or its tortured relationship with sexuality? LGBTQ+ people didn't learn these ideas in a book: We've mastered them in the storm of this complicated thing called life. These values have been forged in the fire, and there is no better group to teach and demystify these concepts for existing and emerging leaders than the LGBTQ+ community. That is the heart of LGBTQ+ genius.

In fact, the most powerful leaders have found a way to integrate these ideals and culturally relevant teachings into their leadership toolkit. What we need, however, is not to rely randomly on charismatic and idiosyncratic leaders to pull us forward. Queer poet June Jordan once said: "If humankind is to have not only a future but a destiny, it must consciously and deliberately be designed."

As you move forward in your leadership journey, my invitation to you is to do the following:

1) **Make the commitment to be the best version of yourself.**
    Once you take one step towards your goals, the Universe will take 1,000 steps back towards you. Your reality and perspective will bend to make what seemed unfathomable imaginable.

2) **Visualize the impact you want to create.** Think about the lives you will touch and the ripple effect you will generate beyond your immediate circle. Envision how you will grow and how your transformed leadership practice will benefit your organization, your family, your community, and the world at-large in distinct and tangible ways.

3) **In a moment when you can be discerning, compassionate, and brave, assess the state of your current leadership practice.** Allow yourself time to reflect on areas where you have been effective and areas where you have been ineffective. Notice those occasions where you have been joyous while also acknowledging those areas where you have made yourself "small." Do not settle for the routine or mundane example of the fainthearted. Be a torchbearer who can light the way for others.

4) **Review each of the Queer transformational leadership principles that I have outlined.** Ask yourself: what is my relationship with justice, authenticity, verve, resilience, somatic awareness, perceptiveness, interconnectedness, non-binary thinking, and creativity?

   a) Do you believe in equity and belonging, or are you DEIB resistant?

   b) Do you show up as yourself in your community, or are you borrowing someone else's persona when the pressure becomes too much?

   c) Do you infuse your environment with energy and flair, or do you deflate it with stilted sensibilities?

   d) Does your story inspire people, or does your trauma injure people?

   e) Do you honor the sensory tools provided by your body and mind, or do you rely on hard-edged facts even when they tell only part of the story?

f) Do you know how to read social cues, or do you revel in being oblivious to the realities of others?

g) Do you facilitate a sense of community or do you perpetuate silos, factionalism, and rivalries?

h) Do you applaud binary thinking or are you constrained by outdated rituals, traditions, conventions and lore?

i) Do you stoke or engineer creative pursuits or do you avoid using your talents in an innovative way?

Use the LGBTQ+ cultural values I outlined in this book as a rubric for assessing where you are and how you want to grow.

5) **Choose one area in which you want to grow.** Select one Queer leadership principle that you want to explore and more fully embody. Make the selection based on what feels right for you, but challenge yourself to adopt a thematic area that will stretch you and take you slightly outside of your comfort zone.

6) **Identify one key dimension in your leadership practice that you want to change.** Focus on elevating your skills, behavior, and consciousness in that specific area. Develop metrics for success and a sureproof accountability plan. Perhaps you want to be more creative in your thought process? Maybe you want to rely more on your intuition and innate wisdom in making critical decisions? Or, perhaps you want to bring more of your personal style or flair into your daily interactions? Whatever the Queer leadership principle is, take one concrete action to move you from the place of inaction to a plan of concrete action. The path forward may seem hazy and the results may be inconclusive, but the choices available to you will be much more clear as you allow yourself to be led by a new paradigm.

7) **Finally, as you navigate the world during your evolving leadership journey, stay the course.** Becoming a transformational leader will not require you to abandon who you are.

It will help you to become a higher version of who you've always been. Becoming a transformational leader doesn't mean you have nothing to offer; it means that the most important thing you have to offer is your heart and fervent commitment. The transformational leadership journey will accentuate your existing skills, acumen, and know-how where applicable, and elevate your thoughts and consciousness where necessary. As scary as the transformational journey may seem, just know that it can't be a routine gesture. Entertain the idea that wisdom and growth can also come from joy. Give yourself credit for deciding that you and the world deserve better. Know that the LGBTQ+-informed leadership journey you are on is one that has been supported, nurtured, and crafted by every self-respecting Queer person in the world in search of their higher self. Our humble march towards liberation has set an example for every other person on the planet to seek their own liberation and liberate others in the process. You are not in a unique or solitary space. In fact, you are in good and abiding company.

If we don't resolve right now to learn from the LGBTQ+ community, we will have missed a great opportunity to right the ship and avoid the point of no return. Our society can't wait. Our children can't wait. Future generations can't wait.

As global citizens, we need to be more intentional in building a world that supports our collective aspirations. If everyone can adopt a little LGBTQ+ magic into their personal leadership practice, we can address our global issues more effectively. We can rediscover our collective ability to evolve at a time when it feels like the world is regressing. And in the end, we can finally affirm one truth that some of us already knew: the wisdom of the LGBTQ+ community can be resonant for everyone. If you are someone who is struggling to find your voice, if you're a leader who feels stuck and uninspired, if you're searching for a way to deal with adversity, or if you're a Queer person in any part of the world struggling to see your own light, I'll leave you with the words I wrote to myself as a young leader:

Baby boy

It will be alright
If no one asks you to dance
If no one puts you first in a popularity contest
Mom said it best
When she said don't attest
To anybody's truth but your own

Peculiar boy

If no one stands to walk by your side
Abide
By the singular notion that
Love is raining for your benefit
Don't be counterfeit

Lonely boy

If camaraderie becomes
Politicized
If no one asks you to poeticize
Or join in the pickup games
To drop dimes
Be kind
To yourself
In truth, there is wealth

Beautiful boy

If no one says:
I want to hear your voice
If no one says:
I want to hear your opinion
Dominion
Means dwelling in every atom of yourself
So if people split you
You become seeds
And bleed forever into the soil
The toils
of your life
Will make for great reading
As long as you're not plagiarizing
Sacrificing
yourself to star in somebody else's fiction
Individuality is conviction
When asked what is the toughest brand
Survey says
I am second to none
I have only ridiculously begun
To be...
Me

If a Queer middle-class black boy raised in the inner city in the Upper Midwest—one whose inner world did not always comport with the outer reality, one with a strong Mama whose words carried me throughout the day but whose arms couldn't protect me forever, and one whose unapologetic nature left him outside of homogenous Black and Gay spaces—can transform his leadership style, so can you. If nothing else, transformational leadership frees the individual to know their values, to understand their worth, and to fulfill their purpose. Through its sacrifice and by its example, the LGBTQ+ community has painted a beautiful portrait of transformational leadership. Let us create a grand opportunity in this present moment to use LGBTQ+ wisdom to help the world to be more beautiful, safe, and just. LGBTQ+ wisdom asks us to be more **L**oving, **G**enerative, **B**old, **T**ransformative, and **Q**ueer-minded. But remember: the world will not become beautiful, safe, and evolved on its own; it will only become transformed by leaders who themselves have been re-defined, newly-created, and personally transformed. It is up to each of us to introduce to the world the leadership possibilities that the Queer community has been diligent enough to envision, embody, and manifest for everyone to see.

References

"A Leader's Best Bet: Exercise." Center for Creative Leadership, 2022.

Abadi, M. (2018, March 18). "11 American work habits other countries avoid at all costs." https://www.businessinsider.com/unhealthy-american-work-habits-2017-11

"About Cecilia Chung." http://www.ceciliachung.com/bio Retrieved 2022-08-14.

Abraham, S. (2009). Strategic Essentialism in Nationalist Discourses: Sketching a Feminist Agenda in the Study of Religion. *Journal of Feminist Studies in Religion, 25*(1): 156–161. doi:10.2979/fsr.2009.25.1.156

Abramson, A. (2022, January 1). "Burnout and stress are everywhere." American Psychological Association. https://www.apa.org/monitor/2022/01/special-burnout-stress

Abstinence-only Education Is a Failure. (2017, August 22). Columbia Mailman School of Public Health. https://www.publichealth.columbia.edu/public-health-now/news/abstinence-only-education-failure

Accelerating Acceptance 2021. Gay and Lesbian Alliance Against Defamation. https://www.glaad.org/publications/accelerating-acceptance-2021

Adam, B. D. (1978). *The survival of domination.* New York, NY: Elsevier.

Adeagbo, O. (2016). 'Love beyond colour': the formation of interracial gay men's intimate relationships in post-apartheid South Africa. *National Identities, 18*(3), 241–264. doi:10.1080/14608944.2014.990957

Adkins, Amy. "Only 35% of U.S. Managers Are Engaged in Their Jobs." Gallup. April 2, 2015.

Alimi, Bisi. "If you say being gay is not African, you don't know your history." The Guardian. September 9, 2015. https://www.theguardian.com/commentisfree/2015/sep/09/being-gay-african-history-homosexuality-christianity

Altman, D. (1997). Global gaze/global gays. *GLQ: A Journal of Lesbian and Gay Studies, 3*(4), 417–436. doi:10.1215/10642684-3-4-417

Angelo, P. J. & Bocci, D. (2021, January 29). The Changing Landscape of Global LGBTQ+ Rights. *The Council on Foreign Relations.* https://www.cfr.org/article/changing-landscape-global-lgbtq-rights

Anonymous. (n.d.) The Loneliness Epidemic Is So Bad World Leaders Have Been Forced to Intervene. https://melmagazine.com/en-us/story/the-loneliness-epidemic-is-so-bad-world-leaders-have-been-forced-to-intervene

Anonymous. (n.d.) Phobias. John Hopkins Medicine. https://www.hopkinsmedicine.org/health/conditions-and-diseases/phobias

Ansolabehere, S., Schaffner, B. F. (2017). "CCES Common Content, 2016." [Data set]. Cooperative Congressional Election Survey. https://doi.org/10.7910/DVN/GDF6Z0

Appleby, G. A. (2001). Ethnographic study of Gay and Bisexual working-class men in the United States. *Journal of Gay and Lesbian Social Services, 12*(3–4), 51–62. doi:10.1300/J041v12n03_04

Arekapudi, Nisha & Recavarren, Isabel Santagostino. (2020). "Sexual harassment is serious business." World Bank Blogs. https://blogs.worldbank.org/developmenttalk/sexual-harassment-serious-business

Aristotle. (1994). *Aristotle's "De Anima."* Leiden; New York: E.J. Brill.

Ashkanasy, N. M., Wilderom, C. P. W., & Peterson, M. F. (2000). *Handbook of Organizational Culture & Climate.* Thousand Oaks, CA: Sage Publications, Inc.

Aspan, M. (2020, June 16). Fortune 500 CEOs praise landmark LGBTQ+ antidiscrimination ruling.

Atkinson, B. (Ed.) (2000). *The Essential Writings of Ralph Waldo Emerson.* New York, NY: The Modern Library.

Balch, O. (2016, Feb. 10). Does a pretty office make a productive workspace? The Guardian. https://www. theguardian.com/sustainable-business/2016/feb/10/ office-beautiful-pretty-views-employees-productive

Baldwin, J. and Troupe, Q. (2014). James Baldwin: The Last Interview and Other Conversations. Brooklyn, New York: Melville House Publishing, pp. 62–63.

Baker, P. (2002). *Fantabulosa*: *A Dictionary of Polari and Gay Slang.* London, England: Continuum.

Banks, J., & McGee-Banks, C. (1989). *Multicultural Education: Issues and Perspectives* (8th ed.). London, England: Wiley.

"Barbara Jordan Chairline" *History, Art & Archies of the United State House of Representatives.* https://history.house.gov/People/ Detail/16031

"Barbara Jordan's Ideals," 19 January 1996, New York Times, A28.

Bawer, B. (2013, March). "Just What is Gay Culture in 2013?" *Forbes.* Retrieved from http://www.forbes.com/sites/ realspin/2013/03/19/what-exactly-is-gay-culture-in-2013/#6c2ee1d653ce

Bearak, M. & Cameron, D. (2016). Here are the 10 countries where homosexuality may be punished by death. *Washington Post.* Retrieved from https://www.washingtonpost.com/news/ worldviews/wp/2016/06/13/here-are-the-10-countries-where-homosexuality-may-be-punished-by-death-2/?utm_term=. d563b5acc7e8

Beard, K., Eames, C. & Withers P. (2017). The role of self-compassion in the well-being of self-identifying gay men. *Journal of Gay & Lesbian Mental Health, 21*(1), 77–96. doi:10.1080/19359705.2016.1233163

Belk, R. W. (1984). Cultural and historical differences in concepts of self and their effects on attitudes toward having and giving. In T. C. Kinner (Ed.), *Advances in Consumer Research Volume 11,* Provo, UT: Association for Consumer Research.

Bellamy-Walker, T. (2022). *Russian court dissolves country's main LGBTQ rights organization.* Retrieved from NBC News website: https://www.nbcnews.com/nbc-out/out-news/russian-court-dissolves-countrys-main-lgbtq-rights-organization-rcna25874

Bergland, Christopher. "How do neuroplasticity and neurogenesis rewire your brain?" Psychology Today. (2017).

Bernstein, R. (2017, March 28). 7 Cultural Differences in Nonverbal Communication. Retrieved from https://online.pointpark.edu/business/cultural-differences-in-nonverbal-communication/

Blashill, A. J., & Powlishta, K. K. (2009). Gay stereotypes: The use of sexual orientation as a cue for gender-related attributes. *Sex Roles, 61,* 783–793. doi:10.1007/s11199-009-9684-7

Bordieu, P. (1972). *Outline of a theory of practice.* Cambridge, UK: Cambridge University Press.

Bouranova, Alene (2022). Explaining the latest Texas Anti-Transgender Directive. BU Today. https://www.bu.edu/articles/2022/latest-texas-anti-transgender-directive-explained/

Boyatzis, R. E. (1998). *Transforming qualitative information: Thematic analysis and code development.* Thousand Oaks, CA: Sage Publications.

Brammer, John P. "Three decades later, men who survived the 'gay plague' speak out." NBC News. December 1, 2017.

"Brands should take a stand on a social issue that is important to their customers." (2020, August 17). YouGov. https://yougov.co.uk/topics/resources/articles-reports/2020/08/17/brands-should-take-stand-social-issue-important-th

Branigin, A., & Kirkpatrick, N. (2022, October 14). Anti-trans laws are on the rise. Here's a look at where—and what kind. The Washington Post. https://www.washingtonpost.com/lifestyle/2022/10/14/anti-trans-bills/

Bravata, D. M. et al (2020), "Prevalence, Predictors and Treatment of Imposter Syndrome: A Systematic Review." J. Gen Intern Med.

Brennan, D. J., Ross, L. E., Dobinson, C., Veldhuizen, S., & Steele, L. S. (2010). Men's sexual orientation and health in Canada. *Canadian Journal of Public Health.*, *101*(3), 255–258.

Bresiger, G. (2014, February 2). "Millions of Americans skipping lunch to work: study." https://nypost.com/2014/02/02/millions-of-americans-skipping-lunch-to-work-study/

Brown, J. (2016). *Inclusion: Diversity, the new workplace, and the will to change.* Charleston, SC: Advantage Media Group.

Bruni, F. (2018, April 28). The extinction of gay Identity. *The New York Times.* Retrieved from https://www.nytimes.com/2018/04/28/opinion/the-extinction-of-gay-identity.html

Bullock, Andrew. (2022, June 20). "Pride and Prejudice: Indian royal Manvendra Singh Gohil on being the world's first openly gay prince." *Tattler.* https://www.tatler.com/article/prince-manvendra-singh-gohil-gay-indian-royal-interview

Burford, Joshua. Interview with WFAE on January 8, 2018. SouthBound Preview: Historian Joshua Burford Recalls Trans Woman's Courage In 1960s Charlotte. https://www.wfae.org/tags/maxine-perkins

Burton, Neal. "Gender Variation and Same Sex Relations in Precolonial Times." Psychology Today. April 25, 2020. https://www.psychologytoday.com/us/blog/hide-and-seek/201707/gender-variation-and-same-sex-relations-in-precolonial-times

Busch, Wolfgang. How Do I Look (2006) (film). Wolfgang Busch.

Butler, J. (1990). *Gender trouble: Feminism and the subversion of identity*. New York, NY: Routledge.

Cain, A. (2017, July). "The Trump Administration declared that a landmark federal law doesn't protect LGBT employees from workplace discrimination." *Business Insider*. Retrieved from http://www.businessinsider.com/trump-doj-lgbt-employment-discrimination-civil-rights-act-2017-7

California Secretary of State (2017). *Report of Registration*. Retrieved from http://elections.cdn.sos.ca.gov/ror/ror-pages/ror-odd-year-2017/county.pdf

Cass, V. (1984). Homosexual identity formation: A concept in need of definition. *Journal of Homosexuality, 20*(2–3), 105–126. doi:10.1300/J082v09n02_07

Catalyst. (2017, May 30). Lesbian, Gay, Bisexual and Transgender workplace issues. Retrieved from http://www.catalyst.org/knowledge/lesbian-gay-bisexual-transgender-workplace-issues.

Catechism of the Catholic Church (2nd ed.). Libreria Editrice Vaticana. 2019. Paragraph 2351.

CBC News. August 16, 2017. https://www.cbc.ca/news/health/loneliness-public-health-psychologist-1.4249637

Centers for Disease Control and Prevention. (2011). *Sexual Identity, Sex of Sexual Contacts, and Health Risk Behaviors Among Students in Grades 9–12 in Selected Cities—Youth Risk Behavior Surveillance, United States, 2001–2009*. (Report No. 60(SS07)). Retrieved from http://www.cdc.gov/mmwr/preview/mmwrhtml/ss6007a1.htm

Chard, A. N., Finneran, C., Sullivan, P. S., and Stephenson, R. (2015). Experiences of homophobia among gay and bisexual men: results from a cross-sectional study in seven countries. *Culture, Health, and Sexuality, 17*(10), 1174–1189. doi:10.1080/13691058.2015.1042917

Chatterjee, Rhitu. (2018). "A new survey finds 81 percent of women have experienced sexual harassment." NPR. https://www.npr.org/sections/thetwo-way/2018/02/21/587671849/a-new-survey-finds-eighty-percent-of-women-have-experienced-sexual-harassment

Chatzipapatheodoridis, C. (2014). "The politics of a global Gay identity: Towards a universal history." *Rupkatha Journal of Interdisciplinary Studies in Humanities, 6*(1), 39–48.

Chauncey, G. (1994). *Gay New York: Gender, urban culture, and the making of the Gay male world, 1890–1940*. New York, NY: Basic Books.

Chee, A. (2015, June). What will gay culture look like in 2035? *New Republic*. Retrieved from https://newrepublic.com/article/122120/what-will-gay-culture-look-2035

Cherry, Kendra. (2021, August 6). "The Dunning-Kruger Effect." VeryWellMind. https://www.verywellmind.com/an-overview-of-the-dunning-kruger-effect-4160740

Chiam, Z., Duffy, S., González Gil, M., Goodwin, L., Mpemba Patel, N. T. (2019). Trans Legal Mapping Report: Recognition before the law (3rd ed.). *International Lesbian & Gay Association*. https://ilga.org/downloads/ILGA_World_Trans_Legal_Mapping_Report_2019_EN.pdf

Chirkov, V. I., Ryan, R. M., Kim, Y., & Kaplan, U. (2003). Differentiating autonomy from individualism and independence: A self-determination theory perspective on internalization of cultural orientations and well-being. *Journal of Personality and Social Psychology, 84*, 97–110. doi:10.1037/0022-3514.84.1.97

Chodorow, N. (1978). *The Reproduction of Mothering: Psychoanalysis and the Sociology of Gender*. Berkeley, CA: University of California Press.

Chopra, D., & Tanzi, R. E. (2018). *The healing self: A revolutionary new plan to supercharge your immunity and stay well for life*. New York, NY: Random Books.

Clark, Maria. (2021). "70+ Sexual Harassment in the Workplace Statistics." https://etactics.com/blog/sexual-harassment-in-the-workplace-statistics

Claudia López: Colombia's capital elects gay woman as mayor. (2019, October 28). BBC News. https://www.bbc.com/news/world-latin-america-50205591

"Code-Switching By Gender." Gender From the Trenches. https://medium.com/gender-from-the-trenches/code-switching-by-gender-a611ee212fd9

Coehlo, L. A. L. (2002). Tal objeto tal dono. In L. P. M. Lopes & L. C. Bastros (Orgs.) *Identidades: recortes multi interdisciplinares.* Campinas, BR: Mercado das Letras.

Conron, Kerith J., Goldberg, Shoshana K., and O'Neill, Kathryn (2020). "Religiosity Among LGBT Adults in the US." UCLA School of Law Williams Institute. https://williamsinstitute.law.ucla.edu/wp-content/uploads/LGBT-Religiosity-Oct-2020.pdf. Accessed March 9, 2022.

Coon, H., & Kemmelmeier, M. (2001). Cultural Orientations in the United States: Re-examining differences among ethnic groups. *Journal of Cross-Cultural Psychology, 32*(3), 348–364. doi:10.1177/0022022101032003006

Creswell, J. W. (2013). *Qualitative inquiry & research design: Choosing among five approaches.* London, England: Sage Publications.

Cronbach, L. (1975). Beyond the two disciplines of scientific psychology. *American Psychologist, 30*(11), 116–127. doi:10.1037/h0076829

Cross, M., & Epting, F. (2005). Self-obliteration, self-definition, self-integration: Claiming a Homosexual identity. *Journal of Constructivist Psychology, 18*(1), 53–63. doi.10.1080/10720530590523071

Crossland. (2018, Nov. 18). "Transphobia rife among UK employers as 1 in 3 won't hire a transgender person." Retrieved

from https://www.crosslandsolicitors.com/site/hr-hub/
transgender-discrimination-in-UK-workplaces

Cullen, C. (2021). *Color*. Berkeley, CA: West Margin Press.

Czyzselska, Jane. "Lesbophobia is homophobia with a side
order of sexism." The Guardian. July 9, 2013. https://
www.theguardian.com/commentisfree/2013/jul/09/
lesbophobia-homophobia-side-order-sexism

D'Andrade, Roy G. (1992). Schemas and motivation. In R. G.
D'Andrade & C. Strauss (Eds.), *Human motives and cultural
models*. Cambridge, England: Cambridge University Press.

Damen, Louise. (1987). *Culture learning: The fifth dimension in the
language classroom*. Reading, MA: Addison-Wiley.

Datz, T. (2015, Oct. 26). Green office environments linked with
higher cognitive function scores. Harvard T. H. Chan School
of Public Health. https://www.hsph.harvard.edu/news/
press-releases/green-office-environments-linked-with-higher-
cognitive-function-scores/

Dave Leip's Atlas of U.S. Presidential Elections. (n.d.) Retrieved
from https://uselectionatlas.org/RESULTS/

Davies, D., & Neal, C. (1996). An historical overview of
homosexuality and therapy. In D. Davies & C. Neal (Eds.),
*Pink therapy: A guide for counsellors and therapists working with
lesbians, gay, and bisexual clients* (pp. 66–85). Buckingham,
England: Open University Press.

Deen, Brian. "Social Network Usage & Growth: How
Many People Use Social Media in 2022?" Backlinko.
October 10, 2021.

D'Emilio, J. (1983). *Sexual politics, sexual communities: The making
of a homosexual minority in the United States, 1940–1970*.
Chicago, IL: University of Chicago Press.

Dentato, Michael P., Ph.D., The minority stress perspective.
Psychology and AIDS Exchange Newsletter. American
Psychological Association. April 2012.

Derksen, S. (2022, March 1). "Being and Doing: Integrating Masculine and Feminine Energies." Living Well Counseling Services. https://livingwellcounselling.ca/integrating-masculine-feminine-energies/

DeSantis, L., & Ugarriza, D. N. (2000). The concept of theme as used in qualitative nursing research. *Western Journal of Nursing Research, 22*(3), 351–372.

Deutsch, James. "Are You a Friend of Dorothy? Folk Speech of the LGBT Community." Folklife Magazine. Smithsonian Center for Folklife & Cultural Heritage. October 25, 2016. https://folklife.si.edu/talkstory/2016/are-you-a-friend-of-dorothy-folk-speech-of-the-lgbt-community

Diaz, Jaclyn. "Social Media Hate Speech, Harassment 'Significant Problem' For LGBTQ+ Users: Report." National Public Radio. May 10, 2021. https://www.npr.org/2021/05/10/995328226/social-media-hate-speech-harassment-significant-problem-for-LGBTQ+-users-report

Dilworth-Anderson, P., & Gibson, B. E. (1999). Ethnic minority perspectives on dementia, family caregiving, and interventions. *Generations, 23*(3), 40–45.

DiPlacido, J. (1998). Minority stress among lesbians, gay men, and bisexuals: A consequence of heterosexism, homophobia, and stigmatization. In G. M. Herek (Ed.), *Psychological perspectives on lesbian and gay issues, Vol. 4. Stigma and sexual orientation: Understanding prejudice against lesbians, gay men, and bisexuals.* Thousand Oaks, CA: Sage Publications Inc. doi:10.4135/9781452243818.n7

Discrimination in America: Experiences and views of LGBTQ+ Americans. (2017). National Public Radio, the Robert Wood Johnson Foundation, and the Harvard T. H. Chan School of Public Health

Djudji, D. (2021, August 26). "The Story of Polaroid: From Empire to Bankruptcy and Back Again." Photography. https://www.

diyphotography.net/the-story-of-polaroid-from-empire-to-bankruptcy-and-back-again/

Dockray, Heather. "Gayborhoods aren't dead. In fact, there are more of them than you think." Mashable. March 12, 2019. https://mashable.com/article/gayborhoods-changing-amin-ghaziani

Doherty, E. (2022). *The number of LGBTQ-identifying adults is soaring.* Retrieved from Axios: https://www.axios.com/2022/02/17/lgbtq-generation-z-gallup

Doonan, S. (2012). *Gay men don't get fat.* New York, NY: Blue Rider Press.

Douglas, C., & Turner, E. (2017, April 20). How Black boys turn blue: The effects of masculine ideology on same-gender loving men. *Psychology Benefits Society.* Retrieved from https://psychologybenefits.org/2017/04/20/the-effects-of-masculine-ideology-on-same-gender-loving-black-men/

Dowsett, G. (1996). *Practicing desire.* Stanford, California: Stanford University Press.

Duncan, P. (2017, July 27). Gay relationships are still criminalized in 72 countries, report finds. *The Guardian.* Retrieved from https://www.theguardian.com/world/2017/jul/27/gay-relationships-still-criminalised-countries-report

Durbin, D. J. (2010). Using multi-voiced poetry for analysis and expression of literary transaction. Paper presented at the American Educational Research Association Annual Conference, Denver, CO.

Edelstein, M. (2022, Jan. 10). "LGBTQ+ People Experience Higher Unemployment as a Result of COVID-19, Impacting Health." Rutgers University. https://www.rutgers.edu/news/lgbtq-people-experience-higher-unemployment-result-covid-19-impacting-health

Epstein, Rob. "What Harvey Milk Tells Us About Proposition 8." HuffPost. December 22, 2008.

Erasure of Bisexuality. GLAAD. https://www.glaad.org/bisexual/bierasure

Erickson, F. (1986). Qualitative methods in research on teaching. In C. M. Wittrock, *Handbook on research on teaching* (3rd ed.). New York, NY: Macmillan Publishing.

Factbox: Stateless groups around the world. (2011, August 23), *Reuters*. Retrieved from https://www.reuters.com/article/us-stateless-groups/factbox-stateless-groups-around-the-world-idUSTRE77M2AS20110823

Facts about Suicide. (2016). Retrieved from Trevor Project Website: http://www.thetrevorproject.org/pages/facts-about-suicide

Faderman, L. (1985). The "new Gay" Lesbians. *Journal of Homosexuality, 10*(3–4), 85–96. doi:10.1300/J082v10n03_12

Fair representation might lead to better outcomes in times of crisis. (2020, April 7). Out Leadership

Fang, Tony. "Yin Yang: A New Perspective on Culture." Management and Organization Review. 8.1 (2015): 25–50.

Fein, S. B. & Neuhring, E. M. Intrapsychic effects of stigma: A process of breakdown and reconstruction of social reality. *Journal of Homosexuality,* 1981, *7*, 3–13. doi:10.1300/J082v07n01_02

Felix, M. S. (2014). Stigma as part of identity development of Gay men in Penang: A qualitative study. *Pertanika Journal of Social Sciences & Humanities, 22*(1), 365–377.

Felix, M. S. (2016). Nature of nurture: A qualitative study of the source of Homosexuality. *Pertanika Journal of Social Sciences & Humanities, 24*(4), 1445–1463.

Fenton, S. (2017, December 6). The 74 countries where it's illegal to be gay. *The Independent.* Retrieved from http://www.independent.co.uk/news/world/gay-lesbian-bisexual-relationships-illegal-in-74-countries-a7033666.html

Ferdman, B. M. & Gallegos, P. I. (2001). Racial identity development and Latinos in the United States. In C. L. Wijeyesinghe, B. W. Jackson, III (Eds.), *New perspectives on racial identity development: A theoretical and practical anthology.* New York, NY: New York University Press.

Ferguson, A. (1990). Is there a Lesbian culture? In J. Allen (Ed.), *Lesbian Philosophies and Cultures: Issues in philosophical historiography.* Albany, NY: State University of New York Press.

Fidas, D., Cooper, L. (2019). A workplace divided: Understanding the climate for LGBTQ+ workers nationwide. Human Rights Campaign Foundation.

Fiske, S. T. (2002). What we know about bias and intergroup conflict, the problem of the century. *Current Directions in Psychological Science, 11*(4), 123–128. doi:10.1111/1467-8721.00183

Flood, Allison. (2019, May 19). "Binyavanga Wainaina, Kenyan author and gay rights activist, dies aged 48." The Guardian. https://www.theguardian.com/books/2019/may/22/binyavanga-wainaina-kenyan-author-and-gay-rights-activist-dies-aged-48

Florida, R. (2016, May 25). San Francisco's increasing dominance over U.S. innovation. *Citylab.* Retrieved from https://www.citylab.com/life/2016/05/san-franciscos-increasing-dominance-over-us-innovation/484199/

Fone, B. (2000). *Homophobia: A history.* New York, NY: St. Martin's Press.

Foucault, M. (1978). *The history of sexuality (Vol. 1).* New York: Pantheon Books.

Foucault, M. (1980). *The history of sexuality, Vol 1.: An introduction.* New York, NY: Vintage Books.

Foucault, M. (1988). *Polemics, Politics and Problematizations.* In P. Rainbow (Ed.), *Essential Works of Foucault, Vol. 1,* New York, NY: The New Press.

Fowler, J. H., & Christakis N. A. Dynamic spread of happiness in a large social network: longitudinal analysis over 20 years in the Framingham Heart Study. BMJ. 2008 Dec 4; 337:a2338. doi:10.1136/bmj.a2338. PMID: 19056788; PMCID: PMC2600606.

France, D. (2020, Ap. 13). "The Activists: How ACT UP—the coalition that fought against AIDS stigma and won medications that slowed the plague—forever changed patients' rights, protests, and American political organizing as it's practiced today." The New York Times. https://www.nytimes.com/interactive/2020/04/13/t-magazine/act-up-aids.html

Frayser, S. (1985). *Varieties of sexual experience: An anthropological perspective on human sexuality.* Santa Barbara, CA: Human Relations Area Files.

Gagnon, J. & Simon, W. (1973). *Sexual Conduct: The Social Sources of Human Sexuality.* Chicago, IL: Aldine.

Gates, G. J. (2015). Marriage and family: LGBT Individuals and same-sex couples. *The Future of Children. 25*(2), 67–87. doi:10.1353/foc.2015.0013

Gay and Lesbian Alliance Against Defamation (2018). Accelerating Acceptance Executive Summary: A survey of American acceptance and attitudes towards LGBTQ Americans. Retrieved from https://www.glaad.org/files/aa/Accelerating%20Acceptance%202018.pdf

Geertz, C. (2017). *The Interpretation of cultures.* New York, NY: Basic Books, Inc.

Gemini, R. (2016, July 29). "Why Are Queer People Creative?" https://www.rigelgemini.com/home/2016/7/29/why-are-queer-people-creative

Ghosal, N. (2016, February 20). *Lesbian, Bisexual and Queer Women in Kenya.* Retrieved from: https://www.hrw.org/news/2016/02/20/lesbian-bisexual-and-queer-women-speak-out-kenya

Giddens, A. (2002). *Runaway world: How globalization is reshaping our lives.* New York, NY: Routledge.

Gittelson, Natalie. The Erotic Life of the American Wife, Delacorte Press (1972), pg. 222.

Giroux H. (1983). *Theory and resistance in education.* South Hadley MA: Bergin and Garvey.

Goffman, Erving. (1963). *Stigma: notes on the management of spoiled identity.* Englewood Cliff, N.J.: Prentice-Hall.

Goodenough, W. H. (1957). Cultural Anthropology and Linguistics. *In* P. L. Garvin, ed., Report of the Seventh Annual Round Table Meeting on Linguistics and Language Study. Washington, Georgetown University Monograph Series on Languages and Linguistics No. 9.

Goodenough, W. H. (1981). Culture, language, and society, 2nd Ed. Menlo Park, CA: Benjamin/Cummings Pub. Co.

Gray, M. (2015, February 5). The World's Largest Stateless Nation? *Inside Story.* Retrieved from http://insidestory.org.au/the-worlds-largest-stateless-nation/

Green, Emma. "America Moved On From Its Gay-Rights Movement—And Left a Legal Mess Behind." The Atlantic. August 17, 2019.

Greenesmith, Heron. "We Know Biphoba Is Harmful. But Do We Know What's Behind It?" Rewire News Group. April 25, 2018.

Grimes, William. "George Weinberg Dies at 87; Coined 'Homophobia' After Seeing Fear of Gays." New York Times. March 22, 2017.

Gryboski, Michael. "Religious Exemption in Employment Non-Discrimination Act 'Terribly Broad,' Denounced NYT Editorial." Christian Post. November 6, 2013.

Guba, E. G., & Lincoln, Y. S. (1994). Competing paradigms in qualitative research. In N. K. Denzin & Y. S. Lincoln (Eds.), *Handbook of qualitative research.* Thousand Oaks, CA: Sage Publications.

Haas, A. P., Eliason, M., Mays, V. M., Mathy, R. M., Cochran, S. D., D'Augelli, A. R., Silverman, M. M., Fisher, P. W., Hughes, T., Rosario, M., Russell, S. T., Malley, E., Reed, J., Litts, D. A., Haller, E., Sell, R. L., Remafedi, G., Bradford, J., Beautrais, A. L., Brown, G. K.,

Diamond, G. M., Friedman, M. S., Garofalo, R., Turner, M. S., Hollibaugh, A., Clayton, P. J. (2011). Suicide and suicide risk in lesbian, gay, bisexual, and transgender populations: Review and recommendations. *Journal of Homosexuality, 58*(1), 10–51. doi:1090/00918369.2011.534038.

Hains, Tim. "Bill Maher on Dave Chappelle/Trans Issues: The Word 'Phobia' Has Seen A Lot of Mission Creep." RealClear Politics. November 18, 2021. https://www.realclearpolitics. com/video/2021/11/18/bill_maher_on_dave_chappelle_and_ trans_issues_the_word_phobia_has_seen_a_lot_of_mission_ creep.html

Hall, S. & du Gay, P. (2011). *Questions of cultural identity*. London, England: Sage Publications.

Halperin, D. (2002). *How to do the history of homosexuality*. Chicago: University of Chicago. Press.

Halperin, D. (2012, June). Normal as Folk. *New York Times*. Retrieved from http://www.nytimes.com/2012/06/22/opinion/ style-and-the-meaning-of-gay-culture.html?mcubz=3

Halperin, D. (2014). *How to be Gay*. Boston, MA: Belknap Press.

Hamer, J. S. (2003). Coming-out: gay male's information seeking. *School Libraries Worldwide, 9*(2), 73–89.

Han, Enze & Joseph O'Mahoney. *British Colonialism and the decriminalization of homosexuality: Queens, crime and empire*. Routledge (May 2018).

Hart, J., & Richardson, D. (1981). *Theory and practice of homosexuality*. Sydney, AU: Law Book Co. of Australasia.

Harter, J. (2021, November 18). Manager Burnout Is Only Getting Worse. Gallup. https://www.gallup.com/workplace/357404/ manager-burnout-getting-worse.aspx

Hauwa, A. (2021, March 16). "How the Biden Administration Can Tackle America's Turnout Problem." Center for American Progress. Retrieved from https://www.americanprogress. org/article/biden-administration-can-tackle-americas-voter- turnout-problem/

Headland, T. N., Pike, K. L., and Harris, M. (Eds.). (1990). *Emics and etics: The insider/outsider debate.* Newbury Park, CA: Sage Publications.

HeartMath Institute. https://www.heartmath.org/articles-of-the-heart/science-of-the-heart/the-energetic-heart-is-unfolding/

Heifetz, R. A., Linksy, M., & Grashow, A. (2009). *The practice of adaptive leadership.* Cambridge, MA: Harvard Business Review Press.

Hentze, Iris, and Tyus, Rebecca. (2021). "Sexual harassment in the Workplace." National Conference of State Legislatures. https://www.ncsl.org/research/labor-and-employment/sexual-harassment-in-the-workplace.aspxHerdt, G., & Lindenbaum, S. (Eds.). (1992). *The time of AIDS: Social analysis, theory and method.* Newbury Park, CA: Sage Publications.

Herek, G. M. (1984). Beyond "Homophobia": A social psychological perspective on attitudes towards Lesbians and Gay men. *Journal of Homosexuality, 10*(10), 1–21. doi:10.1300/J082v10n01_01

Herek, G. M. (2004). Beyond "Homophobia": Thinking about sexual prejudice and stigma in the twenty-first century. *Sexuality Research & Public Policy, 1*(2), 6–24.

Herek, G. M., & Garnets, L. D. (2007). Sexual orientation and mental health. *The Annual Review of Clinical Psychology, 3*(3): 53–75. doi:10.1146/annurev.clinpsy.3.022806.091510

Herek, G. M., & McLemore, K. A. (2013). Sexual prejudice. *Annual Review of Psychology, 64*, 309–333. https://doi.org/10.1146/annurev-pscyh-113011-143826

Heron, J. (1986). *Co-operative inquiry: Research into the human condition.* London, England: Sage Publications, Inc.

Herr, K., & Anderson G. (2015). *The action research dissertation: A guide for students and faculty.* London, UK: Sage Publications.

Herrick, A. L., Lim, S. H., Wei, C., Smith, H., Guadamuz, T., Friedman, M. S., & Stall, R. (2011). Resilience as an untapped resource in behavioral intervention design for gay men. *AIDS and Behavior, 15,* 25–29.

Hewlett, S. A., Marshall, M., & Sherbin, L. (2013, December). How diversity can drive innovation. *Harvard Business Review.* Retrieved from https://hbr.org/2013/12/how-diversity-can-drive-innovation

Hinzmann, D. (2017, July). "Chechen President Denies the Existence of Gay Men Again, Calls Them Devils." *Out Magazine.* Retrieved from https://www.out.com/news-opinion/2017/7/14/chechen-president-denies-existence-gay-men-again-calls-them-devils

Hitlin, S., & Piliavin, J. (2004). Values: Reviving a dormant concept. *Annual Review of Sociology, 30*(1), 359–393. doi:10.1146/annurev.soc.30.012703.110640

Holmes, E. (2004). *This thing called you.* New York, NY: Penguin Books.

Holt-Lunstad J, Smith TB, Baker M, Harris T, Stephenson D. Loneliness and social isolation as risk factors for mortality: a meta-analytic review. Perspect Psychol Sci. 2015 Mar;10(2):227–37. doi:10.1177/1745691614568352. PMID: 25910392.

Honan, Edith & Mason, J. "Obama in Kenya says gays need equality, draws African criticism." Reuters. July 25, 2015. https://www.reuters.com/article/us-obama-africa-gay/obama-in-kenya-says-gays-need-equality-draws-african-criticism-idUSKCN0PZ0MZ20150725

Horowitz, J. L., & Newcomb, M. D. (2001). A multidimensional approach to homosexual identity. *Journal of Homosexuality, 42*(2), 1–19. doi:10.1300/J082v42n02_01

Hottes, T. S, Bogaert, L., Rhodes, A. E., Brennan, D. J., & Gesink, D. (2016). Lifetime prevalence of suicide attempts among sexual minority adults by study sampling strategies: Systematic review and meta-analysis. *American Journal of Public Health, 106*(5), e1–12. doi:10.2105/AJPH.2016.303088

Hughes, L. (1994). *I, Too, Am America. The Collected Poems of Langston Hughes*. New York, NY: Vintage Books.

Hughes, L. (1967). *The panther & the lash (Vintage classics)*. New York, NY: Vintage Books.

Hull, G. T., & Scott, P. B., & Smith, B. (1993). *All the Women Are White, All the Blacks Are Men, but some of us are brave*. New York, NY: Feminist Pres at CUNY.

Human Rights Campaign Fund. (2022, November 22). United Against Hate™—Fighting Back on State Legislative Attacks On LGBTQ+ People. Retrieved from https://www.hrc.org/campaigns/the-state-legislative-attack-on-lgbtq-people

Human Rights Campaign Fund. (2021, November 17). *Marking the Deadliest Year on Record, Human Rights Campaign Announces Release of Annual Report on Violence Against Transgender and Gender Non-Conforming People* [Press Release]. Retrieved from https://www.hrc.org/press-releases/marking-the-deadliest-year-on-record-hrc-releases-report-on-violence-against-transgender-and-gender-non-conforming-people

Human Rights Campaign. (2015, December 10). 2015: A year in review of LGBTQ equality worldwide. Retrieved from https://www.hrc.org/blog/2015-a-year-in-review-of-lgbt-equality-worldwide

Hunt, V., Yee, L., Prince, S., & Dixon-Fyle, S. (2018). *Delivery through diversity*. New York, NY: McKinsey & Co.

Hurston, Z. N. (1998). *Their Eyes Were Watching God*. New York, NY: HarperCollins.

Hyde, J. S. (2005). The Gender Similarities Hypothesis. *American Psychologist*, *60*(6), 581–592. doi:10.1037/0003-066X.60.6.581

"[Infographic] Workplace Harassment: Understand the Numbers." Team True Office Learning (2019). https://www.trueofficelearning.com/blog/workplace-harassment-understand-the-numbers

Inglehart, R. (1990). *Cultural change in advanced industrial societies.* Princeton, NJ: Princeton University Press.

Interview by Sara Sidner with "Margarita," a Mother of two and Ukrainian refugee. CNN Newsroom with Fredericka Whitfield, Interview with Broadcast. March 5, 2022. 8:54a.m. PST.

Ipsos Poll Conducted for Reuters. "Stonewall Anniversary Poll 06.06.2019."

Iudici, A., & Verdecchia, M. (2015). Homophobic labeling in the process of identity construction. *Sexuality & Culture, 19:* 737–758. doi:10.1007/s12119-015-9287-0

Jagose, A. (1996). Queer *theory: An introduction.* New York, NY: New York University Press.

James, S. "Queer People of Color Led the L.G.B.T.Q. Charge, but Were Denied the Rewards." New York Times. June 22, 2019.

Johansen, B. (2020). *Full-Spectrum Thinking: How to Escape Boxes in a Post-Categorical Future.* Oakland, CA: Berrett-Koehler, 7.

Johansson, Warren. (1990). Sex Negative, Sex Positive. In W. R. Dynes (Ed.)., *Encyclopedia of Homosexuality* (pp. 1182–1183). New York, NY: Garland.

Johnson, C. "10 years later, firestorm over gay-only ENDA vote still informs movement." Washington Blade. November 6, 2017.

Johnson, D. K. The Lavender Scare: The Cold War Persecution of Gays and Lesbians in the Federal Government. Chicago: University of Chicago Press, 2009.

Jones, M. (2007). Hofstede—Culturally questionable? Paper presented at Oxford Business & Economics Conference. Oxford, England. Abstract retrieved from http://ro.uow.edu.au/cgi/viewcontent.cgi?article=1389&context=commpapers

Jingfeng, Xia. An anthropological emic-etic perspective on open access practices. *Journal of Documentation, 67*(1), 75–94.

Kanuha, V. K. (2000). "Being native" versus "going native": Conducting social work research as an insider. *Social Work, 45,* 439–447. doi:10.1093/sw/45.5.439

Kates, S. M. (2002). The protean quality of subcultural consumption: An ethnographic account of Gay consumers. *Journal of Consumer Research, 29*, 383–399. doi:10.1086/344427

Katz, J. N. (1976). *Gay American history*. New York, NY: Crowell.

Kazin, M. (2013, April 2). "Gay Rights Before Stonewall." *Dissent*. Retrieved from https://www.dissentmagazine.org/blog/gay-rights-before-stonewall

Kearl, H., Johns, N. E., & Raj, A. (2019). Measuring #metoo: A national study on sexual harassment and assault. Available from Stop Street Harassment: http://www.stopstreetharassment.org/wp-content/uploads/2012/08/2019-MeToo-National-Sexual-Harassment-and-Assault-Report.pdf

Kegan, R. (2000). What "form" informs? A constructive-developmental approach to transformational learning. In: J. Mezirow & Assoc. *Learning as transformation*. San Francisco, CA: Jossey-Bass.

Kim, B. S., Yang, P. H., Atkinson, D. R., Wolfe, M. M., Hong, S. (2001). Cultural value similarities and differences among Asian American ethnic groups. *Journal of Cultural Diversity and Ethnic Minority Psychology, 7*(4), 343–361. doi:10.1037/1099-9809.7.4.343

Kippix, S., Connell, R. W., Dowsett, G. G., & Crawford, J. (1993). *Sustaining safe sex: Gay communities respond to AIDS*. London, England: Taylor & Francis.

Knox, H. "Unholy Religious Exemptions." The Baltimore Sun. December 9, 2013.

Kottak, C. (2006). *Mirror for Humanity*. New York, NY: Mc-Graw-Hill.

Kroeber, A. L., & Kluckhorn, C. (1952). *Culture: A critical review of concepts and definitions*. Cambridge, MA: Peabody Museum of Archaeology and Ethnology.

Kulick, D. (2000). Gay and lesbian language. *Annual Review of Anthropology, 29*, 243–285.

Kunjufu, J. (1986). *Preparing Black youth for success.* Chicago, IL: African American Images.

Kwiatkowski, M., & Janicka, I. L. (2015). Personality of Polish gay men and women. *Current Issues in Personality Psychology, 3*(4), 242–252. doi:10.5114/cipp.2015.55648

Larsen, Nella. (2003). *Passing.* New York, NY: Penguin Books.

LaSala, M. C. (2003). When interviewing "family": Maximizing the insider advantage in the qualitative study of Lesbians and Gay men. *Journal of Gay & Lesbian Social Services, 15*(1–2), 15–30. doi:10.1300/J041v15n01

Lavers, M. K. (2016, December 29). Top 10 international stories of 2016. *The Washington Blade.* Retrieved from http://www.washingtonblade.com/2016/12/29/top-10-international-stories-2016/

Lederach, J. P. (1995). *Preparing for peace: Conflict transformation across cultures.* Syracuse, NY: Syracuse University Press.

Lee, R. M. (2013). The transracial adoption paradox: History, research, and counseling Implications of cultural socialization. The Counseling Psychologist, *31*(6), 711–744. doi:10.1177/0011000003358087

Leonhardt, D., & Miller, C. C. (2015, March 20). The metro areas with the largest, and smallest gay populations. *The New York Times.* Retrieved from https://www.nytimes.com/2015/03/21/upshot/the-metro-areas-with-the-largest-and-smallest-gay-population.html

Levy, D. L., & Johnson, C. W. (2011). What does the Q mean? Including Queer voices in qualitative research. *Qualitative Social work, 11*(2), 130–140. doi:10.1177/1473325011400485

Life Before Stonewall. (1994, July 3). *Newsweek.* Retrieved from http://www.newsweek.com/life-stonewall-189962

Lister, Kate. "The lesbian 'blood sisters' who cared for gay men when doctors were scared to."

Livingston, Jennie. Paris Is Burning (1990) (film). Jennie Livingston & Barry Swimar.

Lorde, Geraldine Audre. (1984). Sister Outsider: Essays and Speeches. Berkeley, CA: Crossing Press.

Lowder, J. B. (2015, May). "What was Gay?" *Slate*. Retrieved from http://www.slate.com/articles/news_and_politics/history/2015/05/can_you_be_homosexual_without_being_gay_the_future_of_cruising_drag_and.html#lf_comment=309848829

MacKinnon, C. (1989). *Towards a Feminist theory of the state*. Cambridge, MA: Harvard University Press.

Manalansan, M. F. (2003). *Global divas: Filipino Gay men in the Diaspora*. Durham, NC: Duke University Press.

Mangan, Dan. "Hate crimes against Asian and Black people rise sharply in the U.S., FBI says." CNBC. August 30, 2021.

Margolin, Emma. "Religious liberty bill opens door for LGBT discrimination." MSNBC. February 6, 2014. <http://www.msnbc.com/msnbc/bill-opens-door-lgbt-discrimination>

Marín, G., & Marín, B. V. (1991). *Research with Hispanic Populations*. London, England: Sage Publications.

Markowitz, M. (1999). Sexing the Anthropologist: Implications for ethnography. In F. Markowitz and M. Ashkenazi (Eds). *Sex, sexuality and the anthropologist*. (pp. 161–174). Chicago, IL: University of Illinois Press.

Markus, H., & Kitayama, S. (1994). A collective fear of the collective: Implications for selves and theories of selves. *Personality and Social Psychology Bulletin, 20,* 568–579.

Marloff, Sarah. "The Rise and Fall of America's Lesbian Bars." Smithsonian Magazine. January 21, 2021. https://www.smithsonianmag.com/travel/rise-and-fall-americas-lesbian-bars-180976801/

Martin, L. H., Gutman, H., and Hutton, P. H. (Eds.). (1988). *Technologies of the self: A seminar with Michael Foucault,* Amherst, MA: University of Massachusetts Press.

Masci, D., Sciupac, E., & Lipka, M. (2017). *Gay Marriage Around the World*. Retrieved from Pew Center website: http://www.pewforum.org/2015/06/26/gay-marriage-around-the-world-2013/

Maslow, Abraham (1943). "A Theory of Human Motivation." Psychological Review (50), pp. 370–396.

Mazar, A., & Wood, W. (2018, November 9). Defining Habit in Psychology. https://doi.org/10.31234/osf.io/kbpmy

Maylon, A. K. (1982). Psychotherapeutic implications of internalized homophobia in gay men.*Journal of Homosexuality*, 7(2–3), 59–69. doi:10.1300/J082v07n02_08

McAllister, J. (2013). Tswanarising global gayness: the 'UnAfrican' argument, Western gay media imagery, local responses and gay culture in Botswana. *Culture, Health & Sexuality*, 15(1), S88–S101. doi:10.1080/13691058.2012.742929

McCarn, S. R., Fassinger, R. E. (1996). Revisioning sexual minority identity formation: A new model of Lesbian identity and its implications for counseling and research. *The Counseling Psychologist, 24*(3), 508–534. doi:10.1177/0011000096243011

McCarthy, J. (2021). *Record-High 70% in U.S. Support Same-Sex Marriage*. Retrieved from Gallup website: https://news.gallup.com/poll/350486/record-high-support-same-sex-marriage.aspx

McCracken, G. (1990). *Culture and Consumption*. Bloomington, IN: Indiana University Press.

McFarland, Dr. Willi, MD, PhD (Ed.). City & County of San Francisco. "Atlas of HIV/AIDS in San Francisco 1981–2000." https://www.sfdph.org/dph/files/reports/RptsHIVAIDS/HIVAIDSAtlas1981-2000.pdf

McIntosh, M. (1968). The homosexual role. *Social Problems, 16,* 182–192.

McKay, M., & Davis, M., Fanning, P. (1995). Messages: The Communication Skills Book. Oakland, CA: New Harbinger.

McLelland, M. (2000). Is there a Japanese "Gay identity?" *Culture, Health, & Sexuality, 2*(4), 459–472. doi:10.1080/13691050050174459

McSweeney, B. (2000). The Fallacy of National Culture Identification. 6th Interdisciplinary Perspectives on Accounting Conference, Manchester, England.

McSweeney, B. (2002). Hofstede's model of national cultural differences and their consequences: A triumph of faith—a failure of analysis. *Human Relations, 55*(1), 89–118. doi:10.1177/0018726702551004

Meckler, L. "Religious Exemptions at Center of ENDA Debate." The Wall Street Journal. Washington Wire. November 1, 2013. <http://blogs.wsj.com/washwire/2013/11/01/religious-exemptions-at-center-of-enda-debate/>

Merriam, S. B., & Tisdell, E. J. (2016). *Qualitative research: A guide to design and Implementation* (4th ed.). San Francisco, CA: Jossey-Bass.

Merriam-Webster's dictionary of English usage. (2021). Springfield, Mass.: Merriam-Webster, Inc.

Mehrabian, A. (1972). *Nonverbal Communication.* New Brunswick: Aldine Transaction.

Meyer, I. H. (1995). Minority Stress and Mental Health in Gay Men. *Journal of Health and Social Behavior, 36*(1), 38–56. doi:10.2307/2137286

Middleton, D. R. (2002). *Exotics and erotics: Human cultural and sexual diversity.* Long Grove, IL: Waveland Press, Inc.

Minton, H. L., & McDonald, G. J. (1984). Homosexual identity formation as a developmental process. *Journal of Homosexuality, 9*(2–3), 91–104.

Miss Rosen. (2021, Sep. 6). "How ACT UP Transformed the Landscape of Art and Activism in the Age of AIDS." Blind Magazine.

Moore, C. (Ed.) (2006). Leo Tolstoy: Spiriting Writings. Maryknoll, New York, NY: Orbis Books.

Morris, M. W. (2014). Values as the essence of culture: Foundation or fallacy? *Journal of Cross-Cultural Psychology, 45*(1), 14–24. doi:10.1177/0022022113513400

Morris, R. T. (1956). A typology of norms. *American Sociology, 21*(5), 610–613.

Mosher, J. (2001). Setting free the bears: Refiguring fat men on television. In J. E. Braziel and K. Lebesco (Eds.), *Bodies out of bounds: Fatness and transgression.* Berkeley, CA: University of California Press.

Murray, S. (2000). *Homosexualities.* Chicago, IL: University of Chicago Press.

Neel, Joe. "Poll: Majority of LGBTQ+ Americans Report Harassment, Violence Based on Identity." National Public Radio. November 21, 2017. https://www.npr.org/2017/11/21/565327959/poll-majority-of-LGBTQ+-americans-report-harassment-violence-based-on-identity

Nodjimbadem, Katie. "The Long, Painful History of Police Brutality in the U.S." Smithsonian Magazine. July 27, 2017.

Oakley, M., Farr, R. H., & Scherer, D. G. (2017). Same-sex socialization: Understanding Gay and Lesbian parenting practices as cultural socialization. *Journal of GLBT Family Studies, 13*(1), 56–75. doi:10.1080/1550428X.2016.1158685

Offord, B., & Cantrell, L. (1999). Unfixed in a fixated world: Identity, sexuality, race, and culture. *Journal of Homosexuality, 3*(4), 207–220. doi:10.1300/J082v36n03_13

Ogola, E. A. (2022). *#JusticeForSheila: Kenyan anger after lesbian's murder.* Retrieved from BBC website: https://www.bbc.com/news/world-africa-61192594

O'hara, M. E. "Study: Bisexual community faces more poverty than lesbians and gay men." them. https://www.them.us/story/bisexual-community-poverty

Ohnuki-Tierney, E. (1984). "Native" anthropologists. *Journal of the American Ethnological Society, 11*(3), 584–586. doi:10.1525/ae.1984.11.3.02a00110

Olie, R. (1995). The 'culture' factor in personnel and organization policies. In A. Harzing et al. (Eds.), *International Human Resource Management: An integrated approach* (pp. 124–143). London, England: Sage Publications: 124–143.

"Opponents seek responses amid court setbacks." Associated Press. San Francisco Chronicle. February 16, 2014, p. A14.

Ortiz, D. R. (1993). Creating Controversy: Essentialism and Constructivism and the Politics of Gay Identity. *Virginia Law Review,* 1833–1857.

Owen, J. (2015, June 26). "Beyond Sex: What Is Gay?" *Huffington Post,* Retrieved from http://www.huffingtonpost.com/james-owens/beyond-sex-what-is-gay_b_6951926.html

Pachankis J. E., Bränström, R. (2019) How many sexual minorities are hidden? Projecting the size of the global closet with implications for policy and public health. PLoS ONE 14(6): e0218084. https://doi.org/10.1371/journal.pone.0218084

Parker, Priya. (2008). *The Art of Gathering: How We Meet and Why it Matters.* New York: Riverhead Books.

Parker, R. G. (1998). *Beneath the equator: Cultures of desire, male homosexuality, and emerging gay communities in Brazil.* New York, NY: Routledge.

Parker, R. G. & Carballo, M. (1990). Qualitative research on homosexual and bisexual behavior relevant to HIV/AIDS. *The Journal of Sex Research, 27,* 497–525.

Parker, R. G. & Easton, D. (1998). Sexuality, culture, and political economy: Recent developments in anthropological and cross-cultural sex research. *Annual Review of Sex Research, 9,* 1–19.

Parker, R. G., & Gagnon, J. H. (Eds.). (1973). Conceiving sexuality: Approaches to sex research in a postmodern world. New York, NY: Routledge.

Patton, M. Q. (2015). *Qualitative research and evaluation Methods* (4th ed.). Thousand Oaks, CA: Sage Publications.

Pereira, S. J. N., & Ayrosa, E. A. T. (2012). Between two worlds: an ethnographic study of gay consumer culture in Rio de Janeiro. *Brazilian Administrative Review, 9*, 211–228. doi:10.1590/S1807-76922012000200006

Pew Research Center (2013). A Survey of LGBT Americans. Retrieved from http://www.pewsocialtrends.org/2013/06/13/a-survey-of-lgbt-americans/

Phillips, A. (2010). What's wrong with essentialism? *Distinktion: Scandinavian Journal of Social Theory, 11*(1), 47–60. doi:10.1080/1600910X.2010.9672755

Phinney, J. (1996). When we talk about American Ethnic groups, what do we mean? *American Psychologist, 51*(9), 918–927. doi:10.1037/0003-066X.51.9.918

Plummer, K. (1975). *Sexual Stigma: An Interactionist Account.* London, England: Routledge.

Popov, I. & Salviati, C. (2019, March 24). "Traffic, Trains, or Teleconference? The Changing American Landscape." Apartment List. https://www.apartmentlist.com/research/traffic-trains-or-teleconference-the-changing-american-commute

[Press Release]. Retrieved from https://www.hrc.org/press-releases/marking-the-deadliest-year-on-record-hrc-releases-report-on-violence-against-transgender-and-gender-non-conforming-people

Quotations from Jordan and Hearon, "Barbara Jordan: A Self-Portrait: 10–11." 7 January 1979, Washington Post Magazine, 6–11.

Rainbow Welcome Initiative (n.d.). *What does LGBT mean?* Retrieved from http://www.rainbowwelcome.org/faq

Rallis, S. F., & Rossman, G. B. (2003). Mixed methods in evaluation contexts: A pragmatic framework. In A. Tashakkori & C. Teddlie (Eds.), Handbook of mixed methods in social & behavioral research (pp. 491–512). Thousand Oaks, CA: Sage Publications, Inc.

Rao, Rahul (2020). Out of Time: The Queer Politics of Postcoloniality. Oxford University Press.

Raymond, D. (1994). Homophobia, identity, and the meanings of desire: Reflections on the cultural construction of Gay and Lesbian adolescent sexuality. In J. M. Irvine (Ed.), *Sexual cultures and the construction of adolescent identities.* (pp. 115–150). Philadelphia, PA: Temple University Press.

Redpath, L., & Nielsen, M. O. (1997). A comparison of native culture, non-native culture, and management ideology. *Canadian Journal of Administrative Sciences, 14*(3), 327–339. doi:10.1111/j.1936-4490.1997.tb00139.x

Reiss, I. (1960). *Premarital sex standards in America.* Glencoe, IL: Free Press.

Reiss, I. (1967). *The Social Context of Premarital Sexual Permissiveness.* New York, NY: Holt, Rinehart, & Winston.

Rich, A. (1980). Compulsory heterosexuality and Lesbian experience. *Signs: Journal of Women in Culture and Society,* 5(4), 631–660. doi:10.1086/493756

Robinson, H. (2016) Dualism. In E. N. Zalta (Ed.). The Stanford Encyclopedia of Philosophy. Stanford, CA: The Metaphysics Lab.

Rodden, J. (2018, November). Keeping Your Enemies Close: Electoral Rules and Partisan Polarization. Stanford University. https://ces.fas.harvard.edu/uploads/files/events/rodden_anxieties_november2018.pdf

Rofel, L. (2007). *Desiring China: Experiments in neoliberalism, sexuality, & public culture.* Durham, NC: Duke University Press.

Rosenfeld, Dana. "The AIDS epidemic's lasting impact on gay men." The British Academy. February 19, 2018. https://www.thebritishacademy.ac.uk/blog/aids-epidemic-lasting-impact-gay-men/

Rosqvist, H. B., Arnberg, K. (2015). Ambivalent spaces-the emergence of a new gay male norm situated between notions of the commercial and the political in the Swedish gay press,

1969–1986. *Journal of Homosexuality, 62*, 763–781. doi:10.1080/00918369.2014.998958

Rubin, G. S. (1984). Thinking sex: Notes for a radical theory of the politics of sexuality. In C. S. Vance (Ed.)., *Pleasure and danger: Exploring female sexuality* (pp. 267–319). London, England: Routledge.

Russell, S. T., & Joyner, K. (2001). Adolescent sexual orientation and suicide risk: Evidence from a national study. *American Journal of Public Health, 91*(8), 1276–1281. doi.org/10.2105/AJPH.91.8.1276

"Russia: Court rules against LGBT activist." (2016, February 3). Retrieved from https://www.hrw.org/news/2016/02/03/russia-court-rules-against-lgbt-activist

Saldaña, J. (2013). *The coding manual for qualitative researchers.* Thousand Oaks, CA: Sage Publications, Inc.

Satell, G. (2014, September 5). "A Look Back At Why Blockbuster Really Failed and Why It Didn't Have To." Forbes. https://www.forbes.com/sites/gregsatell/2014/09/05/a-look-back-at-why-blockbuster-really-failed-and-why-it-didnt-have-to/?sh=3ad82eb11d64

Schein, E. (2017). *Organizational culture and leadership* (5th ed.). Hoboken, New Jersey: Wiley & Sons, Inc.

Schmidt, Samantha. "1 in 6 Gen Z adults are LGBT. And this number could continue to grow." Washington Post. February 24, 2021. https://www.washingtonpost.com/dc-md-va/2021/02/24/gen-z-lgbt/

Schneider, B. (Ed.) (1990). *Organizational climate and culture.* San Francisco, CA: Jossey-Bass, Inc.

Schwartz, S. H. (1999). A theory of cultural values and some implications for work. *Applied Psychology: An International Review, 48*(1), 23–47.

Scott, B. A., & Barnes, C. M. (2011). A multilevel investigation of emotional labor, affect, withdrawal, and gender. Academy of Management Journal, 54, 116–136.

Scott, J. W. (1996). *Only paradoxes to offer: French feminists and the rights of man*. Cambridge, MA: Harvard University Press.

Seidman, S. (2011). Theoretical perspectives. In S. Seidman & N. Fischer & C. Meeks (Eds.), *Introducing the new sexuality studies* (2nd ed.). (pp. 3–12). New York, NY: Routledge.

Seltzer, L. F. (2008, September 10). The path to unconditional acceptance: How do you fully accept yourself when you don't know how? *Psychology Today*. Retrieved from https://www. psychologytoday.com/us/blog/evolution-the-self/200809/ the-path-unconditional-self-acceptance

Serano, J. Whipping Girl: A Transsexual Woman on Sexism and the Scapegoating of Femininity. Seal Press, 2007.

"Sexual harassment of LGBT people in the workplace." (2019). Trades Union Congress. https://www.tuc.org.uk/sites/default/ files/LGBT_Sexual_Harassment_Report_0.pdf

Shaffer, E. & Neal, S. (2021). Why leaders must connect more during times of crisis. Catalyst.

ShareAmerica (2016). The "I" in LGBTI stands for Intersex: Here's what it means. Retrieved from https://share.america.gov/ what-does-it-mean-to-be-intersex/

Shareef, M. "Black and Queer in the Harlem Renaissance." Queer Majority. https://www.queermajority.com/essays-all/ black-and-queer-in-the-harlem-renaissance

Shostak, M. (1981). Nisa: *The life and words of !king woman*. Cambridge, MA: Harvard University Press.

Singh, S. & Durso, L. E. (2017, May 2). Widespread Discrimination Continues to Shape LGBT People's Lives in Both. Subtle and Significant Ways. *Center for American Progress*. Retrieved from https://www.Americanprogress.org/ issues/lgbt/news/2017/05/02/429529/widespread-discrimination-continues-shape-lgbt-peoples-lives-subtle-significant-ways/

Smith-Rosenberg, C. (1975). The Female World of Love and Ritual. *Signs, 1*(1), 1–29.

Søndergaard, M. (1994). "Hofstede's consequences: A study of reviews, citations and replications." *Organization Studies,* *15*(3), 447–456.

Spanjart, Jasper. "Engagement issues: Europe has the least engaged employees in the world." Totalent. August 16, 2021.

Spitko, E. G. (1996). A Biologic Argument for Gay Essentialism-Determinism: Implications for Equal Protection and Substantive Due Process. University of Hawai'i Law Review *18*: 571–622 (1996).

Spradley, J. P. (1979). *The Ethnographic Interview.* Belmont, CA: Wadsworth.

Stabbe, O. (2016, April 11). *"Queens and queers: The rise of drag ball culture in the 1920s."* National Museum of American History. https://americanhistory.si.edu/blog/queens-and-queers-rise-drag-ball-culture-1920s

Stitch, Stephen S. & Warfield, T. A. (Eds.) (2002). *The Blackwell Guide to Philosophy of Mind.* Hoboken, NJ: Wiley.

Stotzer, Rebecca L. (September 2017). "Data Sources Hinder Our Understanding of Transgender Murders". American Journal of Public Health. 107 (9): 1362–1363. doi:10.2105/AJPH.2017.303973. ISSN 0090-0036. PMC 5551619. PMID 28787204.

Stringer, P. & Grygier, T. (1976). Male homosexuality, psychiatric patient status, and psychological masculinity and femininity. *Archives of Sexual Behavior, 5*(1), 15–27. doi:10.1007/BF01542237

Stryker, Susan. *Transgender History.* First Printing edition. Berkeley, CA: Seal Press, 2008.

Sue, D. W. *Microaggressions In Everyday Life.* Hoboken, NJ: John Wiley & Sons, Inc., 2010.

Sue, D. W., Capodilupo, C. M., Torino, G. C., Bucceri, J. M., Holder, A. M. B., Nadal, K. L., & Esquilin, M. (2007). Racial microaggressions in everyday life: Implications for clinical practice. *American Psychologist, 62*(4), 271–286. https://doi.org/10.1037/0003-066X.62.4.271

Swierad, E. M., Vartanian, L. R., & King, M. (2017). The influence of ethnic and mainstream cultures on African Americans' health behaviors: A qualitative study. *Behavioral Sciences, 49*(7). doi:10.3390/bs7030049.

Tamale, S. (2014). "Exploring the contours of African sexualities: Religion, law and power." African Human Rights Law Journal, 14(1). http://www.ahrlj.up.ac.za/tamale-s

Thomas, D. C., Elron, E., Stahl, G., Ekelund, B. Z., Ravlin, E. C., Cerdin, J., Poelmans, S., Brislin, R., Pekerti, A., Aycan, Z., Maznevski, M., Au, K., and Mila B. Lazarova, M. B. (2008). *International Journal of Cross Cultural Management 8*; 123–143. doi:10.1177/1470595808091787

Thompson, P., & Gunter, H. (2011). Inside, outside, upside-down: The fluidity of academic researcher 'identity' in working with/in school. *International Journal of Research & Method in Education, 33*(1), 17–30. doi:10.1080/1743727X.2011.55230

Thoreson, R. (2018, February 19) Human Rights Watch. All We Want Is Equality: Religious Exemption and Discrimination against LGBT people in the United States. Retrieved from https://www.hrw.org/report/2018/02/19/all-we-want-equality/religious-exemptions-and-discrimination-against-lgbt-people

Ting-Toomey, S., Yee-Jung, K. K., Shapiro, R. B., Garcia, W., Wright, T. J., & Oetzel, J. G. (2000). Ethnic/cultural identity salience and conflict styles in four US ethnic groups. *International Journal of Intercultural Relations, 24*(1), 47–81. doi:10.1016/S0147-1767(99)00023-1

Torres, L. (2009). Latino definitions of success: A cultural model of intercultural competence. *Hispanic Journal of Behavioral Science, 31*(4), 576–593. doi:10.1177/0739986309349186

Triandis, H. C. (1990). Cross-cultural studies of individualism and collectivism. In J. Berman (Ed.), *Nebraska Symposium on Motivation, 1989.* (pp. 41–133). Lincoln, NE: University of Nebraska Press.

Triandis, H. C., Marín, G., Betancourt, H., Lisansky, J., & Chang, B. (1982). *Dimensions of familialism among Hispanic and mainstream Navy recruits.* Chicago: University of Illinois, Department of Psychology.

Troiden, R. R. (1988). Homosexual identity development. *Journal of Adolescent Health, 9*(2), 105–113. doi:10.1016/0197-0070(88)90056-3

Troiden, R. R. (1989). *Gay and lesbian identity: A sociological analysis.* New York, NY: General Hall.

UCLA School of Law Williams Institute. (2019, December 9). LGBT Discrimination costs South African more than $300 million per year. Retrieved from https://williamsinstitute.law.ucla.edu/press/cost-discr-south-africa-press-release/

U.S. Bureau of Labor Statistics. (2022) Table 4. [Quit levels and rates by industry and region, seasonally adjusted]. *Economic News Release.* https://www.bls.gov/news.release/jolts.t04.htm

Vance, C. S. (1991). Anthropology rediscovers sexuality: A theoretical comment. *Sociological and scientific medicine, 33*, 875–884.

Villareal, Daniel. "We're Loving the Push to Revive the Hanky Code for a New Queer Community." Hornet. August 20, 2021. https://hornet.com/stories/new-hanky-code/

Walters, K. L., & Simoni, J. M. (1993). Lesbian and gay male group identity attitudes and self-esteem: Implications for counseling. *Journal of Counseling Psychology, 40*(1), 94–99. doi:10.1037/0022-0167.40.1.94

Wang, J., Plöderl, M., Häuserman, M., & Weiss, M. G. (2015). Understanding suicide attempts among gay men from their self-perceived causes. *Journal of Nervous and Mental Disease, 203*(7), 499–506. doi:10.1097/NMD.0000000000000319

Wang, Stephanie Yingyi. (2019). When Tongzhi Marry: Experiments of Cooperative Marriage between Lalas and

Gay Men in Urban China. *Journal of Feminist Studies:* 45(1), 13–35. https://doi.org/10.15767/feministstudies.45.1.0013

Wareham, J. (2020, September 30). New Report Shows Where It's Illegal To Be Transgender in 2020. *Forbes.* https://www.forbes.com/sites/jamiewareham/2020/09/30/this-is-where-its-illegal-to-be-transgender-in-2020/?sh=58550f8e5748

Weeks, J. (1977). *Coming out: Homosexual politics in Britain from the 19th century to present.* London, England: Quartet Books.

Weeks, J. (1986). *Sexuality.* London, England: Tavistock.

Weinthal, B. (2021). *Treatment of LGBTQ people across Middle East examined in new report.* Retrieved from the Jerusalem Post: https://www.jpost.com/middle-east/treatment-of-lgbtq-people-across-middle-east-examined-in-new-report-689123

Werder, Corrine. "Queer Women History Forgot: Barbara Jordan." 15 March 2017, GOMAG. http://gomag.com/article/queer-women-history-forgot-barbara-jordan/

West, R. F., Meserve, R. J., & Stanovich, K. E. Cognitive sophistication does not attenuate the bias blind spot. J Pers Soc Psychol. 2012;103:506–19. https://doi.org/10.1037/a0028857

Westhaver, R. (2011). Gay men dancing: Circuit parties. In S. Seidman & N. Fischer & C. Meeks (Eds.), *Introducing the new sexuality studies* (2nd ed.). (pp. 390–397). New York, NY: Routledge.

"What Black History Month Doesn't Teach You About the Harlem Renaissance." 2012, Feb. 24. Black Youth Project. Retrieved from http://blackyouthproject.com/what-black-history-month-doesnt-teach-you-about-the-harlem-renaissance/

Where We Are On TV—2020. Gay and Lesbian Alliance Against Defamation. https://www.glaad.org/whereweareontv20

"Why anti-gay sentiment remains strong in much of Africa." The Conversation. June 10, 2015. https://theconversation.com/why-anti-gay-sentiment-remains-strong-in-much-of-africa-42677

Wilkerson, W. (2008). *Ambiguity and Sexuality: A theory of sexual identity.* Basingstoke, England: Palmgrave Macmillan.

Wilkinson, S. & Kitzinger, C. (1995). *Feminism and discourse: Psychological perspectives.* London, England: Sage Publications.

Williams. R. M., Jr. (1970). *American society: A sociological interpretation* (3rd ed.). New York, NY: Knopf.

Williams, W. L. (1992). *Spirit and the Flesh: Sexual Diversity in American Indian Culture.* Boston: Beacon Press.

Williams Institute. UCLA School of Law. October 2, 2020. https://williamsinstitute.law.ucla.edu/press/ncvs-lgbt-violence-press-release/

Williams Institute. UCLA School of Law. "How many people are Lesbian, Gay, Bisexual, and Transgender." April 2011. https://williamsinstitute.law.ucla.edu/publications/how-many-people-lgbt/

Williamson, I. (2000). Internalized homophobia and health issues affecting lesbians and gay men. *Health Education Research.* *15*(1), 97–107. doi:10.1093/her/15.1.97

Wong, S. (2022, September 20). *55% experienced workplace discrimination in Singapore: AWARE survey.* yahoo!news. https://news.yahoo.com/workplace-discrimination-singapore-aware-survey-130324125.html

Yoshino, Kenji & Deloitte University (2016). "Uncovering Talent: A New Model of Inclusion."

Zheng, L. (2020, January). We're entering the age of corporate social justice. *Harvard Business Review.* https://hbr.org/2020/06/were-entering-the-age-of-corporate-social-justice

Zinn, M. B. (1979). Field research in minority communities: Ethical, methodological and political observations by an insider. *Social Problems, 27*(2), 209–219. doi:10.2307/800369

About the Author

Dr. Joel A. Davis Brown is the Chief Visionary Officer of Pneumos LLC ("Pneumos"). Joel works strategically with a variety of non-profit organizations, Fortune 500 companies, and other institutions to build consciousness, capacity, community, and collective esteem. His work spans 6 continents, and his mission is to facilitate liberation for every global citizen. As an internationally recognized leader in Organizational Development, Change Management, and Global Inclusion, he is a professor at the IESEG management School in Lille and Paris, France. Additionally, Joel is a certified leadership coach and a member of the Forbes Coaches

Council. Joel graduated magna cum laude from the University of Minnesota with a double major in Political Science and Philosophy and a double minor in African-American studies and Spanish. Joel also received his law degree from the University of Virginia, as well as a doctorate in leadership and adult education from Saint Mary's College of California. In the creative realm, Joel is also a well-respected storyteller and spoken word artist.